ALL THE BIRDS
OF THE AIR

ALL THE BIRDS OF THE AIR

The names, lore and literature of British Birds

Francesca Greenoak
Illustrated by Alastair Robertson

ANDRE DEUTSCH

First published 1979 by
André Deutsch Limited
105 Great Russell Street London WC1

Filmset in Monotype Bembo 270
by A. Brown & Sons Ltd., Hull, England.

Printed in Great Britain by
Tonbridge Printers Ltd
Tonbridge

ISBN 0 233 97037 1

Contents

Acknowledgements

This book has been a friend from the first and made more pleasurable by the enthusiasm of those who saw me through it; in particular Adrian Greenoak, Loraine Greenoak, Gus Clutton, Robin Hamilton, and Kevin and Heinke Woodbridge. Peter Sommer helped with staunch practical advice. Special thanks to Richard Mabey who listened, advised and ploughed through almost unreadable early drafts, and to my best and oldest friend Jacquie Meredith for immensely supportive comments and brisk typing of the manuscript, and to John Kilpatrick for devoted kindness and help at every stage. Thanks are due too, to Anthony Cheke of the Armitage Library, the British Trust for Ornithology at Tring and to Berkhamsted Library for their remarkably speedy and always good-tempered service in retrieving many obscure and recondite books. And, not least, a word of appreciation for my editor Piers Burnett.

Acknowledgement must be made to Ted Hughes for permission to quote from his poem 'Swifts', from *Season Songs,* published by Faber and Faber and to Mr T. Poyser who was kind enough to send me the appendix of names from *The Hen Harrier* by Donald Watson (T. & A. D. Poyser) before publication.

The British Isles are very rich in birds. The total number of bird species recorded in Britain is in the region of five hundred but this includes a great many obscure subspecies and rare vagrants, known only to the more practised of ornithologists. There are, however, many birds which people have noticed and talked about, written of and depicted in art and story, and drawn upon for the imagery in their poetry, from as far back as we have records. People of different regions accorded more or less attention to certain birds, depending on their religious, superstitious, or practical significance; and they were called by names which evolved out of their various roles. Linguistic borrowings from other countries and dialect adaptations increased the variation, and today our heritage is a rich abundance of bird names which tell us much about the birds and about the people who have observed them through our history.

The practice of having a standardised form of name is a comparatively recent one, brought about largely through the large-scale production of field guides which met (and played its part in creating) an increased interest in bird life. The old ornithologies cite several common names for the birds they describe, not specially, I think, because they were concerned with keeping alive the old names, but because, before modern communications, they would probably not have been comprehensible in some parts of the country had they tried to use a single name. In the past, species definitions were not as clear as they are now (and taxonomic classifications are still changing in the light of new knowledge). Including a range of common names along with a 'main' name made it clear not only which species was being referred to, but that birds known by other names were also of that species. Until the middle of the nineteenth century for instance, there was a certain amount of confusion about the diver family, males and females sometimes being thought to be different species because of the striking difference in plumage.

There are many birds names which have been with us for well over a thousand years. A list of Anglo-Saxon names includes quite a few still used as a standard form: Swan, *Wuducocc* (Woodcock), *Goldfinc* (Goldfinch), *Ganot* (Gannet), *Hrafn* (Raven) and *Nihtegale* (Nightingale). A number of the common names have as long a pedigree as their standard counterparts. Names like *Hicemase* (Bluetit) and *Mushafoc* (Kestrel) are lost to those of us who have computed our course entirely by field guides. But these old names still echo down through the centuries in certain regional names. In Devon the Blue Tit is known as Hickymouse and Yorkshire names for a Kestrel are Mouse Hawk and Mouse Falcon. One or two names seem to have been completely lost; regrettably the marvellously bold *Tysca,* the Old English name which was superseded by the Frenchified 'Buzzard', but these are surprisingly few in number.

The interest and pleasure which people have in birds, still strong today, echoes continuously through our language and our literature. It is strongly present in the earliest Anglo-Saxon writing such as *The Seafarer* and *The Wanderer* and *Beowulf* and in Bede's beautiful metaphor of the sparrow, and something of the old intimacy lingers in the old names. Often beautiful and resonant in form, these names offer us real perceptions. Take for instance the range of names for the Goldeneye; between them, they alert you to all the field guide features. Even without the equipment indispensable to the modern birdwatcher, and scientific methods of classification and recording, birds have been closely and accurately observed. Chaucer, for instance, was quite aware that the Dunnock was one of the most frequent hosts to Cuckoo fosterlings.

Strong feelings have been aroused over the

observational side of bird behaviour. It is only in the last few years that it has been established that Woodcock really do sometimes carry their young in flight. People who recorded this in the past have been thought fanciful, or even wilfully misleading. In the late eighteenth century controversy raged over the observations of the doctor and orfnitho-logist Edward Jenner (the man who pioneered the practice of vaccination in Britain). In 1788, he published the first account of how the nestling Cuckoo ejected the young of the foster bird. This aroused angry and disbelieving opposition from other naturalists, particularly the influential Charles Waterton. However, in 1808 Colonel George Montagu in the introduction of his *Ornithological Dictionary* wrote a painstaking and carefully substantiated piece of work which confirmed Jenner's, and he added a general observation which in the spirit of the best ornithologists spoke for a sense of wonder and imagination to be joined to the spirit of scientific enquiry.

> Too apt are some persons to wonder at and disbelieve any things seemingly out of the ordinary course of nature; whereas it should only excite our admiration. To disallow things because our contracted comprehensions and confined ideas are limited within so small a compass savours of atheism.

In the case of the Cuckoo, it must be admitted that the truth of its cycle of behaviour is no less extraordinary than the various superstitions and stories which have grown up about it. However, the folklore of birds is interesting in its own right. Many old names still in use, such as Rain Goose (Red-throated Diver) and Devil's Bird (Yellow Wagtail), and bird superstitions, relate to customs and ancient beliefs, some of which may be traced back into prehistory. Edward Armstrong in his brilliant investigation into the origins of bird folklore observed the remarkable persistence of the past which lingers in our language and in our superstitions, without our recognising these 'ancient notions living a ghostly underground existence may survive for centuries after they have ceased to be philosophically acceptable or theologically orthodox.'

One of the most enjoyable aspects of investigating the names of birds is that you find an unpredictable and haphazard richness. On the one hand, there are names with a pedigree of perhaps a thousand years or more, drawn from the very roots of our language, others may be traced to the influence of early invaders such as the Vikings, or from later ones like the Normans of William the Conqueror (though there was considerable cultural interchange between Britain and France before the actual conquest). Mixed in with these one comes across what the nineteenth century ornithologist Alfred Newton disparagingly called 'book-names', things which appealed to the most orderly-minded of ornithologists and led to earnest literal compounds such as Short-heeled Field Lark (Tree Pipit) or Red Coot-footed Tringa (Red-necked Phalaraope) or Newton's particular aversion, *Garganello* or Garganey for the little duck he knew as Summer Teal. From the same stable there are some peculiar names for a few waders; Red-legged Horseman for Redshank, Green-legged Horseman for Greenshank, which only become clear when you look at the French where a whole group of long-legged waders which includes various species of sandpipers, –shanks and Yellowlegs are called *Chevaliers*. Edward Albin writing his three volumes *Natural History of Birds* in the early eighteenth century must have felt that the French epithet commended itself over the existing alternatives and introduced the 'horseman' names to Britain – but they were never in common usage.

Dialect often exerts its influence upon a traditional name, sometimes quite simply as in the transformation of an Ouzel (Blackbird) into a Zulu in Somerset. In other instances, an old meaning is forgotten and a name altered and 'rationalized' into a recognisable form. In this way, the Anglo-Saxon *Hyghwhele* became, among other things,

High Hoe and Hew-hole, and the tiny *Titmase* became Titmouse.

Many of the names are enormously rich in their associations; Hew-hole and Titmouse come from very old words, but have been reshaped to correspond to the way the birds behave. Similarly, in the folklore there are usually details which connect with some actual point of the birds' behaviour. There is also a large number of names which are purely descriptive, and by coupling an imaginative name to a characteristic feature, bring the bird vividly to mind. It may be a call or song as in Too-zoo for the Woodpigeon or Little-bit-of-bread-and-no-cheese for the Yellowhammer; or a characteristic noise of the wings as in Rattlewings or Sounder (Goldeneye and Mute Swan); or a cry of anger as in the Sussex names Shreitch and Shriek for the Mistle Thrush. Plumage details and habitat are also common themes for names. There are marvellous riches, the associations and observations of centuries of birdwatchers, to be discovered bound up with the names they gave the creatures they saw.

It would give rise to geographical error to translate the regional sources for the names, from old books, into the new post 1972 county rearrangement so I have retained the old county names.

I have listed the names in a rough order, in which names which seem to relate to one another are placed together. For instance, Hernshaw; Heronseugh (Yorkshire); Hernshaw; Heronshaw (Nottinghamshire) — all French derived names for the Heron, are clearly related, although I have only traced definite regional attributions for two of them, (in brackets after the name). Where names are separated by a comma rather than a semi-colon, as with Hegrie, Hegril's Skip (Shetland) both names are (or have been) in known usage in this locality. The birds themselves are taken in Wetmore order (rearranged slightly according to the BTO Species List: 13) which is the way that most of the good field guides are arranged.

These lists of names are as comprehensive as I could make them (excluding obvious archaisms) but I have no doubt that there are many which I have not been able to trace. Harking back to a venerable tradition by which readers customarily made marginal notes, my publishers have considerately provided a wide margin for any reader who wishes to add extra names or comments—or to take issue with what I have written. Finally, if any reader would care to write to me, I should be pleased to hear about names and derivations not included in this book.

A Chronological List of the Principal Works Referred to

ARISTOTLE The History of Animals (lived 384–322 BC)

PLINY *Historia Naturalis* Book X (lived 27–79 AD)

The Exeter Book, *Riddles* (copied c 975, probably from a much earlier original, perhaps eighth century)

The Exeter Book, *The Seafarer* and *The Wanderer* (also perhaps eighth century or a little earlier)

Beowulf (eighth century, written down in tenth century)

BEDE *Historia Ecclesiastica Gentis Anglorum* (731)

Life of Saint Cuthbert (based on an anonymous Life by a monk of Lindisfarne, written about 699)

AELFRIC ABBOT OF EYNSHAM, (The 'Grammarian') Glossary (998)

GERALD OF WALES (also known as Giraldus Cambrensis) *Topographia Hibernica* (1185)

JOHN OF GUILDFORD The Owl and the Nightingale (c 1200)

CHAUCER, GEOFFREY The Romaunt of the Rose (1369)
    Parlement of Foules (1382)
    Canterbury Tales (1386–1391)

TURNER, WILLIAM *Avium Praecipuarum Historia* (1544) includes 112 English names

GESNER, CONRAD *Historiae Animalium (Liber III qui est de Avium Natural)* (1555)

KAY, JOHN *Britanni, de Rariorum Animalium* (1570)

ALDROVANDRUS, U. *Ornithologiae, hoc est de Avibus historiae* (1599)

CAREW, R. Survey of Cornwall (1602)

DRAYTON, MICHAEL Poly-Olbion (1613)

SHAKESPEARE, WILLIAM Poems and Plays

BROWNE, SIR THOMAS Notes and Letters on the Natural History of Norfolk (1662–8)

MERRETT, CHRISTOPHER *Pinax Rerum Naturalium Britannicarum . . .* (1667) This is the second edition (the first is dated 1666) and it contains a list of some 170 species of birds, for some of which English names are given

WILLUGHBY, FRANCIS and RAY, JOHN Ornithology in Three Books, wherein all the Birds hitherto known, being reduced into a Method suitable to their natures, are accurately described, translated into English and enlarged by John Ray (1978)
    (Originally published in Latin in 1676 four years after

Willughby's death. John Ray probably did much of the work on this also.)

ALBIN, E. Natural History of Birds (1738)

PENNANT, T. British Zoology (1776–1777)

LATHAM, JOHN A General Synopsis of Birds (1781–1790)

WHITE, GILBERT Natural History and Antiquities of Selborne (1789)

BEWICK, THOMAS History of British Birds (1797–1804) (Text of Vol I by Beilby, of Vol II by Bewick, much assisted by Mr Cotes of Bedlington.)

MONTAGU, G. Ornithological Dictionary (1802 Supp. 1813)

SELBY, P. J. Illustrations of British Ornithology (1825–33)

JENYNS, L. Manual of British Vertebrate Animals (1835)

MACGILLIVRAY, WILLIAM History of British Birds 1837–1852)

YARRELL, WILLIAM History of British Birds (1843–1856)

HARTING, J. E. The Ornithology of Shakespeare (1871) Handbook of British Birds (1872)

SWAINSON, REVEREND CHARLES Provincial Names and Folk-Lore of British Birds (1886)

NEWTON, A. Dictionary of Birds (1893–1896)

HETT, C. L. Glossary of Popular, Local and Old-fashioned Names of British Birds (1902)

COWARD, T. A. The Birds of the British Isles (1920)

SHARROCK, J. T. R. The Atlas of Breeding Birds in Britain and Ireland (1977)

CRAMP, STANLEY and SIMMONS, K. E. L. Handbook of the Birds of Europe, the Middle East and North Africa: The Birds of the Western Palearctic, Volume I (1977)

Lumme
Speckled Loon
Lesser Imber
Northern Doucker
Herring Bar (Sussex)

Black-throated Diver
Gavia arctica

Loon; Loom
Ring-necked Loon (East Lothian; Cork Harbour)
Immer, Ember, Immer Goose (from *himbrini,* Icelandic for
    this bird) (Orkney)
Imber Diver (Ireland)
Gunner
Naak (Scotland); Nauk (Northumberland)
Cobble
Holland Hawk (Ballantrae)
Great Doucker

Great Northern Diver
Gavia immer

Speckled Diver; Speckled Loon
Mag Loon = *magpie* (Norfolk)
Rain Goose (Caithness; Shetland)
Loon, Lune (Devon; Cork; Wexford)
Loom (Shetland)
Cobble
Silver Grebe (Kent)
Burrian (Ballantrae)
Galrush (Dublin Bay)
Arran Ake (Dumbarton)
Sprat Loon; Sprat Borer (Essex)
Spratoon (Norfolk; East Lothian)

Red-throated Diver
Gavia stellata

Divers are probably the most primitive family of
birds known in Europe and this is borne out by
their appearance which conveys a sense of the
prehistoric. They are superbly built for diving;
Diver is not only the standard name, but, with its
dialect variant Doucker, forms part of a number of
local names. Divers outswim the fish on which
they feed, their large bodies are streamlined for
speed, their legs set well back for maximum thrust.
They can remain under water for periods of several
minutes and go down to considerable depths.
Juvenile Red-throated Divers are known as Sprat
Loons or Sprat Borers, as they are partial to these
small fish, but adult birds of all three species will

17

take much larger fish, such as haddock and trout, as well as crustaceans, molluscs and a fair amount of vegetable matter.

In his book *Great Northern* about the biggest of the Divers, Arthur Ransome calls them simply 'the great birds' a fitting title for creatures powerful both in myth and in their build. They seem eternal as the sea itself; even in rough waters, the Great Northern Diver appears stable, like some black rock, the snaky line of the back, neck and head, and the mighty wedge of a beak, immobile among the thrashing waves. During the winter months, Divers may come inland on storms and by an odd quirk of coincidence, on the day I was preparing to write about them, a Great Northern Diver came to Wilstone reservoir in Hertfordshire, just across the way from where I live. Having spent a solid morning with books, reasearching the mythology attached to Divers, I went out for a walk to clear my thoughts and, as I came over the reservoir embankment, found myself within yards of 'the great bird' itself. In the circumstances it was uncanny. But, my own astonishment apart, the presence of this large reptilian seabird, seemed to produce a disquieting effect on the whole countryside round about. It transformed the atmosphere of the place, as much as if a battleship had appeared on this quiet inland water. This event made the Diver lore, which is very ancient and widespread, suddenly comprehensible to me, even in terms of a modern landscape.

The Divers are on the edge of their breeding range in Britain. (The Great Northern breeds here only rarely, the Black-throated in small numbers, the Red-throated more frequently – but still only in the region of about 750 pairs.) The powerful folklore of the Divers is also on the edge of its range in Britain. Considerable attention is devoted to the Rain Goose by Edward Armstrong in his remarkable book which explores the mythology of birds over many centuries and in many cultures. He suggests that the Diver lore and superstitions, which in Britain mostly take the form of telling the weather, are not to be taken literally but seen in a wider context of ancient tradition and belief, dating possibly from the Old Stone Age. Divers play an important part in several myths about the creation of the world; they dived beneath the waters to bring up the mud which formed the basis of the earth. All over 'the crown of the world', in the mythologies of the Eskimo, North American Indian, Siberian and Scandinavian peoples, there are stories about Divers which echo each other. In Norway, it is considered impious to kill a Diver, and that there was some cross cultural transference is clear from the fact that our word Loon and other variant names come from the Old Norse. There is also an area of rough moorland scattered with lochans in Mainland, Orkney (where Red-throated Divers are known to breed) which is called The Loons.

Though the calls of Divers differ from one species to another, their calls all have an unearthly, wailing character. These sounds are particularly eerie because they have something of a human quality to them and have drawn a special attention to the birds. In a number of primitive legends, Divers adopt the form of humans, and the reverse. They are also believed to wail as they accompany the souls of the dead (or, in Norway, before a death), and the heads of Divers were carried by Eskimos as talismans. The Thompson Indians believe that the power of the Great Northern Diver was such that, further to its cry portending rain, it could actually cause it, and even a human being imitating the cry could do likewise. In Shetland, as in Norway, there is a tradition that when the Black-throated Diver or the Red-throated Diver (the Rain Goose) are especially vocal, bad weather will follow. But there is also a Shetland rhyme which in certain circumstances (for example when Divers call noisily inland) could offer a contradiction to this:

> If the rain gose flees to da hill,
> Ye can gang to da heof when ye will;
> But when sho gangs to da sea,
> Ye maun draw yir boats an flie.

In the Faeroes there are more complicated degrees of weather prognostication based on different kinds of cry made by Red-throated Divers. The comparative abundance of weather sayings, the multiplicity of the signs and interpretations and the lack of specificity to a single species, point to the likelihood that they might have diffused from a main source rather than risen from separate observations. There is in any case very little in actual Diver behaviour which could be brought forward to support any of the traditional folklore.

The tendency of the Divers to attract strange observations continued on into later times. Thomas Pennant, who would surely have described himself as 'a man of science', in his *British Zoology* published in 1777, repeated the tale in currency in the Faeroes, that 'the Immer is thought to hatch its young in a hole formed by nature under the wing for that purpose.' Another modern 'myth' came about through the early ornithological illustrators drawing from bird corpses and attempting to reassemble an injured beast back into a lifelike posture for their portrait. A Diver is, in fact, incapable of achieving the proud upright stance, tiptoe on its webs, as pictured in Bewick's 'The Lesser Imber', and many other Diver and Grebe illustrations.

Because of the differences between summer and winter plumage there was considerable confusion about the identification of various Divers among early ornithologists. The Great Northern was recognised as a separate species in 1634 and the distinction between Black- and Red-throated was made in the eighteenth century. Though Bewick had not come by this information by the time of the 1826 edition of his *British Birds* where he says of his 'Lesser Imber' (a Black-throated Diver in winter plumage) 'we have little doubt that this, and the bird described in former editions under the name of Imber, are the young of the Great Northern Diver.'

Crested Doucker (E Lothian)
Horned Doucker
Greater Copped Doucker; Great Diver (Cheshire)
Greater Dobchick; Greater Dabchick
Greater Loon (Norfolk; W Ireland)
Ash Coloured Loon; Ash Coloured Swan; Grey Loon
Gaunt (Lincolnshire)
Arsefoot
Molrooken (Lough Neagh)
Car Goose
Tippet Grebe
Satin Grebe

Great Crested Grebe

Podiceps cristatus

Before the latter half of the eighteenth century, the Great Crested Grebe was fairly widely distributed over Britain, a not uncommon sight on shallow lakes and ponds. But by 1860, a total count of the species came to a lamentable forty-two pairs. The soft white breast plumage of the Grebe had become fashionable in the trimmings of clothes and hats. At first 'grebe fur' was imported from the continent but soon, wholesale slaughter of British birds was under way and the unfortunate birds became known as Satin Birds and Tippet Grebes. A cotton cloth with a downy surface on one side was even sold as 'grebe cloth'. However, the story does not end there. Recolonization began and was aided by the passing of the Bird Protection Acts. In 1867 there was only one breeding pair of Great Crested Grebes at the Tring reservoirs, and by 1884 there were seventy-five pairs, and they spread out from Hertfordshire over the rest of Southern England.

There was also a positive human reaction to the decline of the Great Crested Grebe. As many of the women on whose behalf the 'grebe fur' clothes were fashioned became aware of the massacre behind the finery, they banded together in vigorous protest. In 1889, a small group of ladies pledged themselves 'to refrain from wearing the feathers of any birds not killed for the purpose of food'. By the end of its first year that small group which had called itself The Fur, Fin and Feather Folk, had a membership of over five thousand which is some measure of the strength of feeling which lay behind it. They later changed their

21

name, and from 1904 were known as the Royal Society for the Protection of Birds. Bird sanctuaries were established by the RSPB and other protectionist societies and by private landowners like Charles Waterton. There is no doubt that the heightened private watchfulness and public awareness achieved by these people helped to some extent to restrict the widespread breaking of the Bird Protection Acts.

It was at Tring that Julian Huxley made the observations on the courting behaviour of the Great Crested Grebe, later published as a short book, of literary as well as scientific excellence. Even in October when they are in plain winter plumage (lacking the pronounced 'horns' and striking chestnut brown frill of cheek feathers) a pair will sometimes indulge in a few of the courtship actions, swimming towards one another, necks outstretched, to rear up opposite each other, satin breast to satin breast, shaking their heads gently. It is usually only in the spring that they dive and offer each other pieces of weed. These Grebes (also called Divers and Douckers) have an easy rolling dive, slipping gently but strongly under the water to catch the small fish which form the mainstay of their diet. They rarely fly, except during the height of the spring courtship; they need a long take-off and seem heavy and rather laboured in the air. They make a floating nest in reeds at the water's edge, and hardly come to land at all; their legs are designed for swimming rather than walking, placed far back on the body, as expressed succinctly in the name Arsefoot.

Greve (Yorkshire)
Rolling Pin (Sussex)

Red-necked Grebe
Podiceps grisegena

Dusky Grebe
Horned Grebe
Magpie Diver (Sussex)
Small Diver (E England)
Hell Diver
Black-and-white Dabchick

Slavonian Grebe
Podiceps auritus

Black Grebe
Eared Grebe
Lesser Crested Grebe
Rolling Pin (Sussex)

Black-necked Grebe
Podiceps nigricollis

Until this century none of these three birds was recorded as breeding in Britain or Ireland, and they are still better known to us as winter visitors, though small numbers of Slavonian and Black-necked now regularly have their young in these islands. It is a shame that these charming birds have been accorded such unimaginative standard names. Black-necked Grebe is a direct translation of the scientific name *nigricollis*. This made a contrast with the Red-necked Grebe which used to be called *rubricollis* or *ruficollis* which, however, has now been given to the Dabchick. As this jumble of names suggests, early ornithologists, confused by similarities between the species and by the differences in summer and winter plumages, were perplexed as to how many species and subspecies of Grebe there were. The scientific names have undergone a number of changes, but it is more difficult to re-route a common name once it has gone into use.

By the time of Yarrell's *History of British Birds* (1843) the five species of Grebe were listed as they are now with the same vernacular names, with the one exception that the Black-necked Grebe was called, as it still is in many parts of the country, the

Eared Grebe. Early this century, the British Ornithologists Union attempted to re-allocate the name Eared Grebe to the Slavonian Grebe to match the transfer of its scientific name *auritus* (=eared). In this case common usage was against them and Slavonian Grebe (as recorded in Montagu's *Ornithological Dictionary*, 1802) was retained. As a matter of observation, the Black-necked or Eared Grebe in breeding plumage has golden-red feathers which extend across the ear-coverts and back over the cheeks, The Slavonian Grebe has a rufous sweep which starts at the base of the bill and ends in two erectile tufts: from whence the name Horned Grebe. The name Rolling Pin which is applied in Sussex to Great Crested, Red-necked and Black-necked Grebes probably alludes to the habit, common to Grebes and Divers, of rolling nonchalantly on their sides to preen their silky white underfeathers.

Dabchick
Tachybaptus ruficollis

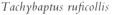

Diver (Renfrewshire)
Diedapper (Dorset; Hampshire; Norfolk)
Dabber (Berkshire; Buckinghamshire)
Divedapper, Divedop (Lincolnshire)
Dive an' Dop, Divy Duck (Norfolk)
Doucker (Shropshire; Perthshire)
Jack Doucker (Shropshire)
Small Doucker, Little Doucker (East Lothian)
Dobchick
Spider Diver

others:
Arsefoot
Bonnetie (Forfar)
Black Chin, Black Chinned Grebe (Berkshire)
Drink a Penny (Loch Strangford)
Loon
Mither o' the Mawkins (Stirling)
Penny Bird (Loch Morne; Carrickfergus)
Little Grebe (General)
Tom Puddin' (Shropshire; Toome, Antrim)

Rather than fly, a Dabchick will dive for safety. Usually, it will surface under cover of reeds or the dense foliage of a bankside until it judges things to be calm again. Even when there is no ready cover (this is rare, for Dabchicks are very cautious animals) a Dabchick will still dive if it senses danger, then rise slowly to lie semi-submerged, head and neck just breaking the surface, watching. Even when you know what it is, you are still deceived into believing that it is a piece of driftwood, except that driftwood does not disappear into a slow dive before your eyes.

In his poem *Poly-Olbion,* Michael Drayton drew attention to the incessant activity of the 'diving Dobchick':

> Now up, now down again that hard it is to prove
> Whether under water most it liveth, or above.

It is not surprising that names for the Dabchick: Dive Dapper, Doucker, Divedop and so on, make reference to its diving. Nor, I think, is it too far-fetched to hear in the plosive repetition of 'd's and 't's of the names, an echo of the sharp splash of the water breaking and closing with the Dabchick's dive.

Shakespeare does not concern himself particularly with the exploration of the world of birds. They figure largely in his imagery, but they are incidental; their purpose is literary, enriching the writing, but not offering startlingly new perceptions of the birds themselves. There are, however, places where the character of the bird comes through, notably in *Venus and Adonis* when the nervous Adonis is being wheedled into seduction by Venus

> Upon this promise did he raise his chin
> Like a dive-dapper, peering through a wave
> Who being look'd on, ducks as quickly in;

a nice description of the Dabchick's alert watchfulness.

Fulmar

Fulmarus glacialis

Malmock, Malduck, Mallemock, Mallimoke (Shetland)
Molly-mawk, Mallimack (Orkney)
Mollemoke, Mollemawk (Yorkshire)

The places of origin of the Fulmar names show quite clearly the northerly locations in which the bird has its longest history. It is only very recently that we have been able to see Fulmars in Wales, Cornwall, Essex and Norfolk. There has been a continuous population increase over the last two centuries and now Fulmars have colonized nearly all the suitable cliffs of Britain and Ireland.

The most famous Fulmars are those of the island of St Kilda, where they have probably lived and been hunted for nearly a thousand years. The ornithologist William MacGillivray visiting the island in 1840 reported that the Fulmar 'forms one of the principal means of support to the islanders, who daily risk their lives in its pursuit.' There is, however, strong evidence to show that the present great Fulmar spread is not of St Kildan birds, but a population overspill from Iceland. A piece of weather lore from St Kilda says that if a Fulmar seeks land it is a sign that the west wind is far away, that is that there will be bad weather. This could well be so for the St Kildan birds, who nest almost exclusively on coastal cliffs and are rarely seen over land and it would be a matter for remark to see them over land. The Fulmars of Icelandic descent are much more adaptable in their colonizing. In Orkney, they often fly inland and they nest on chimney stacks and at the bottom of dry stone walls.

The Fulmar sits very tight on its lovely, large, chalky-white egg. To the point of stupidity, according to Fulmar hunters, and this, it is suggested, may be the origin of the Mallimoke group of names, derived from the Dutch *mal* = foolish, *mok* = gull. If you approach gently, you can usually get within a metre of a sitting bird which will watch you warily and 'kek-kek' a warning. If provoked, as hunters and bird ringers know, the bird will eject a stream of oily secretion and half-digested food at the attacker, forcibly enough to be on target for about a metre and a half. The Fulmar, Foul Maa, or Foul Gull is so-named because of this pungent oily spew. It is a very ancient name, probably going back to before our earliest record of it which occurs in an Icelandic saga written by a tenth century satirist called Hallfredh.

Baakie Craa (Shetland)
Cocklolly (Pembroke)
Crew, Cockthroden (Scilly Isles)
Cuckee, Cuckles (Pembroke)
Mackerel Cock
Lyre; yrie (Orkney; Scotland; Shetland)
Sea Swift; Skidden; Skinner
Scraber (Hebrides)
Manx petrel; Manx puffin
Night bird (Skellig Island)
Booty (Shetland)

Manx Shearwater

Puffinus puffinus

H. Kirke Swann quotes a proverbial northern saying 'to gan as licht's a lyrie' which draws its simile from the graceful, beautifully controlled glide of the Shearwater. It skims the water, banking steeply first one way, then the other, displaying alternately, the black of its back and upper wing, then the white of the underwing and breast. Skimming almost at right angles to the water, the 'shear-water' seems to cut through the waves with its long straight wings, in an action similar to that of a ploughshare on the land. Both 'shear' and 'share' originate from the Anglo-Saxon *scieran*. Manx Shearwaters are brilliantly adept at riding the winds and can glide considerable distances without beating their wings. They alter the angle of flight or create a moderate impetus by flicking the primary feathers of the wingtips only, but in a low wind or when travelling purposefully as when on migration, they move the whole wing in a steady beat.

Like other 'tube-nosed' birds, the petrels and albatrosses, who spend nearly all their lives at sea, the Manx Shearwaters have difficulty moving about on land, and come to shore only at breeding time. They make their nests in underground burrows like Puffins do, but unlike them, Manx Shearwaters come to their burrows only at night, hence the name Night Bird. Manx Shearwater parents share the family duties, both male and female taking their turn in the long incubation of their single egg, and in feeding the young bird. Shearwaters nest in colonies and when the visitations are being made at the dead of night, the nesting 'village' rings with their loud cries. A typical utterance was rendered 'cack-cack-cack-carr-hoo' by R. M. Lockley and these crowing and cackling cries have given rise to a number of 'cock' and 'crow' names.

The characteristic noise and their nocturnal habits seems to have made an impression on generations very much earlier than ours. It is likely that a Shearwater colony was the original inspiration for a passage in an old Icelandic poem of the early eleventh century, Njal's Saga. Two chieftains, Osprak and Brodin, had a quarrel which was to culminate in the Battle of Clontarf, and the noise of the Shearwaters, here called 'ravens', is used as a metaphor of the coming battle.

> The third night the same clamour was heard. Ravens came flying at them with beaks and talons which seemed made of iron.

This scene takes place when the ships of both chieftains were anchored near to the Calf Sound in the Isle of Man, the traditional colony which gave the Shearwater its standard name. The earliest written British record of the Manx Shearwater is in Camden's Britannia (1586) and in 1652, James Chaloner ventured a brief description of the 'Manks Puffin'. A few years later Willughby and Ray called the bird 'The Puffin from the Isle of Man'. In fact, for a period of 150 years the Manx Shearwaters did not breed in this ancient site but, since 1967, they have returned and there is now once again a colony on the southernmost tip of the island.

There are also colonies in Shetland, islands off the West of Scotland, the Faeroes and a few places

on the Irish coast-line. The Hebridean name
Scraber derives from the Faeroese *Skapur*. The
colony on the West Wales island of Skokholm has
been made famous through Lockley's book
Shearwaters and several echoic names hail from this
region. The Scillies have the extraordinary
imitative name Cockthroden for the Manx
Shearwater.

Some books give as an explanation for the name
Mackerel Cock that feeds upon mackerel fry, but
the *Birds of the Western Palearctic* does not mention
these as an item of diet and it is possible that the
name originated because migrating Shearwaters
and mackerel shoals more or less coincide in their
spring arrival (the Wryneck is also a Mackerel Bird).

Manx Shearwater

Storm Petrel
Hydrobates pelagicus

weather names:
Stormy Petrel
Storm Finch (Orkney)
Witch; Waterwitch
Assilag (from Gaelic *easchal* = storm) (Hebrides)

*The bird ever on the wing – apparently from the Italian
    ala = wing and* monte = *to mount:*
Alamonti (Orkney)
Allamotti
Alamouti (Shetland)
Mitey; Mitty

other names:
Gourder; Gourdal (Kerry)
Hornfinch
Little Peter
Martin-oil (Ireland)
Mother Carey's Chickens
Sea Swallow; Swallow (Shetland)
Spence, Spencie (Hebrides)
Tom Tailor
Oily-mootie (Foula)

One of the most devoted observers of the petrel
family, R. M. Lockley, wrote of the Storm Petrel
'I have a great affection for this little bird which is
no bigger than a sparrow and yet can ride out the
endless hurricanes of the Atlantic winter.' They are
associated with storms because in the heaviest

29

weather, they are swept inland by the gales and sometimes 'land-wrecked' many miles from the coast: so they are 'storm birds' for the people who find them.

Storm Petrels are very much birds of the ocean. The people most familiar with them are sailors and many of the beliefs connected with Storm Petrels are nautical in character. It is held that Storm Petrels are the restless spirits of skippers who have ill-treated their crews. Another legend says they are the damned souls of mariners. A French name for them is *Ames damnées*; this and the Alamouti, Mitey, Mitty names probably refer to the way a Storm Petrel flits and flutters continually over the water, never at rest.

The flight of a Storm Petrel is not unlike that of a hirundine, hence Sea Swallow and Martin-oil. Small and black, it is not unlike a House Martin in appearance, an impression enhanced by the white blaze on the tail (which however is not forked). The 'oil' suffix of Martin-oil owes its origin to the bird's habit of discharging a jet of malodorous stomach oil at an aggressor (as do Fulmars and other related species).

The Storm Petrel straddles a contradictory mixture of associations. One school of thought believes Mother Carey to be an ancient witch, another that it is a name derived from *Mater Cara*, possibly a title of the Virgin Mary. Neither version is authenticated. Its names are also Witch and Waterwitch; it is a damned soul and *Satanique*. Yet the Storm Petrel is called Little Peter, or Petrel, because as it flies over the surface of the waves, it drops its legs, as if attempting to walk on the water, like St Peter on the Lake of Galilee.

Gan (Wales)
Mackerel Gant (Yorkshire)
Solan Goose
Soland (Lowlands of Scotland)
Bass goose, Basser (Forfar)
Herring Gant (Norfolk)
Channel Goose (Devon)
Sula (North Country)
Spectacled Goose

Gannet
Sula bassana

The Gannet is a large and splendid seabird. It has complete mastery of the air; the straight blade-like wings measure nearly two metres at full stretch and carry it along in buoyant powerful flight. The Gannet spends most of its life on the open sea except during the breeding season, feeding on shoaling fish such as Herring and Mackerel (hence Herring Gant and Mackerel Gant). Gan and Gant are old forms of Gannet. It sometimes dives for fish from a considerable height, folding back its wings to form a 'W' with the pointed tail, and plunging into the sea with a tremendous splash. The plumage varies from the very dark young birds to the predominantly white mature adults. Adult plumage is attained at about four years or so; some of the two- and three-year-old Gannets have an extremely attractive black and white mottle as rich and thick as ermine. Mature birds have buff-yellow shading on their heads, bluish-white bills and a curious ring of blue skin around the eye, which gives them the name Spectacled Goose. The wings are liberally tipped with black.

The name Gannet has a long lineage, ultimately deriving from the same root as goose and gander. It has been is use since Anglo-Saxon times. The Poet of *The Seafarer*

> . . . had for amusement the cry of the gannet
> And the trill of whimbrels instead of the laughter of
> men
> The kittiwakes' song in place of mead.

Gannets are silent except during the breeding season so the poet must have been near a sea-bird colony. James Fisher, making his deductions from the range of species represented in the poem and what is known of the extent of the Anglo–Saxon realm of the eighth century, concluded that the scene might have been set at Bass Rock in East Lothian, which is even today very much a Gannet stronghold. The Gannet is still known as the Bass Goose or Basser in the north and the scientific epithet is *bassana* from the same origin. It is also called Solan Goose, Solan or Soland, from the Icelandic *Sula,* a name still in use in the north of Scotland.

The Gannet also features in the seventh century epic poem *Beowulf* which like *The Seafarer* is set against a background of the seas. Sometimes the adjectives stress the extent of the waters as in 'wide seas' and 'broad seas' but in the moving scene where Beowulf is taking his leave of his friend the old King Hrothgar, whom probably he will not see again, the hero wishes to soften the blow of his departure and make light of the distance soon to separate them and then he calls the sea the *ganotes baeth,* the Gannet's bath.

Cormorant

Phalacrocorax carbo

Sea Crow
Coal Goose (Kent)
Scart (Lancashire; N Ireland; Orkney)
Gorma; Gormer (Northumberland)
Hibling; Palmer; Scarf (Orkney)
Loering (Shetland)
Cowe'en Elders (Kirkcudbright)
Mochrum Elders (Wigtown)
Isle of Wight Parsons

young:
Brongie (Shetland)

I came across my first Cormorants in quite unexpected circumstances. They were dotted all over the trees on a small island in the middle of a Tottenham reservoir. Not half a mile away, heavy traffic made its way in and out of London on the A10. The Cormorants looked strange, black and angular, clasping the branches of the wintry trees, in contrast to several Herons who looked quite at home and had formed a breeding colony on this urban refuge.

There is another man-made site where I regularly watch Cormorants in winter. Some thirty to forty of them exploit the outflow rig of the cooling system of Sizewell nuclear power station. The conspicuous black figures line the upper railings sharply outlined against the winter greys of the North Sea. They look uncomfortably perched, but they are sitting over a sure supply of food, the mashed fish who were lucklessly sucked into the filters of the cooling system.

I have been watching wintering Cormorants in various places in the South of England for several years, but it was only travelling up through Northeast Scotland recently, that I felt that I really saw Cormorants for the first time. It was an immediate and joyful recognition. There were Cormorants on a jut of rocky coastline, black as the rock itself; they seemed almost an extension of it as they preened, slept and watched the sea. Large craggy birds, Cormorants are always impressive but here they did not stand out; they were perfectly identified with this wild landscape.

Milton recognised something sinister and primeval in the Cormorant. In Book III of *Paradise Lost,* he chooses it for a simile for Satan as he plans the downfall of Adam and Eve in the Garden:

> . . . on the Tree of Life,
> The middle tree and highest there that grew,
> Sat like a cormorant; yet not true life
> Thereby regained, but sat devising death.

The name Cormorant is from the Latin *Corvus marinus* = sea raven; the Raven, of course, is also a bird of sinister reputation. Andrea Mantegna (1431–1506) used the Cormorant in a satanic role, not in the Fall, but in his picture *The Agony in the Garden*. In stony bleak Gethsemane, Christ kneels praying. Behind him the Cormorant, perched in a bare tree, sits staring down.

In the sixteenth century, the word Cormorant was used in Britain as a synonym for insatiable appetite. James I kept Cormorants (as well as Otters and Ospreys) on the Thames at Westminster. These birds were trained into a semi-domesticated condition and would fish for their masters. The Master of Cormorants was a member of the Royal Household. In the Bibliothèque Nationale there is a picture of Japanese fishermen, fishing by night with the aid of lanterns, and using Cormorants. These birds have had a ring placed round their necks as a precaution against the birds swallowing their prey, and in this picture the fishermen in the leading boat are holding the Cormorants on long reins which are paid out or pulled in according to the birds' movements.

The association of Cormorants and greed dates back at least four hundred years and there are a number of passing literary references to this, such as Shakespeare's 'light vanity, insatiate cormorant' in Richard II. It is however interesting that there is virtually no folklore in Britain attached to the Cormorant. References play upon the actual appearance or behaviour of the bird, rather than drawing on any symbolic meaning. The local names, are in the main, quite literal, as in Sea Crow or Coal Goose. There are several spiced with malicious funpoking and it must be admitted that there is more than a little resemblance between these lanky black-frocked birds and the stock figure of a parson or an elder of the kirk.

Shag
Phalacrocorax aristotelis

plumage:
Crested Cormorant
Tufted Skart
Skart (Orkney)
Scarf (Shetland)
Cole Goose
Colmorn

others:
Crane (Northumberland)
Green Cormorant (Ireland)

The Shag is slighter and smaller than the Cormorant, otherwise similar in shape. It is a dark greeny-black all over, except for the bright yellow at the base of the bill and, until recently, Green

Cormorant was a widely used alternative for Shag. *Skegg* the Old Norse, meaning 'beard' gives us the name now in general use, which alludes to the upright crest which crowns the head of the Shag in breeding plumage.

The Shag is almost exclusively a bird of rocky coasts. It fishes in deeper water than the Cormorant and rarely uses estuaries, rivers or reservoirs as a food reserve. The dark shapes of the Shag are seen flying low over the waves, sinuous–necked on the water or perched on a rocky promontory. Where Cormorants and Shags nest together on one cliff, it is noticeable that the Cormorants will take the higher, more exposed places, whereas Shags will search out shady crevices, narrow concealed ledges or caves. R. M. Lockley who watched Shags on his island home of Skokholm, remarked on how like reptiles the birds sometimes seemed, especially when engaged in courtship, gaping their large hooked yellow beaks at each other.

Nobody who has studied these great birds wedged in their narrow crannies, fails to report on the awful smell of the nests which are built of twigs and wet and rotting seaweed which becomes increasingly pungent as time passes. Although obviously disturbed by any intrusion Shags will sit very close on the nest. T. A. Coward gives a sympathetic impression of their agitation, 'They sit on the ledges, swinging their heads from side to side if approached and croak dismally.'

The Shag usually carries its beak at a slightly uptilted angle which gives it a faintly anxious, enquiring air. In contradistinction to the image of its close relative the Cormorant which is seen in a sinister role, the Shag is a bird of appealing aspect. Oliver Postgate seized on this when he featured a noble and helpful Shag called Graculus in a children's television story *Noggin the Nog*. (Graculus was the second part of a scientific name given by Linnaeus to the Shag, *Phalacrocorax graculus,* now superseded by *Phalacrocorax aristotelis*).

Heron

Ardea cinerea

Harn (Norfolk)
Hernser (Suffolk)
Harnsey (Norfolk)
Hernsew; Heronseugh (Yorkshire)
Hernshaw; Heronshaw (Nottinghamshire)
Huron (Roxburgh)
Herald (Forfar)
Hegrie, Skip Hegrie, Hegril's Skip (Shetland)
Ern (Somerset); Varn, Yarn (Cheshire)

familiar names:
Jack Hern (Sussex)
Moll Hern (Midlands)
Jenny Crow (North)
Jemmy Heron (Kirkcudbright)
Tammie Herl (Perth)
Jemmy Lang Legs; Jemmy Lang Neck (Lancashire)

from the cry:
Frank (Suffolk)
Frank Hanser (Fens)
Diddleton Frank (Fens)
Joan-na-ma-crank (Cumberland)

'long neck' names:
Longie Crane (Pembroke)
Long-necked Heron (Ireland)
Lang-necket Haaran (Berwickshire)
Long Necky (Dumfries)
Long Neck (Yorkshire)
Longnix (Cheshire)

young:
Brancher

These large and impressive birds have been with us since well before historical times. Herons were among the bird fauna of Clevedon Cave which may date as far back as the Mindel Glacials, about 400,000 years ago. Bronze Age Herons have also been found. Today, Herons are still widespread and fairly numerous over Britain and Ireland though the drainage of land has destroyed a great deal of their erstwhile habitat. Written reference to Herons dates back to the eighth century, though the word Heron itself is a Norman-French import. The Old English name was *Hragra,* still preserved in Shetland as Hegrie and Hegril's Skip.

By Chaucer's time, however, the name Heron

was in common use. Hawking for Herons was extremely popular: 'a marvellous and delectable pastime' according to Harting (*Ornithology of Shakespeare*, 1871). It was due to hawking that Herons were accorded a reputation for cowardice. They flew high and tried to avoid conflict rather than fight the adversary. A play was made on this by the exiled Robert of Artois who presented Edward III with a dish of roast Herons, signifying that they were cowardly birds for the cowardly king who did not invade France.

Not only the word *Hiron* was adopted from the French, but their word for a young Heron: *Hironceau*. When it crossed the Channel, it became more general in its meaning, and Heron and the variants of *Hironceau* (Hernsaw, Hernser, Heron-shaw) are used interchangeably with Heron. Shakespeare chooses to use a *Hironceau* form in the famous lines from Hamlet's assumed ravings:

> I am but mad north-north-west: when the wind is southerly I know a hawk from a handsaw.

The metaphor is sustained from an earlier part of the scene where Polonius plots with the King and Queen to discover if Ophelia can be the cause of Hamlet's eccentric behaviour. The words Polonius chooses are from the falconer's vocabulary, 'At such a time I'll loose my daughter to him', as if she were a tame dove to be used as a decoy. So Hamlet's speech, though directed exclusively at Rosencrantz and Guildenstern, also refers obliquely back to the previous passage. He can tell the hunter from the prey; at least he can sometimes, when the wind is right. At this time, at the very beginning of the seventeenth century, anti-French feeling was running high which may account for the thoroughly Anglicised version of *Hironceau*, like Handsaw. It is thought that at this time the word Dauphin was similarly converted in an English 'daw-fin'.

In early times there were still Cranes in Britain, and both Cranes and Herons appeared on the menus of banquets held during the Middle Ages. These lists and household accounts, such as those of

37

the Lestranges of Hunstanton which comments 'A young Heron is lighter of digestion than a Crane', clearly use the two names to refer to different species. However, by the nineteenth century when John Clare wrote *The Shepherd's Calendar,* the Crane was extinct in Britain and both names were applied to the Heron.

> While far above the solitary crane
> Swings lonly to unfrozen dykes again
> Cranking a jarring mellancholy cry
> Thro the wild journey of the cheerless sky.

As one would expect with a bird of such majestic stature, Herons have a large number of names which relate to their physical appearance, principally the long sinuous neck, so powerful and devastating in its lightning strike for a fish or eel. It also has several voice names, imitative of the hollow 'Frank' cry. It may seem a little incongruous that such large birds elect to nest aloft, but the majority of heronries are in trees. Thomas Pennant wrote in 1769 to Gilbert White of a spectacular Heronry at Cressi's Hall near Spalding. Pennant records that it was 'the greatest curiosity in these parts' and indeed it must have been, for the eager observer counted no less than eighty nests in a single oak. Gilbert White with characteristic consideration and without evincing disbelief, politely presses his friend who is sometimes given to exaggeration for more details of this phenomenon.

It seems as if in past times the Heron was thought to have a sympathy with the moon. In Angus, there is a tradition that the Heron waxes and wanes with the moon; being plump when the moon is full and lean at the crescent. Old medicine too, took account of lunar cycles and receipts often prescribe the picking of a herb only when the moon is at its fullest. In the North of Ireland, the fat of a Heron killed at full moon was believed to be a remedy for rheumatism.

Bittour (Northumberland)
Buttal (Norfolk)
Butter Bump; Bottle Bump (Yorkshire)
Bitter Bum; Bumble
Bumpy Cors (*Bwmpygors* = boom of the marsh) (Wales)
Bumpy Coss
Bitterurne (Surrey)
Bog Bumper (Scotland)
Bog Blutter; Bog Jumper
Bog Drum (Ireland; Scotland)
Boom Bird (Wales)
Bull of the Bog (Roxburgh)
Bull of the Mire (Northumberland)
Heather Bluiter, Heather Blutter (Scotland)
Miredrum (Northumberland)
Clabitter (Cornwall)

Bittern
Botaurus stellaris

The Bittern is not only one of our rarest birds, it is one of the most elusive. The mottled brown and black plumage is scarcely discernible against the reedbed background which the Bittern has made its home for over a thousand years. They are large bulky birds (only a little smaller than a Heron) but they can slip through the reeds like wraiths. G. K. Yeates lovingly observed Bitterns on the Norfolk Broads; here he describes a nesting female:

> A reed-bed is the most difficult place in the world in which to move quietly. A human being who *tries* to be quiet cannot do so. A bittern is a large bird, yet only the most intensive listening will give a clue of her coming – usually the slight splashes of water drops. Frequently the first warning I got was a long neck with thick orange bill coming through the screen of reeds behind the nest. It would be followed by a green foot which did not seem to mind if it were placed actually on the eggs; and at last the heavy, fat body.
>
> A Bittern can change its shape more completely than any bird I know. The normal incubating bird is a heavy thickset fowl, neck tucked into body. Every now and then, to pick up a floating reed or to arrange the nest, the bull-like neck is stretched out until it becomes a long, thin, scraggy thing of astonishing length. But

39

this is as nothing to the attenuation which occurs when a human being approaches. At such times she may slip off quietly and retire through the reeds, but at others, she will raise herself on tiptoe, make slim even her fat body and extend her neck bolt upright to an extent that only seeing will believe. Then is seen to advantage the wonderful adaptive coloration of the streaks on her throat and neck, which merge perfectly with the surrounding reeds. Then too is seen the comical sight of her binocular vision, as, bill pointing skywards, she turns her eyes to see straight before her, round and under her bill. Truly a remarkable bird.

(*Bird Haunts in Southern England*)

The wide range of local names for the Bittern give us some idea of how abundant a bird it used to be. Neolithic Bitterns have been preserved in the surface peat over many regions of England and Wales. Yet, with the draining of so much wetland and considerable pressure from shooting and egg collecting, by the latter part of the nineteenth century the Bittern was extinct as a British breeding bird. John Clare wrote of a Bittern in Whittlesey Mere

. . . the bushy clump down by the river
And the flags where the butter-bump hides in

just a few years before the mere was drained and the birds deprived of their habitat. It is only comparatively recently that recolonization (by continental birds) has begun again, principally in East Anglia. An odd instance of a 'name from nature' occurs along the Suffolk coast where ship's foghorns are called sea bitterns. In southern England, the number of Bitterns is swelled in winter by migrants, but the total breeding population is probably less than a hundred pairs.

Nowadays, you will be very lucky to hear the springtime calling of the male Bittern which gives rise to most of its local names. The resonant 'booming' is not particularly loud but it has a remarkable carrying power. It is also mysteriously difficult to locate, seeming to come from no precise direction. This 'booming' or 'bumping' is a strange and uncanny sound and folklore has it that to hear it was bad luck. Willughby and Goldsmith identified the Bittern with the ominious 'Night Raven' of mythology, probably on the grounds that it calls sometimes at night and when it does may cause superstitious dismay (a 'thing which went bump in the night' perhaps). Another belief which says that the Bittern only booms in odd numbers, has an element of truth in it. The three-fold boom appears to be the commonest, and nine has been recorded (probably made by two birds) though twos and fours are not uncommon. Pliny referred to the Bittern as *taurus* and a few local names allude to the bullishness of the roaring, and the scientific first name plays on this with a mixture of *bos* = ox plus *taurus* = bull.

It used to be thought that the Bittern thrust its bill into the marsh to make its booming. Chaucer uses this image to good effect in *The Tale of the Wife of Bath* where he tells the tale of how asses' ears grew on King Midas. His wife confides the secret to the marsh rather than tell it to another human being and betray her husband:

> Doun to a mareys faste by she ran
> Til she came there, hir herte was a-fyre
> And, as a bitore bombleth in the myre,
> She leyde hir mouth unto the water doun.

Dryden's rendition of the same tale (1700) contains a more sophisticated image: that of a Bittern pushing its bill into a reed and blowing it like a trumpet. However, James Thomson in 'Spring' (1728) the third of the *Seasons* poems to be published, goes back to the original version, when he writes of the way that wintry weather keeps breaking back when one expects Spring to arrive

> . . . so that scarce
> The Bittern knows his time with bill engulphed
> To shake the surrounding marsh.

Mallard
Anas platyrhynchos

Wild Duck
Common Duck
Mire Duck (Forfar)
Moss Duck (Renfrew; Aberdeen)
Muir Duck (Stirling)
Grey Duck (Lancashire; Dumfries)
Stock Duck (Orkney; Shetland)

There can scarcely be anything more male than a Mallard in either its name or its behaviour. The first syllable is derived from the Latin *masculus,* via Old French. The ending '-ard' comes from an Old High German suffix *hart* = hardy or bold, denoting a male creature. Mallard as a species name is, in fact, a usage from the Middle Ages which has only fairly recently come back into fashion. During the nineteenth century and the first half of the twentieth century, this species was known simply as the Wild Duck, the male Wild Duck only being called a Mallard.

Mallard live on nearly every park lake and farm duck, not only in Britain, but in the world. Tame Mallard live on nearly every park lake, and farm pond. They have been managed and specially bred to produce entirely domestic forms, of which the Aylesbury duck is one. In domestic or semi-domestic conditions, more than in the wild, Mallards live up to their 'male-chauvinist' name. There is no finesse in the pursuit flight of the Mallard; lovemaking drakes will attack female ducks vigorously and if, as is often the case in parks, the females are outnumbered, several males may make repeated assaults, sometimes actually killing the duck. This violent behaviour is probably due to overcrowding and seems not to be a modern phenomenon. In Chaucer's *Parlement of Foules,* the drake is introduced as a 'stroyer of his owne kind' and when he uncomprehendingly mocks the devoted fidelity of the turtle doves, is denounced in no uncertain fashion by the Tercel who says rudely that speech like the Mallard's 'comes out of a dunghill', as one might expect—

Thy kind is of so a wrecchednesse,
That what love is, thou canst not see ne gesse.

42

'Wild' Wild Duck are rather different in behaviour from their domesticated cousins. No angling with bread will convince a real wild Mallard of your friendly intentions; you will be lucky to get within half a kilometre without scaring them away. And, in the wild, on the moors, lakes and marshes, courtship is taken at a more relaxed pace, beginning in October when the birds come into breeding plumage and begin to pair off.

During the thirteenth century, Pope Gregory IX preached a crusade against a Friesland community, whom it was believed, worshipped the devil 'Asmodi' who appeared to them in the form of a duck, a goose or a youth, during special rites. After the worshippers had danced around him and kissed him, he enveloped them in darkness under cover of which everyone gave themselves up to orgiastic rout. This event might have been some kind of fertility ritual, the bird forms of the supernatural apparition having an obviously sexual significance.

Other supernatural powers attributed to both the duck and the goose are those of augury. The 'picking of the wishbone' and a smattering of weather lore may be the last living tokens of early beliefs which carried much more important meaning. Nowadays, most people simply break the wishbone and wish on the larger piece but in the past, the bone was carefully examined for signs which, among other things, would forecast the weather. Colour was an important feature, as may be seen in this quotation from *Notes and Queries* (at as late a date as 1875).

In Richmondshire, some persons say that the breastbone of ducks after being cooked are observed to be dark-coloured before a severe winter, and much lighter coloured before a mild winter.

The behaviour of the living creatures is also significant as in this Scots rhyme:

When ducks are driving through the burn
That night the weather takes a turn.

Another relic of the past is a festival held at All Souls' College, Oxford, known simply as 'The Mallard'. A 'Lord Mallard' is elected and with a band of Fellows, he 'hunts the Mallard' through every chamber of the College. The custom is said to be as old as the College itself; the tradition is that during the digging of the College foundations a Mallard 'grown to a vast bigness' was found trapped in an underground drain, and that ever after the Mallard ceremony was enacted annually, every 14 January. The first actual reference to the custom is in 1632 when Archbishop Abbot wrote reprovingly that 'Civil men should never so far forget themselves under pretence of a foolish mallard, as to do things barbarously unbecoming.' Proceedings which were obviously riotous and possibly pagan in their early origins clearly provoked the churchmen. Over a century and a half later, Bishop Heber observed the 'orgies' of 'Lord Mallard and the forty fellows in a kind of procession on the library roof with immense lighted torches'. It was clearly an occasion for unrestrained revelry and it was not without its sexual aspects, as may be seen in the 'Merry Old Song of the All Souls Mallard' which is sung as an accompaniment to the searching and celebrates the prodigious exploits of the bird, as in this verse which plays on the legend of Leda and the swan. (An old meaning of the word swap was 'to throw down', 'to strike upon, or fix upon something' or someone, and in the spirit of this song, it probably has sexual connotations.)

> The poets feign Jove turned into a swan,
> But let them prove it if they can:
> As for our proof 'tis not at all hard,
> For it was a swapping, swapping Mallard.
>
> Oh! by the blood of King Edward,
> Oh! by the blood of King Edward,
> It was a swapping, swapping Mallard.

Jay Teal (Kirkcudbright)
Tael Duik (Scotland)
Throstle Teal (Lancashire)
Speckled Teal

Teal
Anas crecca

Considering that Teal have certainly been with us since the time of Neolithic man, as we know from remains preserved in peat deposits, it is surprising that there are so few names known for this beautiful little duck. It is the smallest duck to frequent the waterways of Britain and Ireland and one of the most appealing. Teal are dabbling ducks and their small busy figures are to be found along the shorelines of lakes and boggy pools, especially during winter months when the numbers are increased by migrants, and they are less secretive than they are during the breeding season. The musical calling of the winter flocks of Teal, the high flutes of the males blending with the rhythmical chirruping of the females, has a wistful soothing quality to it as it echoes over the water. The collective name, a spring of Teal, is nicely descriptive of their quickness to start into flight. They take to the air almost vertically and the flight itself is swift and marvellously precise. The male in breeding plumage is very handsome, the mottled pastel grey and buff, offset by striking markings of chestnut green, black and white. Though the contrasting colours are different in the Jay the tonal impression is quite similar and may account for the name Jay Teal. Teal have a surprisingly wide distribution over the British Isles but their actual numbers are quite small, even in Scotland where they are at their most populous and have two local names.

45

Garganey

Anas querquedula

Pied Wigeon; Pied Wiggon
Garganey Teal
Summer Teal (Somerset; Norfolk)
Summer Duck
Cricket Teal (Hampshire)

There seem to have been no written British records for the Garganey before the 1660's. Among the first writers to describe it was Christopher Merrett who introduces it as 'a kind of Teale which some fowlers call Crackling Teale from the noyse it maketh'. We still have an echoic name for the Garganey in Cricket Teal, which represents the rapid, low-pitched cracking calls of the male. The female has a low quack which perhaps finds its echo in the specific term of the scientific name *querquedula*.

The Garganey is unique among British duck in that it is a summer migrant. It arrives in Spring and departs about September so the vernacular Summer Teal and Summer Duck are most appropriate names for this rather special summer-time duck which is smaller than a Wigeon but bigger than a Teal, though related to both these dabbling ducks (and borrowing names from both). The standard name Garganey is a slightly arbitrary one. It comes from the Italian *Garganello,* and came to us via the German-Swiss naturalist Conrad Gesner who listed it as such in his *Historiae Animalium* (1555), an early work which was much respected by seventeenth century British ornithologists. Willughby (1678) lists both Garganey and Summer Teal but a much later ornithologist, Alfred Newton, was not so accomodating, remarking disparagingly that Garganey was a 'bookname for the duck generally known as a Summer Teal'.

Garganey are delicate in form with beautifully coloured plumage, the female an exquisite brown and creamy-white mottle, the male considerably more colourful with elegantly sickle-shaped 'scapular' feathers which spring from the shoulder and curve down the back. It is probably the contrasting of the drake's brighter colours with the white of the eyestripe and the grey-white on his side which gave rise to the 'pied' names for the Garganey.

Grey Duck
Rodge
Sand Wigcon (Essex)
Gray

Gadwall
Anas strepera

The Gadwall is not common as a breeding bird but numbers increase in winter with visitors from western Europe and Iceland. It is a freshwater dabbling duck. The drake is the most quietly coloured of all the dabbling ducks, predominantly a Grey Duck or Gray, as its names suggest. Gadwall are only a little smaller than Mallard but they are sleeker in appearance, their beaks dainty, their bodies slender by comparison.

There is no conclusive argument about how the Gadwall came to be so-called. The first reference is in Merrett's list of birds in 1666. Over a century later, a Kentish physician and ornithologist John Latham (1740–1837) traced a possible origin of the name to *quedul,* a gentle onomatopaeic Latin quack, found also in the scientific name for Garganey *Anas querquedula.*

Wigeon

Anas penelope

call names:
Whistler
Whim
Whewer; Whew Duck *female*
Pandle Whew; Grass Whew (Yorkshire)

plumage names:
Bald Pate
Golden Head, Yellow Poll *male* (Ireland)
Black Wigeon *female*
Lady Fowl *female;* Lady Duck (Lancashire)
Easterlings *young males*

others:
Half Duck
Smee Duck (Norfolk)
Cock Winder (Norfolk)
Winder (Eastern England)

Wigeon used to be almost entirely seaside duck, roosting peacefully in large packs on even the roughest seas, and coming to shore to feed upon *Zostera* grass *(Zostera marina),* in some places called Wigeon grass. They are less exclusive in their diet than Brent Geese who feed almost entirely on *Zostera*, and when this grass was badly hit by disease in 1930, and again in the 1970s, Wigeon suffered much less than the Brents, adapting their feeding habits to what was available and moving to freshwater lakes and reservoirs inland. Though the breeding population of Wigeon is small, the number of wintering birds is increasing, especially on reserves.

Since the Brent Goose was given special protection in 1954, Wigeon have been a chief quarry of wildfowlers on coastal marshes. At one time, in past days, they were sold extensively in markets all over Europe. Two names Easterlings and Lady Fowl are recorded by the ornithologist John Latham (1740–1837), for young male and young female Wigeon respectively, on sale in London. About the middle of the eighteenth century, there occurs another use of Wigeon; when applied to a person it meant a fool or simpleton. Wigeon are not notably foolish in their behaviour, but they are very gregarious, and in the context of a duck shoot, they were particularly

vulnerable. Another 'market' name was Half Duck, signifying that a Wigeon, being smaller than a Mallard was worth only half the price.

Wigeon have two particularly striking characteristics, one visual, one auditory, and both commemorated in their common names. The males have a high whistling call, quite beautiful to hear when a large pack is all together. Whistler and Whewer obviously come from this call, and it possible that the name Wigeon itself also does. Wigeon are also called Golden Head or Yellow Poll, again from the male who had a vivid orange-yellow streak which stands out brilliantly on his chestnut head.

---

from the 'pin tail':
Sea Pheasant (Hampshire; Dorset)
Sprig Tail

others:
Cracker
Harlan (Wexford)
Winter Duck
Thin Neck (North)
Lady Bird (Ireland)

Pintail
Anas acuta

The Pintail is the rarest dabbling duck to breed in Britain and Ireland. It is, however, a very common duck in Europe, second only to the Mallard in numbers. Winter visitors to Britain are regular and fairly numerous and the bird is known as Winter Duck in some parts. Pintail are shapely and elegant duck; the northern name of Thin Neck is practically slanderous. The graceful tilt of the slender neck makes a perfect balance with the 'sprig' of long tail feathers. Sea Pheasant is still a well used alternative name and conveys something of the exotic appearance of the bird as well as its

49

Pintail

predilection for coastal haunts. Like Pheasants, too, the male Pintail is very strikingly coloured in contrast to the browny female. The name Cracker probably refers to the male's courtship call though it is perhaps more a croak than a crack.

Shoveler
Anas clypeata

Shovel Bill
Broad Bill; Beck (Norfolk)
Shovelard (Norfolk)
Spoon Bill; Spoon Beak (Norfolk)
Whinyard (Waterford)
Scopperbill (Norfolk)
Sheldrake (Waterford)
Blue Winged Shoveler
Blue Winged Stint

others:
Maiden Duck (Ireland)
Kirk Tullock; Kertlutock

We can see Shoveler all the year round in Britain, but it is a changing population because they are strictly migratory. The birds which nest in Britain and Ireland will winter in France and Spain, and the large packs of Shoveler which winter here have migrated from Scandinavia and Russia. The males are very striking in their colours, with a glossy green head, white breast and chestnut flanks, and it has the name Sheldrake meaning, as in Shelduck, a 'sheld', or variegated, plumage. Both male and female have a wide sky-blue wingbar which shows both at rest and, very conspicuously, when the birds are flying. In flight the body of the male makes a dramatic pattern, a white diamond enclosing two smaller black diamonds.

The most distinctive feature of Shoveler is of course the shovel bill and the common names make a varied range of allusion to it, such as Spoonbill, Scopperbill, Broad Bill and Whinyard, the latter named after a knife similar in shape to the Shoveler's bill. Shoveler feed as they swim. They sieve particles of food and little aquatic creatures from the surface film of the water with the fine comb-like 'lamellae' on both the upper and lower parts of the beak. Shoveler hold the fore part of the body low down in the water for easy 'filter feeding' and this attitude and the angle of the heavy bill contrive to give them a gentle trusting expression.

Scaup Duck
Mussel Duck (Norfolk)

Scaup
Aythya marila

plumage names:
Green-headed diver (Belfast)
Black-headed Diver; Black Duck (Somerset)
Golden-eyed Diver
Black-Headed Wigeon
Blue Neb (Northumberland)
Spoonbill Duck (E Lothian)
Grey Backed Curre (Scotland)
Silver Pochard (Yorkshire)
Frosty-back Wigeon

female only:
Bridle Duck (Dublin)
White-faced Duck
Dun Bird (Essex)

others:
Holland Duck (Forfar)
Mule (Wexford)
Norway Duck (Belfast)
Norwegian Duck (Banffshire)
Covie Duck (Northumberland)

It is likely that the name Scaup or Scaup Duck is taken from the small molluscs and crustaceans which form its diet and are known as scaup or scalp in the North. The Scaup is also known as the Mussel Duck. The Scaup has a typical diving-duck shape, small and compact. It is very much a saltwater duck, a deep water feeder, diving down as far as six metres, and entirely untroubled by rough water. Scaup only rarely breed in Britain, but considerable numbers come southwards from their summer territories in Iceland to spend the winter here. There are a number of foreign place names incorporated into Scaup local names,

51

as with many migratory birds. Most of the other common names refer to one detail or another of the plumage, indeed pretty well covering the Scaup's every feature, the grey-black head and the golden eye, the broad blue bill, and the silvery grey mantle. The female is also well served with names; a Blue Neb like the male, she has a patch of white which extends around the base of the bill which gives her the names Bridle Duck and White-faced Duck; otherwise she is a browny-dun in colour, slightly lighter on the breast and flanks.

Tufted Duck
Aythya fuligula

White-sided Duck; White-sided Diver (Armagh)
Magpie Diver
Black Poker (Norfolk)
Black Curre (Hampshire)
Black Topping Duck (Yorkshire)
Black Wigeon; Curre Wigeon (Somerset)
Doucker (Islay)
Crested Diver (Ireland)
Dovver (East)
Gold-eye Duck (Wexford)
Blue Billed Curre (West)
Blue Neb (Northumberland)

This striking black and white Magpie Diver has greatly increased its breeding population in Britain and Ireland over the last century. The first record of a breeding pair was made as late as 1849 in Yorkshire. Now there may be as many as five thousand breeding pairs, well-distributed over lakes, lochs, reservoirs and flooded gravel-pits. Tufted Ducks are compact in outline with a small 'pigtail' of dark feathers on the back of the head (the male's rather longer than the female's), giving us Tufted Duck and Crested Diver. Tufted Duck are expert divers, swooping down to considerable depths tc capture their food, often the introduced 'zebra mussel' common in reservoirs and gravel-pits.

The brick-shaped white patch on each flank of the male White-sided Diver vanishes in the moult and is late to reappear but is very conspicuous during the months of courtship and breeding. The golden eye and blue bill (neb) are registered in the vernacular names Gold-eye Duck and Blue Neb. The Tufted Duck shares with the Goldeneye, the names Curre, or Curre Wigeon, probably echoic in origin, imitating the low purring notes of the flight and alarm calls.

Pochard
Aythya ferina

colour characteristics:
Poker (Lincolnshire; Hampshire)
Poker Duck
Red-headed Poker; Red-eyed Poker
Red-headed Wigeon (North)
Snuff-headed Wigeon
Red-headed Curre
Gold Head (N Ireland)
Red Neck (Cheshire)
Dun Bird (Essex; Dumfries; Ireland) *female*
Dun Curre; Dun Air; Dun Poker (Yorkshire) *female*
Bull-headed Wigeon (N Ireland)
Great-headed Wigeon
Blue Poker

others:
Wigeon Diver (Cork)
Freshwater Wigeon (N Ireland)
Vare-headed Wigeon
Diver; Doucker (Roxburgh)
Smee Duck (Norfolk)
Whinyard (Wexford)
Well Plum

The *OED* gives several pronunciations for the word Pochard: one can quite correctly, it seems, say *potchard, pockard* or *poachard*. This could be an indication of a long history and widespread usage. It is likely that one of the birds mentioned in the glossary of Aelfric, Abbot of Eynsham (c 998) was a Pochard, though not by this name. The dictionary gives no hint as to the derivation of Pochard stopping short at 'origins obscure'. Potter and Sargent in *Pedigree* suggest that it is a bird which 'pokes about' with its beak for weed and molluscs beneath the water. Possibly the word Pochard came to us from *pocher* = 'to poke' in Old French. The name Blue Poker (the Pochard's bill is

53

blue) could be seen as support for this. The first mention of the bird under the name Pochard appears in William Turner's *Avium Praecipuarum* (1544).

Pochard do breed in Britain and Ireland but in relatively small numbers; the large flocks which are a familiar sight on many inland waters are composed largely of winter migrants. About the size of a Wigeon (which is a dabbling duck) and not dissimilar in colour, Pochards are known as Wigeon Divers. Pochards do dive for their food, but not very deep, nor do they stay down for very long. Many of the plumage names refer to the chestnut-red head of the male. He also has a startlingly red eye, which gleams redder still when he is sexually excited. The rather squat shape of the head is also the subject of two names Bull-headed and Great-headed Wigeon. The female whose delicate gradations of brown and grey-brown merge simply into a dark shape at any distance, is called a Dun Poker, Dun Curre or Dun Bird, (the last a name which fowlers sometimes used indiscriminately for any small duck).

Goldeneye
Bucephala clangula

Golden-eyed Garrot; Buffle-headed Garrot
Gowdy Duck (E Lothian; Orkney)
Whiteside (Westmorland)
Pied Wigeon
Grey-headed Duck; Brown-headed Duck *female*
Freshwater Wigeon (Ireland)
Mussel Cracker (Lancashire)

from various sounds associated with the Goldeneye:
Curre
Pied Curre (S and W England)
Rattlewings (Norfolk)
Whistler

as a diver:
Diver, or Doucker (Roxburgh)
Douker (Scotland)
Diving Duck (Shetland)
Popping Wigeon

Though never very numerous, these lively and attractive ducks scatter themselves widely over the waters of the British Isles during the winter months. They are very distinctive in appearance, compact in shape and with a curious, heavy buffel Head (from buffalo head). Male Goldeneye have a moss-green head which, unless you are very close, looks black. But even over a considerable distance the eye is caught by the gleaming black and white contrast of the rest of the plumage. The 'comb' of white against the black back, and the dramatic dash of white at the base of the bill are extremely conspicuous, although only two names, Pied Wigeon and Whiteside, relate specifically to this arresting colouration.

Goldeneye are usually to be seen in small groups on both salt and freshwater; they mostly spend the winter at sea, but come inland to breed in freshwater sites. (The name Freshwater Wigeon comes from the region around Strangford Lough in Ireland, but the species is not known to have bred there.) Goldeneye are enormously active divers, often spending over twenty seconds beneath the water to three or four above. Generally speaking they are rather nervous of people, but the beautiful golden eye which gives the species its most widely used name is very apparent if you can get near enough to see the head clearly. Not notably vocal ducks, Goldeneye occasionally emit a faint 'krrr', from which come the Curre names. A more obvious sound is the noise of its flight which has been described both as a whistle and a rattle. T. A. Coward says that it reminds him of 'the ring of thin ice cracking under the bows of a boat', he once heard the whistling wings of a Goldeneye from fully half a mile away.

Up until 1970 Goldeneye had only twice been reported nesting in Britain, but they now seem to be quite established as a breeding species in Scotland. The *Atlas of Breeding Birds* shows nineteen dots for the Goldeneye (denoting fourteen possible breeding sites, three probable and two confirmed) and since the *Atlas* survey period several more sites have been confirmed. Goldeneye normally nest in deep holes in the stumps of trees but many of the Scottish birds have been raising young in nestboxes, judiciously placed for them in likely places. This is not always a simple procedure as shown by the experience of M. A. Ogilvie with a pair of Scottish Goldeneye:

> They breed in a nest box put up beside what was thought to be a perfectly suitable water. The female Goldeneye, however, has other ideas and each year leads her brood safely over a railway line, a main road and a river, to another loch more than a kilometre away.
>
> (quoted in Sharrock's *The Atlas of Breeding Birds*)

Long-tailed Duck

Clangula hyemalis

Sharp-tailed Duck
Swallow-tailed Sheldrake
Long-tailed Hareld
Sea Pheasant (Northern England)

from the cry:
Caloo; Calaw (Orkney; Shetland)
Darcall
Coldie (Forfar)
Coal and Candlelight (Orkney)
Col-candle Wick (Fife)

others:
Northern Hareld (Aberdeen)
Ice Duck (Northumberland)
Mealy Bird (Norfolk) *young*

Most of the names for the Long-tailed Duck come from the northerly regions where the duck is most plentiful. It is almost exclusively a winter duck as far as we, in Britain, are concerned, except for an occasional few seen in summer in Orkney and Shetland, and it has taken some wintry names such as Ice Duck and Coldie. The long tail of its name is possessed by the male only, and consists of two exceptionally long central tail feathers which may reach a length of twenty-four centimetres. During courtship the male emphasises the length of his tail by tilting forward and holding his tail almost vertically erect.

Hareld comes from *Haveld* the name for this duck in Iceland where it is an abundant breeding bird. The Longtail is the best diver of all sea duck; it can go to an incredible twenty metres in depth, sometimes staying below the water for more than a minute. In fact, when feeding, these duck spend more time below the surface than above. Like other sea duck which congregate in large 'rafts' in the northern seas Long-tailed Duck suffer considerably from the effects of oil pollution.

Caloo, the commonest name for the Long-tailed Duck in Scotland is an imitation of its musical double call. This call will carry over nearly half a kilometre. It is also rendered Coal-and-can-le-licht, which not only contains the sound of the call but carries subsidiary visual associations. The winter bird is charcoal-breasted; it also has white flanks, the colour of tallow, there is some resemblance in the long tail streamers to an old fashioned woven wick for a candle, and the whole shape of the bird is something like an old candle-holder.

Velvet Duck
Black Diver
Great Black Duck
Double Scoter
Astracannet (Northumberland)

Velvet Scoter
Melanitta fusca

Black Duck (Essex; Norfolk; Ireland)
Black Diver (Ireland; Northumberland)
Surf Duck (Scotland)
Sea Duck (Norfolk)
Doucker (Lancashire; Westmorland)
Sea Hen (Northumberland) *female*
Whilk
Scoter Duck; Scoter

Common Scoter
Melanitta nigra

The name Scoter may be derived via the old Norse from the Old English *sceotan* meaning to move rapidly. The Norse have a better acquaintance with these birds than we do, both Common and Velvet Scoters are resident along the northeastern Scandinavian coast. A few Common Scoter breed in Scotland and Ireland but we know them mainly as visitors in winter, when large flocks of these big, black sea ducks come to our coasts. The Common Scoter is the only duck which is black all over. The larger Velvet Scoter, the Great Black Duck, has a small white crescent behind the eye and a white wing bar, but these are not easily visible at a distance.

Willughby differentiates between Common and Velvet Scoter in his *Ornithology* of 1678, but the word Scoter was well known before that, at least since 1537, and at that time probably denoted both birds. The French call the Scoter *Macreuse* and in Normandy there is a tradition that it may be eaten without qualm during Lent. Hequet, in a book on Lenten dispensations published in 1709, classed the *Macreuse* with beavers and turtles in the amphibia: 'ambiguous creatures of doubtfull origin and uncertain genus'. A proverb quoted by Swainson goes '*Il ressemble une macreuse; il n'est ni chair ni poisson.*' (A French equivalent of our common saying, 'neither fish nor flesh—nor good red herring'). This definition was very convenient for the people on a coastline where neither the original Lenten bird-fish the Barnacle Goose, nor a substitute, the Puffin, were likely to be found.

Bewick refers to the custom in his *British Birds* and attempts an explanation; 'these birds and a few others of the same fishy flavour, have been exempted from the interdict [Lenten prohibitions], on the supposition of their being cold-blooded and partaking of the nature of fish.' Bewick also remarks on the diving abilities of the Scoters who 'seldom quit the sea, upon which they are very nimble, and they are indefatigable expert divers . . .' As one would expect, they have several Diver, Douker, Sea, and Surf names.

Scoter are unusual among diving ducks in that they open their wings underwater when diving, though they do not actually 'fly' underwater. The powerful legs, set well back on the body propel the bird with strong, lateral strokes and the partly opened wings are used to stabilize it as it feeds from the bottom. In winter Scoter usually congregate in large flocks. They are vulnerable to oil pollution and five oil spills in the Baltic between 1969 and 1971 were responsible for the death of at least 7,700 Scoter.

Great Black-and-white Duck
Dunter, Dunter Goose (Orkney; Shetland)
Dusky Duck
Colk
Crattick (Scotland)
St Cuthbert's Duck, Cudberduce (Northumberland)
Edder; Eider
Culverts (Northumberland)
Coo-doos
Dunter Duck

Eider Duck
Somateria mollissima

The Eider is a large handsome duck, the most abundant sea duck in the world. The European wintering population alone is about two million. They are resident along our northern coasts, and reach down to more southerly regions in winter. Powerful and adroit swimmers, they pass unconcerned through the most turbulent waters and around spiteful rocks and reefs, diving for molluscs and crustaceans. Food too big to be swallowed comfortably, they break open in the strong, crushing beak. Eiders sometimes climb out of the water to sit peaceably upon the rocks, or at low tide to search for crabs and molluscs. There is an Orkney saying: 'as lazy as an Eider'; this may refer to their resting periods or the drakes' habit (in common with most duck species) of deserting the female during incubation and having no hand in looking after the young.

For the whole of the incubation period which lasts about twenty-six days, the female stays at the nest refusing under almost any circumstances to leave the eggs. Mr W. H. St Quentin noted that well before a captive Eider he was watching got up from the nest, she and the nest had become overgrown with chickweed which had sprung up during the incubation time. When the young are hatched they have to survive a perilous journey to the sea. A mortality rate of over fifty per cent has been estimated for these tiny ducklings in their first dangerous week of life, though their chances of survival improve after this point.

The Great Black-and-white Duck is clearly the male, his flanks, tail and the crown of his elegant wedge of a head, are black, the neck and mantle white. His colouration is more subtle than this name suggests though, a delicate pale green feathering the back of his head and a soft rose shading the lower breast. The Dusky Duck refers to the female, who is dusky dark brown all over with no distinguishing marks, though a barred effect is visible from close to. The birds are called St Cuthbert's Ducks, (sometimes contracted to Culverts) as they are reputed to have been specially beloved of the Saint during his solitude on the Farne Islands. Perhaps he was soothed by the soft crooning calls from which came the name Coo-doos. The name Culvert may have some association with Culver, used for another gentle voiced species the Wood Pigeon.

Eider ducks were always very much sought after for the soft down with which they line their nests. By the end of the eighteenth century, the word eiderdown had assumed the current meaning of quilt (originally of real Eider down, but nowadays of any kind of feather—just as the duvet which used always to contain swan's or duck down has come to mean any kind of continental quilt).

from the bill:
Lesser Toothed Diver
Sawbill (Aberdeen; Stirling; Galway)
Sawneb (Aberdeen)
Sawbill Wigeon (Galway)
Sawyer (Suffolk)
Sandbill (Sussex)
Spear Drake (Sussex)
Spear Wigeon (Sussex)

from the Icelandic haveld = *duck (also Long-tailed Duck):*
Herald (Shetland)
Herald Duck (Forfar; Shetland)
Harle (Orkney)
Herle (Northumberland)
Land Harlan (Ireland)
Earl Duck (Scotland); Yearel (Northumberland)

various:
Bardrake (Co Down)
Rodge
Grey Diver (Islay)
Tuke (Sussex)
Popping Wigeon (Ireland)

Red-breasted Merganser
Mergus serrator

from its bill:
Sawbill (Stirling)
Sawneb (Aberdeen)
Jacksaw (Yorkshire)
Sawyer (Suffolk)

male:
Shell Duck (Ireland)
Pied Wigeon (Shropshire)
Green-headed Goosander

female:
Dun Diver (Sussex) *also immature*
Harle *also immature*
Sparkling Fowl; Sparling Fowl

various:
Land Cormorant (Dublin)
Rantock (Orkney)
Spear Duck (Sussex)
Spear Wigeon (Kerry)

Goosander
Mergus merganser

These two closely related species are similar in appearance and share many of their local names. The male Goosander is a very large duck and

61

differs from the smaller Merganser in having a buff-salmon tint to the white of its breast and flanks, whereas the Merganser has grey flanks and the striking chestnut breast which gives it the epithet Red-breasted. The females with their chestnut heads and grey backs are much more like each other than their respective mates, so much so in fact, that in the eighteenth century it was believed that they were a separate species – the Sparkling Fowl or Sparling (sprat) Fowl.

Both species are in the genus *Mergus* which also forms a part of the Merganser's name: *mergus* = to dive or dip, plus *anser* = goose. Goosander seems to be a hybrid name, possibly composed by the addition of the Scandinavian *gøs* = goose, to the Old Norse *ond* = drake. These duck dive and swim with power and speed. They are largely fish-eaters, and a characteristic of all Merganser species (which includes the Smew) is the sawbill, the serrated edge of the fierce, slim bill, an ideal tool for grasping and holding fish. The Merganser is more of a marine species than the Goosander, mostly fishing in estuaries and bays, except in the breeding season; the Goosander spends much of its life on reservoirs and freshwater lochs.

The Merganser has a much longer recorded history than the Goosander. First mentioned in the ornithological glossary of Aelfric the Grammarian (998), it also has a longer list of names. Many of these are formed from the Icelandic *haveld* = duck (a name also used for the Long-tailed Duck).

In France the standard name for the Merganser is *Harle* and this forms part of a number of British names, both for the Merganser and Goosander, such as Harle itself, Herle, Land Harlan and Earl Duck. The earliest reference to a 'Gossander' is in 1622 but the first record of a successful breeding came as late as 1871 (not the same pair!).

Smee; Smee Duck (Norfolk)
White Nun (Ireland)
White-headed Goosander
White Merganser; White Wigeon (Devon)
Magpie Diver (Ireland; Kent)
Lough Diver *female and immature*
Red-headed Smew *female*
Pied Diver
Vare Wigeon *female and immature*
Weasel Duck (Norfolk; Northumberland)
Weasel Coot (Norfolk)
Small Herring Bar (Sussex)

Smew
Mergus albellus

The Smew is the smallest of the mergansers, and it is likely that the word Smew is an old variant of small. Writers of the seventeenth and eighteenth centuries sometimes used smew adjectivally in compound names such as Smew Merganser or Smee Duck. Though only a winter visitor to England and parts of Scotland and Wales, the Smew is a striking bird and attracted the attention of the early ornithologists, figuring in both Merrett (1666) and Willughby (1678).

As with other mergansers, however, there was considerable question about the sexes. Willughby uses the name Smew but it comes under a main heading White Nun, a name which refers to the male Smew. A white bird marked with a web of black lines, he seems to epitomise winter: white ice cut with black cracks.

The Smew is also called the Magpie Diver. In flight the black of the shoulder and wing primaries is exposed and the male Smew gives a much more pied impression. Like the female Red-breasted Merganser and Goosander, the female Smew is grey, white and chestnut brown. She has, however, a slimmer and more sharply delineated line of chestnut on her head, which sharpens the appearance making it rather weasel-like; hence Weasel Duck and Vare Wigeon, *vare* or *vair* being a Middle English name for a stoat or weasel (it is also used in heraldry to denote ermine).

Shelduck

Tadorna tadorna

Sheldrake
Skeldrake; Scale Duck (Orkney)
Skeel Goose; Skeel Duck (Scotland)
Sheld Fowl (Orkney)
Shell (Yorkshire)

from its nesting place:
Burrow Duck
Bar Gander (Essex); Bar Goose; Bergander
Bar Duck (Ireland)
Bay Duck (Norfolk)

other names:
Links Goose (Orkney)
St George's Duck
Pirennet = *pied ent* = pied duck
Stock Annet (E Scotland)
Sly Goose (Orkney)
Sly Duck (Yorkshire)

Shelduck are large handsome birds, their tortoise-shell colours clearly marked out: white, chestnut, black and a dark green head that looks almost black at a distance. The word 'sheld' is exactly appropriate, a dialect word meaning variegated or particoloured. They are usually found on or near salt or brackish water, although with the increase in breeding numbers some birds have been moving further inland, but seldom more than twenty kilometres from tidal water. The preferred nesting place is a hole or old burrow in a sand dune or bank from which we get the names Burrow Duck, Bar Gander and Bergander.

The males will defend their own territories, an unusual feature in duck, but a number of Shelduck often nest close to each other and there is competition for nest sites. Another unusual point of behaviour is that a 'cuckoo' female without a nest of her own may drop swiftly into another's nest and, stimulated by the sight of eggs, lay her own among them. This process may even happen twice and an average clutch of eleven or so eggs be augmented to perhaps as many as thirty-two, all of which the first female will incubate. Surprisingly, most of them will hatch.

Within a day or two of hatching, the young

Shelduck are led by the parents to the sea. This may be a long journey for ducks with an inland nest. T. A. Coward had personal experience of a family of Shelduck who nested by the edge of a Cheshire mere nine miles from the nearest salt water:

> On one occasion I met the ducklings with their parents just after they had left the burrow, and the inexperienced infants came cheeping to meet me, heedless of the agonised cries and extravagant behaviour of their parents, and allowed me to take them in my hand. Later they learn wisdom and on the shore run with wonderful speed; on the water they dive with skill, and I have seen a brood tire out an energetic retriever and never be in danger.

(The Birds of the British Isles)

Wild Goose
Fen Goose; Marsh Goose
Stubble Goose (East Lothian)
Grey Goose

Greylag Goose
Anser anser

This name is nowadays written as Greylag Goose but in times past it has been Grey Lag Goose and Grey Lag-goose. There are two schools of thought as to the interpretation of this name. The majority opinion seems to be that it came about because the Greylag, our indigenous goose 'lagged behind' when the other kinds of geese took off for other breeding grounds. For no reasons other than intuition, I personally prefer the alternative explanation that it was so called because it was a bird which grazed the field or 'leas'; 'lea-goose' turning with usage into 'lag-goose' in much the same way as the name for a nestling hawk 'a nias' became converted to 'an eyass'. The Greylag is also known as the Stubble Goose and there are many other parallel food names for geese: Bean Goose, Corn Goose, and Ware (seaweed) Goose.

The real Wild Goose population is now quite small, restricted to the very north of Scotland, and even there, the wild stock has been supplemented by released birds. Elsewhere the population is feral, descended at some time in the near or distant past from birds kept in captivity. The colony at Castlecool in County Fermanagh is thought to date from introductions at the beginning of the eighteenth century. The East Norfolk population can be traced back to two geese, unable to fly, brought in during the years of the Second World War. The Greylags which breed at Tring probably come from nearby Whipsnade – where they may return in the winter after having had a summer's freedom.

The Greylag is the traditional 'British Goose' often referred to simply as 'the Goose' in old books. The phrase 'Wild Goose chase' meaning an unsuccessful enterprise has an obvious literal meaning in that geese are extremely alert and liable to fly off at the first hint of danger. There may also be a tenuous association with the legend of the Wild Hunt for there is a strong tradition that it was geese which were the Gabriel hounds (see Curlew).

The words goose and gander are in fact related to each other, though they have taken different paths through the language. They are also associated with the latin *anser* which is preserved intact in Merganser (the 'diving goose'), and which constitutes the scientific name for the Greylag and the generic first name for a number of other geese. Some other European names bridge the gap between goose and gander: Spanish, *Ansar*; Portuguese, *Ganso;* French, *Oie;* Irish, *Goss.* Slavonic forms are: *Gus,* Russian; *Husa,* Czech; western forms: *Gans,* Dutch and *Gås,* Scandinavian. The Old English was *Gos* and it was from this that the baby goose or gosling was formed. All of these words have a dim echo of a 'honking' sound in them.

Geese had a special magico-religious significance in a large number of the earliest cultures from China, over Asia and India to Europe. The two strongest themes, solar symbolism and fertility, are traceable back at least to the land of Sumer (fertility) and ancient Egypt (sun symbolism), the latter from the birds' very high flight. Much later, in the Greek and Roman traditions, the goose had more of an explicitly sexual meaning. The goose was one of Aphrodite's birds and an Apuleian vase in the Fitzwilliam Museum (c 300 BC) shows Eros chasing a goose. The fertility aspect is preserved in some other parts of Europe. George Sand recorded that in villages in Berry, a dead goose was customarily carried in the procession of the bridegroom. We still innocently teach our children the nursery rhyme:

> Goosey goosey gander, whither shall I wander
> Upstairs and downstairs and in my lady's chamber.

Christianity had an uneasy time with the goose. Sometimes it absorbed old rituals. The equinoctial time of the slaughter of beasts which could not be fed during the winter, and the picking out of the stock animals for breeding, became known as the feast of Michaelmas. Dr Hartlieb, physician to the Duke of Bavaria, wrote in 1455 of the way goose was eaten on St Martin's day (on the Continent it was St Martin's feast rather than St Michael's) and he described how the breast bone was retained, and when it had dried, carefully examined. From the state of the bone was determined what kind of weather would follow. The Doctor reports also that he was assured that the Teutonic knights in Prussia waged all their wars by the goose-bone. As the goose-bone predicted, so they used to plan their two annual campaigns, the one in summer and one in winter.

This kind of augury continues, in a weakened form, right through to the present day; as the practice of eating goose diminished, passing to the duck and nowadays to the chicken. Even with the most unnatural of force-fed frozen chickens, most of us 'pick the wishbone'. In Morayshire, the weather predictions take another form:

> Wild geese, wild geese, ganging to the sea
> Good weather it will be;
> Wild geese, wild geese, ganging to the hill
> The weather it will spill.

67

There is also a belief which says that from the formation in which the geese fly, the number of weeks of frost to come can be deduced. Two distinctly different forms of attention to the goose can be found in Britain and Ireland. In the Celtic areas, the goose was a taboo creature, kept in enclosures for the purpose of sacrifice, but never eaten. Julius Caesar comments upon this during one of his campaigns. In other parts, the killing and eating of the goose was an important part of certain festivities. There was a saying 'If you eat goose at Michaelmas, you will not want for money all the year round', perhaps an optimistic survival of the augury which in its ancient form could predict bad times as well as good.

White-fronted Goose
Anser albifrons

White-faced Goose
Bald Goose
Laughing Goose
Tortoise-shell Goose (Ireland)

Giraldus Cambrensis, or more prosaically, Gerald of Wales, c 1146–1220, is one of the few chroniclers of the later twelfth century. He wrote of the Marcher Lords of Wales and their campaigns in Ireland with brilliance (and some say, excessive imagination). But there is no reason to suspect partisanship in his ornithological records and he seems to have been the first to write about the White-fronts. They were not however, called White-fronted Geese until Thomas Pennant named them as such in 1766, after the broad and conspicuous white band at the base of their bills. (White-faced Goose is also a name for the Barnacle Goose.) Another name, Laughing Goose, used by Edwards (1743–64), arose from the loud harsh cries which the geese make and seems to have applied only in the north of England.

White-fronted Geese are winter visitors. They are predominantly bog birds typically preferring to feed on marsh and estuary than in fields, though in recent times they have taken to grass and clover meadows. There was considerable concern among conservationists when a boggy area in southeast Ireland, known as the Slobs, which is the only remaining wintering place of the huge numbers of the Greenland race of Whitefronts, began to be drained and claimed for agriculture. The Irish government bought some of the most important places to maintain as a reserve for the benefit of these Geese but surprisingly (for White-fronts have deserted other drained areas in Ireland) the Slobs colony seemed completely at home on the new agricultural land and had taken to feeding on potatoes, winter wheat, carrots and peas and appear to have benefited from the reclamation of land.

Corn Goose
Wild Goose (Ireland; Scotland)
Small Grey Goose
Grey Goose (Sussex)

Bean Goose
Anser fabalis

Grey Goose (Sussex)
Long-billed Goose (Yorkshire)

Pink-footed Goose
Anser brachyrhynchus

These two species are very similar in appearance and closely related, some authorities regarding the Pink-footed as a subspecies of the Bean Goose. The Bean Goose is a dark bird, with a mainly black bill, crossed by an orange band, and orange legs. The call is a soft 'honk'. It is a fairly uncommon winter visitor to Britain, only perhaps one or two hundred visiting southwest Scotland and Norfolk. They were called Bean Goose by Thomas Pennant from their feeding in the fields on the field bean *(Vivia faba)*, then grown more extensively than it is today. The French name is *Oie de moissons* or Harvest Goose. In Germany and Scandinavia it is *Saatgans* or *Sädgås,* that is 'seed goose' and a Russian name is *Gumennik* or 'thresher bird'. All these names are quite appropriate for this arable goose whose long, strong bill enables it to take grain roots and shoots, probing

Bean Goose
Pink-footed Goose

down for them even through a layer of snow.

There is a record of the Pink-footed Goose being called the Long-billed Goose in Yorkshire. This seems odd considering that the Pink-footed has a short rather ineffectual bill compared to that of the Bean Goose (or indeed many other geese). The Pinkfoot is rather greyer on the back than the Bean Goose. The bill is pink with a black base, and the legs and feet are also pink. Winter visitors, Pink-footed Geese arrive towards the end of harvesting and feed on stubble and grain, moving off to the coast later in the season. During this century they have also learned to like potatoes and Pinkfeet in most areas now feed on potatoes as well.

Brent Goose

Branta bernicla

from its cry:
Rott Goose; Rat Goose
Road Goose; Rood Goose
Clatter Goose (East Lothian)
Quink Goose
Crocker

various:
Brand Goose
Ware Goose (Durham)
Horie Goose; Horra Goose (Shetland)
Brabt (Norfolk)
Black Goose (Essex)
Barnacle (Ireland)

Brent are small attractive geese, hardly as big as Mallard, and in shallow water they are often to be seen 'up-ending' like ducks in order to reach submerged vegetation. Most of Europe's population of Brent Geese move southwards from their breeding territory in the tundra to spend the winter on the British, French and Dutch channel coasts.

The Brent, or sometimes Brant, Goose is so called because it is a dark, charred-looking (or burnt) colour. The call is more of a low cluck than a honk and from this come the several echoic names Rott, Crocker and Clatter Goose. It is also known as Quink and it is possible that the brand of ink of the same name was called after the goose-quills which were used as pens. Brent are geese of the sea and tidal estuaries, feeding on marine vegetation, known as 'sea ware' in the north, mostly eel grass (*Zostera* species) hence the name Ware Goose. The dependence on *Zostera* led to a decline in the population of Brent during the early seventies when a widespread disease killed much of this food. There is now a recovery both of the *Zostera* and the numbers of geese. In some parts the Brent is confused with the Barnacle Goose and both species share the same name. Something of this mistaken identity is reflected in the scientific name for the Brent which is *Branta bernicla*. It is known also as a Black Goose, distinguishing it from 'greys' such as the Greylag, Pink-footed and Bean Geese.

Barnacle Goose
Branta leucopsis

Bar Goose (Essex)
Clakis, Claik (Scotland)
White-faced Barnacle
Norway Barnacle (Ireland)
Rood Goose
Routhecock (Orkney)
Tree Goose

In his *The Herball or General Historie of Plantes* John Gerard reserves for the climax, the final entry, that rather special tree, 'the Goose tree, Barnacle tree, or the tree bearing geese', 'one of the marvels of this land'.

> They are found in the North parts of Scotland and the Islands adjacent, called Orchades, certain trees whereon do grow certaine shells of a white colour tending to russet, wherein are contained little living creatures: which shells in time of maturity doe open, and out of them grow those little living things, which falling into the water do become fowles, which we call Barnacles; in the North of England, brant Geese; and in Lancashire, tree Geese . . .

He goes on to give a personal account of having

71

examined some barnacles, describing in accurate detail the tiny feathery appendage (actually a modified 'leg') with which the barnacle plumes particles of food towards the mouth of its cone, an accurate piece of detailed observation from 1597. But if he was right that 'the first thing that appeareth is the foresaid lace or string' he let common belief rather than his own eyes take him on to write

> next come the legs of the bird hanging out, and as it groweth greater it openeth the shell by degrees, til at length it is all come forth and hangeth onely by the bill: in a short space after it commeth to full maturitie, and falleth into the sea, where it gathereth feathers and groweth to a fowle . . .

Gerard has been censured for prefacing this part with 'What our eies have seen and hands have touched we shall declare . . .' but while there is no gainsaying that what he wrote was not true, it was not an original mendacity. Stylistically, Gerard was echoing an Irishman quoted by Turner (1544) 'he had himself seen with his own eyes and handled with his own hands, birds still half formed' and a much earlier document, Giraldus Cambrensis' *Topographia Hibernica* written in 1185 following an expedition to Ireland with Prince John.

> I have frequently seen with my own eyes, more than a thousand of these small birds, hanging down on the sea-shore from a piece of timber, enclosed in their shells and already formed.

Giraldus also notes that even 'Bishops and religious men in some parts of Ireland do not scruple to dine off these birds at the time of fasting, because they are not born of flesh.' Edward Armstrong quotes several twentieth century sources which show that the Barnacle Goose is eaten still in Ireland during Lent and on Fridays. In places where there were no Barnacle Geese, other 'bird-fish' were adopted in their place; Puffins in Pembrokeshire; in France the *Macreuse,* probably the Velvet Scoter, and in Kent a bird–beast described as a 'Barneta' whose precise identification is obscure. Armstrong has also turned up some very interesting Jewish Rabbinical references which indicate that the question of whether the certain bird was fruit, fish or flesh and how it should be killed, was a matter of importance in the twelfth century.

The very earliest record is contained in Riddle Ten of the Exeter Book which though assigned to the eighth century may have been a written version of a traditional riddle poem of even older lineage.

> My beak was in a narrow place, and I was washed from beneath
> by the watery flood, sunk far
> in the ocean streams; and I grew up in the sea
> covered above by the waves and touching
> a moving piece of wood with my body.
> I was fully alive, when I came in black clothing
> from the embraces of sea and wood.
> Some of my trappings were white
> when the air and wind raised me living
> from the wave, and afterwards carried me far
> over the seal's bath. Say what I am called?

Giraldus Cambrensis is the first to link this bird-fish with the Barnacle Goose. Max Muller put forward the view that the name Barnacle Goose came about through a corruption of the adjective for Irish, *Hibernicae*, Ireland being the place where the legend seems to have had its roots. It is also said that the name of the goose preceded that of the cirriped, but the etymology of the word 'barnacle' is obscure. It is however of interest to see that as early as the tenth century, the word for Barnacle Goose in Irish was *guirann* the same word as is used in Irish and Scottish Gaelic for the barnacle, while the words are also the same in Welsh *(gwyrann)*.

The fact that the words for the Goose and the barnacle were homomorphs so long ago could indicate that the origins of the legendary association reach very far back in time. What is perplexing is that there is no known cosmology against a background of which this story would become explicable. Nor is there anything specific either in appearance or in behavioural characteristics which would link the Barnacle Goose with its namesake.

Several of the common names for Barnacle Goose are however quite easily explained. It is the only goose with a white face (White-faced Barnacle) and its call is a short sharp bark which gives rise to the imitative names Clakis and Claik. It is a winter migrant (not in fact from Norway but from high in the Arctic) to Scotland and Ireland. In some of its Irish wintering places, the Barnacle seems able to sustain itself in places which seem entirely incapable of supporting animals as large as geese. With its stubby but strong bill, it can forage the lowest vegetation; it can graze sea plantain not more than a centimetre high, pecking with extreme rapidity.

Canada Goose
Branta canadensis

Cravat Goose (Southern Scotland)

Canadas are large and impressive looking geese. Looking at the long graceful black neck with the white chinstrap which gives it the name of Cravat Goose, it is easy to see why the nineteenth century naturalist Jenyns, called them Canada Swans. These geese are now a familiar sight all over England and in certain parts of Scotland and Wales. They breed in a large variety of inland waters, not only ornamental lakes but reservoirs, flooded gravel pits, town lakes and large slow-flowing rivers. As one would expect from their standard name, Canada Geese are a North American species, specially introduced into Britain in the seventeenth century to grace ornamental waters.

The population seems to have remained pretty well restricted to parks and estates until well into the 1940s. The first Canada Goose survey was undertaken by the BTO in 1953 and it was about this time that farmers began to complain of them grazing their fields and stamping down the soil. One way of avoiding these problems (apart from shooting, or destroying the eggs) was to round up the geese during their summer moult when they are flightless, and to transport them to other areas, usually those where wildfowling was rife. The whole population of Canada Geese today is very probably composed of the descendants of birds who have escaped or been moved from their ornamental precincts. However, once settled in their new location Canada Geese proved highly uncooperative; unfrightened by human beings they would continue grazing close to the guns, and when persuaded to fly did not take to great heights but flapped languidly at tree height or less. This was not considered to be sporting.

The Canada Goose is now a common sight in England but probably because its increase in population is comparatively recent, it has only two names and both of these are 'book-names' rather than local ones. However, it looks as if the Canada is here to stay and perhaps as its presence becomes more and more familiar new names will be forged for it.

Cob *male*
Pen *female*
Cygnet *young*
Tame Swan
Wild Swan (Sussex)

Mute Swan
Cygnus olor

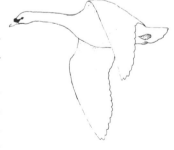

It is strange that since the nineteenth century, we have called this swan 'mute' when the old Anglo-Saxon 'swan' itself means 'sounder' (sound, sonnet, assonance come from the same base). The Mute Swan will give a deep hiss in anger and its vocabulary also extends to a trumpeting grunt and growls. But the true 'sounding' of this species does not refer to vocalized sound but to the strange and beautiful soughing of its wings as it flies. One of the Riddle poems of the Exeter Book, translated by Richard Hamer, describes the wing music:

> My dress is silent when I tread the ground
> Or stay at home or stir upon the waters

Sometimes my trappings and the lofty air
Raise me above the dwelling place of men,
And then the power of clouds carries me far
Above the people; and my ornaments
Loudly resound, send forth a melody
And clearly sing, when I am not in touch
With earth or water, but a flying spirit.

Another translation gives the last two words as 'travelling spirit' which may be linked with belief that the souls of the dead are transported into Swans, or that Swans accompany them to their resting place. In County Mayo it was only pure virgins who took the form of Swans after death, but within living memory there has been an instance of an old woman from the island of Uist, who believed a wounded Swan on Loch Bee to be her grandmother. It was also widely held that to kill a Swan would bring bad fortune, even death. There are many Swan stories and legends involving people turning into Swans, especially in Ireland, the land of Swans. In the story *The Wooing of Etaine*, Midir won the right to clasp King Ecochaid's wife, Etaine, in his arms, and when he did so flew off with her, the two of them in the form of a pair of white Swans.

It is not entirely clear to which species of Swan the myths properly belong. The Swans who lived along the River Avon were more likely to be Mute Swans than anything else, but when Ben Jonson called Shakespeare 'the Swan of Avon' he was alluding to the presence of these beautiful creatures and allying it with the legends of the Swans who held people enthralled with their song.

There may be only a few specific tales, the others being common to all the Swan species. Different versions of some of the stories appear all over Eurasia. There are also depictions of Swans on pottery and metal from the Bronze and Iron Age which indicate that Swan beliefs date at least from these times. A number of the variants of the 'Swan maiden' stories involve an aversion to iron, as for instance in the Welsh story where Wastin of Wastinog watched the Swan maidens for three moonlit nights, one after the other. He captured one of them and she agreed to marry and stay with him unless he struck her with a bridle and when, later, he accidentally did so, she flew off to the lake with their children and plunged in. A very early story, similar to this one, tells of a man whose wife decreed that he should never know her name, nor should he ever strike her with iron. By accident, once again, the fatal mistake was made. He tossed a bridle to her, and the iron bit struck her whereupon she flew away and vanished in the lake. One bold theory about the origins of these stories is that they were mythic interpretations of the Bronze Age peoples of the time when they were overruled and dominated by Iron Age Celtic invaders. But whatever the ultimate origins, the Swan has been an important symbol over centuries. Successive cultures absorbed the old stories and modified them to suit their own requirements. For example, Christianity changed the pathway of a tale by decreeing that swan-protagonists had to be baptised.

Since ancient times, the Swan has been a royal bird. Edward I had a Swan as his badge and on the day he knighted his son, two Swans were brought to Westminster as a part of the ceremony 'gorgeously caparisoned, their beaks gilt' and upon these Edward took an oath against the Scots. (It was also a custom in Germany in early times to swear upon the Swan). In 1387 Edward III passed protective legislation for Swans. They were very highly thought of as table birds and a large flock was very valuable. During the reign of Edward IV it was decreed that besides the King, only substantial freeholders might be granted a Swan mark designating ownership, and Henry VII imposed a sentence of imprisonment for a year and a day, in addition to a fine, for stealing a Swan's egg. To this day, the Crown has retained the right to the Swans on the Thames between London Bridge and Henley-on-Thames which it shares also with the Vintners Company and the Dyers Company. The Swan marks of the owners (nowadays a simple arrangements of 'nicks' or

'V's) are put on the young birds' bills at the annual 'swan-upping'. The mark of the Vintners Company consist of two nicks in the side of the bill and this is said to account for the unusual name given to several pubs in this area of the Thames: The Swan with Two Necks, a corruption of 'two nicks'. Swans are in fact a great favourite for inn names. In his 'The Ornithology of Inn Signs' W. B. Alexander reckoned that over a third of the total number of pubs and inns named after birds consisted of Swan names, more than any other single bird.

Because of the widespread practice of semi-domesticating Swans (in the time of Queen Elizabeth I there were no less than 900 recognised Swan marks), the histories of the tame and the wild birds are not easily distinguishable. Perhaps some of those 'games' of Swans were once wild stock, perhaps semi-tame birds were imported from other parts of Europe. It is now generally believed that all of the birds now living in Britain and Ireland are feral stock, but that there were once wild Mute Swans living here as they still do in Scandinavian countries. The present population has a large range extending to most inland waters; even quite small town ponds often have a resident pair of Swans. There is a wide spectrum of behaviour. Town Swans are often tame enough to take food from the hand, but some of those on the Irish and Scottish islands are as shy and wild as their truly wild Scandinavian relatives.

Whooper Swan

Cygnus cygnus

Whistling Swan
Wild Swan (Sussex)
Elerch (Cornwall)
Elk (Northumberland; Yorkshire)

The Swans who sing sweet songs to each other by the lakeside in Irish legend must take their voices from the Whooper Swans', or possibly the Bewick's, haunting cries. The name Whooper is imitative of the rising double note which takes on a different tone depending on whether the birds are feeding conversationally, calling to each other in flight or sounding in alarm. In the Irish legend *The Children of Lir,* the daughter and two sons of the king were turned into Swans by their wicked stepmother and sentenced to live nine hundred years on the Waters of Moyle. They sang so wonderfully that anyone who heard them fell under the spell of it and other birds would flock around them to listen. There is also a version of the Swan maiden legend which tells of how the hero Caer took the form of a bird and with a hundred and fifty Swans wearing gold coronets and silver chains sang so sweetly that anyone who fell within hearing went into an enchanted slumber for three days and three nights.

One would expect a bird with a beautiful and distinctive voice to be associated with singing and music. In Greece, swans are the birds of Apollo, the inventor of the lyre. As high-flying birds it was also natural that they should be associated with him in his role as the sun god. Swans drew the chariot of Apollo when he sojourned in the north for three months of youth, music and feasting. There is also a more intimate association, for Zeus conceived Apollo and his twin Artemis in the guise of a Swan, and in old astronomical works the Swan is often pictured with the Heavenly Twins.

There is however nothing in natural history to account for the legend that Swans sing before they die. Yet this idea of a swansong, recorded as early as Pliny, has come down to us in a literary tradition and become an idiomatic expression. It is possible that it was a story superimposed on to Swan beliefs by the people of the Mediterranean which was then passed into northern Europe by the way of the classics. Plato thought it an important enough idea to have Socrates speak of it on the day of his death. In the *Phaedo,* Socrates, facing his own end, says that the Swans sing not in grief, but for joy that they are going to meet the god whose bird they are. Apollo himself is interesting for the fact that, although the Greeks made him the son of Zeus and Leto, he was also the god of the Hyperboreans – 'beyond-the-north-wind-men' – whom Hecatus identified as Britons. The cult of Hyperboreans extended southwest to Palestine and northwest to Britain and included Athens, and visits were constantly exchanged between member states.

But if some of the poets took classical allusion for fact, this was not true of Michael Drayton who in lovely measured rational verse gives us his clear, admiring and truthful picture of the Whooper.

Here in my vaster pools, as white as snow or milk
In water black as Styx, swims the wild swan, the ilke
Of Hollanders so termed, no niggard of his breath,
(As poets say of swans who only sing in death);
But, as other birds, is heard his tunes to roat,
Which like a trumpet comes, from his long arched throat.

Bewick's Swan
Cygnus bewickii

Tame Swan (Sussex)

In 1830, two years after the death of Thomas Bewick whose finely drawn illustrations in his *History of British Birds* brought this very popular book into many family libraries, he was paid the compliment of having this Swan named in his honour. The writer of another milestone in ornithological publishing, *Yarrell's British Birds,* proposed that the newly defined species should be called *Cygnus bewickii*.

The Bewick's Swan is slightly smaller than the Whooper with slightly more delicate features, and it is also a winter visitor. They are faithful to their wintering grounds, and at the reserve at Slimbridge where they have been closely studied, individual birds have returned yearly for as long as twelve winters. The yellow and black pattern of the bill varies from bird to bird and many of the Slimbridge birds are known personally and their histories plotted. Some interesting evidence has emerged from this kind of study. One rather disquieting figure is that despite the fact that they are protected birds, over one third of the

---

Black Eagle
Ringtailed Eagle
Mountain Eagle
Erne

Golden Eagle
Aquila chysaetos

After years of watchful care and protection, the population of Golden Eagles, which fell to a dangerously low level about the middle of the nineteenth century, is beginning to pick up again, despite the continuance of illegal persecution. During the last few years the Osprey has rather eclipsed the Golden Eagle in the public eye, but more than any other bird it is still the Golden Eagle which is the symbol of Scotland. In a wider context it represents strength, wildness and freedom to many people who have never seen an Eagle.

Much of our Eagle symbolism comes not from Scotland but from the Middle east (via the Mediterranean) where the Eagle was an important symbol even before the time of the Sumerian civilization. There are Eagle-gods in the legends of Babylon and of ancient India, and double-headed Eagles are known from the city state of Lagash in the land of the two rivers, the Tigris and the Euphrates. Much later the Eagle was the bird sacred to the chief of the Greek gods, Zeus, as it was also to his Roman counterpart, Jove. Coins dating from 400 BC in the Greek city of Elis have Eagles on them. The Roman legions carried Eagle standards. The word Eagle, *Egle* in Middle English, comes to us via the French *Aigle* from the Latin *Aquilus*.

The Eagle is depicted with a snake in art and legend from earliest times. It is predominantly a symbol of light and the sky powers (including storms), whereas the snake represents the earth, and the two together form a kind of yin-yang opposition. It is possible that the Eagle represented on church lecterns has some distant connection with its supposed aversion to serpents. A more obvious explanation is that the four beasts of

81

Revelations were each assigned to an apostle: the lion to St Mark, the calf to St Luke, the beast with the man's head to St Matthew and the eagle to St John. It is therefore fitting that the lectern from which the gospel is read should be fashioned in the shape of the bird dedicated to St John, the bearer of the Word.

All over Europe and in North America there are versions of the story of how the Wren outwitted the Eagle in the election for the king of birds, springing from the Eagle's back at the last minute and flying higher. There is an interesting complementary tale in a fifteenth century manuscript, in which the birds compete a second time, in this instance to see who shall descend the furthest. The Wren wins again, this time by scurrying down a mouse hole. Here again there is opposition between the Eagle, the creature of the heights, and the Wren who flies down low to the ground; the Eagle who is large and conspicuous, the Wren small and secretive. The Eagle was an important bird in southern cultures, the Wren had a strong position in the mythology of northern Europe. Pliny writes of emnity between the Eagle and the Wren and Suetonius records that the Wren predicted Caesar's death. Perhaps, as might also be the case with the Raven and Eagle (see Raven), these legends of the Eagle and the Wren are echoes of an old conflict of beliefs.

But however the Eagle ideas came to us, they are now firmly a part of our own mixed culture. The Eagles of Rome have disappeared, as have those of the Tzars, but the power of America is symbolized in another Eagle, the Bald-headed Eagle. It is also the sign of one of our biggest banking groups. In our everyday language too, we talk of being swift as an Eagle or fierce as an Eagle and of being Eagle-eyed. This is a kind of verbal remnant of the sympathetic magic which enabled a person to take on the power of a bird or animal. This used to be done in a literal way by fletching one's arrows with Eagle feathers to make them fly fast and strong. Sometimes one killed or ate the subject in order to be endowed with its special characteristics. 'Eagle-marrow' was an ingredient for several old cures and prescriptions (despite the fact that it would be impossible to obtain, as Eagles, like all birds, have hollow bones).

Buzzard
Buteo buteo

Bald Kite
Kite (Ireland)
Goshawk (Ireland)
Buzzard Hawk (Forfar)
Gled (North Scotland)
Shreak (Gloucestershire)
Puttock (Scotland)
Puddock
Bascud, Barcutan (North Wales)

Considering that the Buzzard is a large and impressive and relatively abundant bird of prey, it has a scanty group of local names. It may be that most of the powerful folklore was attracted by the Golden Eagle and that preoccupation with falconry concentrated attention on hawks and falcons, and the Buzzard was overlooked. Several of the names used locally for the Buzzard (such as Goshawk and Kite) belong more properly to other birds. It is referred to another species even in its newest name, the Tourists' Eagle, a somewhat sceptical coinage by the Scots, to mark the way that visitors constantly mistake the Buzzards they see for Golden Eagles.

The word Buzzard is a French import which entered Middle English vocabulary as *busard* or *basard* and ousted our Old English name *tysca*. In America people still use Buzzard colloquially, in a derogatory sense, to denote stupidity or worthlessness; a slander upon the Buzzard unless you are speaking from the exclusive and limited point of view of the falconer, which is how the idiom originally came about. The *OED* gives an interestingly ambiguous late seventeenth century example of this usage: 'An Historian and a Libeller are as different as Hawk and Buzzard'.

By far the most fitting and descriptive name for the Buzzard is Gled, the glider, from Old English derivation. Close research on the Buzzard in Britain has shown that it hunts from a favourite perch such as a dead tree, rock or post (or telegraph pole) or hovering low over likely ground. The effortless soaring, on those wonderfully full wide wings, which is so typical of the Buzzard, has nothing to do with the practical business of hunting. Watching the slow graceful gliding on the thermals it is hard to believe that the Buzzard does not itself take delight in its actions, though strict ornithologists will tell you its purpose is entirely territorial display. Contrary to its reputation, the Buzzard usually kills for itself, though it does on occasion make use of a kill by another animal such as a fox, or of a creature which has died in a road accident. Rabbits and voles are important items of prey in the Buzzard's diet. It is called Puttock or Puddock in the East and Midlands indicating a dependence on frogs or toads. The Middle English word for toad is *padde* and in some parts of Scotland frogs are known as puddocks. Buzzards are very versatile hunters and frogs have been noted in the diet, but they usually form only a small proportion.

Sparrowhawk

Accipiter nisus

Blue Hawk (Berkshire; Buckinghamshire; Oxfordshire; West Riding; Stirling; East Lothian)
Blue Merlin (Perth)
Maalin (Shetland)
Gleg Hawk (Renfrew)
Pigeon Hawk (Yorkshire)
Gold Tip (Yorkshire)
Spar Hawk (Surrey; Scotland)
Spare Hawk (Scotland)
Spur Hawk (Scotland)
Stannin Hawk (Yorkshire)
Stone Falcon (Sussex)

You need a sharp eye to pick out the stealthy Sparrowhawk, among the trees in the mixed woodland and farmland which it haunts. Despite the severest persecution from gamekeepers and farmers, the species managed to hold its own and was fairly abundant all over Britain and Ireland until the widespread use of toxic chemicals half-way through this century accomplished in its torturous way what the gun had not. In 1963 the Sparrowhawk was made a protected bird; but, though with the banning of certain pesticides the situation looks brighter and many places are being recolonized, the overall population is still a fraction of what it was thirty years ago and nowhere is it common.

The Sparrowhawk is a small bird but its presence seems to carry with it a charge of excitement. To T. A. Coward it gave 'an impression of nervous tension and capacity for swift movement unequalled in any other raptor'. They are extremely effective hunters, lurking within trees, or flying low behind cover, then with a sudden turn of speed bursting in upon a flock of small birds and with verve and agility, eventually picking one of them off. The male, (the Blue Hawk, from the slatey grey of the wings and tail) is considerably smaller than the female and generally hunts Sparrows and Finches as well as Pipits, Wrens and Larks. The Tree Pipit is particularly vulnerable, especially at the time it is making display flights, fluttering up from an upper branch in a warbling spiral he is as good as advertising an easy breakfast for any lurking Sparrowhawk. The male Sparrowhawk is called a Musket in falconry and the early hand gun used by infantry was named after this (see Hobby for other gun-names). The female Sparrowhawk may be as much as ten centimetres larger than the male. An extremely capable and fierce huntress, she has been known to take Woodpigeons, fast birds and almost twice her weight, and far too large for a male to tackle.

In the case of Sparrowhawks, as with most other raptors which have suffered seriously from human malevolence over the years, the prejudice against them on the part of farmers and gamekeepers is not entirely a rational one. Intensive research shows that game birds form only a very small part of the Sparrowhawk's diet, and that farmers and game-keepers would not be unwise to foster a few of these hawks who catch many Corvids, Wood-pigeons and other seed-eating birds.

Goshawk
Accipiter gentilis

Goosehawk (Scotland)
Great Hawk
Tiercel *male*

This bird, aptly named Great Hawk, is like a huge, fierce Sparrowhawk. It also shares two of its names with the Peregrine falcon: Goshawk itself and Tiercel, and in many of the older records it is difficult to decide which bird is being referred to. James Fisher dates the first record of the Goshawk from Aelfric's *Glossary* (998). It has, however, probably not been numerous in Britain since the huge tracts of forest began to be cleared, though numbers would have been increased by 'escaped' birds from falconry. It became extinct in Britain and Ireland before the Osprey and it is only in the last few decades that it has returned to re-establish itself patchily and in very small numbers.

The word Goshawk itself comes from Old English *gos* = goose and *hafoc* = hawk, the goose being the largest potential prey. The word is now used generally for the species as a whole but falconers used only to call the larger female bird by the name Goshawk (the male was a Tiercel, the same as a Peregrine). In fact, a goose would be a very large victim even for a female to claim. Goshawk have a throaty chattering call and a high, long-drawn-out cry which Sir Walter Scott thought like a whistle, but certainly an evocative sound. . .

> . . . shrill
> As a Goshawk's whistle on the hill.

Red kite
Milvus milvus

Fork Tail (Yorkshire)
Crotch Tail (Essex)
Gled, Glead, Greedy Gled (N England, Scotland)
Puttock
Glead Hawk (Cheshire)
Scoul (Cornwall)
Baegez (Cornwall)
Forky-tailed Kite (Sussex)
Barcud, Bascud, Bascutan (Welsh)
Bod, Bodfforchog = fork-tailed kite; *Bod Wennol* = swallow-tailed kite; *Boda Chwiw* = whistling kite (Welsh)

It is sad that today the only kites to be seen soaring in the skies are the manufactured ones, and not the magnificent bird of prey, once common, after which they are named. Hand-kites were introduced to Britain in the seventeenth century, a time when Red Kites were abundant and widespread and their careless soaring, and easy gliding flight were a frequent sight above cities just as much as over the surrounding countryside. At this time, as in the Middle Ages, Kites were accorded a special tolerance (as are Black Kites in cities such as Cairo), for their scavenging habits made them useful attendants on the drainless and insanitary cities. As late as 1777 Thomas Pennant reports that Kites bred in Grays Inn and were widespread over the rest of the country. A couple of centuries earlier Turner wrote of the Kite as 'abundant and remarkably rapacious'.

Towards the end of the eighteenth century the history of the Kite took a turn which eventually brought it near to extinction in the British Isles. The gradual process of cleaning-up and draining the cities began. In the country, obsessive ideas about the protection of game from its natural predators to allow more scope for its human hunters led to a continuous and savage assault upon the once welcome Kites. The twentieth century was just dawning when a few Welshmen grouped together to defend the last remaining Kites from oblivion. Despite their resourcefulness and continuing patience, it was fifty years before the small population showed any sign of firm increase and even today the population is only shakily holding on at a level of about eighty birds. There are several Welsh names for the Red Kite and in the resurgence of national feeling among the Welsh, it has become something of a national symbol.

Kites are faithful to their traditional breeding territory and this last colony in the retreats of the steep oak-covered hills of Cardiganshire is likely to remain situated in Wales. Nests are made in the crotches of old trees, on the foundations of a previous structure made by a raven, or buzzard. This is repaired and the inside lined with wool, and interwoven with pieces of cloth, and bits of paper and plastic, found or taken from human settlements. That the addition of 'something borrowed' in the nest-materials is not a modern trait is borne out by Autolycus in *The Winter's Tale,* himself 'a snapper-up of unconsidered trifles'. He gives a warning applicable to both himself and the Kite: 'When the kite builds, look to your lesser linen.' If, as Turner says, 'this kind is wont to snatch food out of children's hands in our cities and towns,' Kites probably did snatch the odd item off clothes lines. It makes a poor reflection to contrast this past boldness with the nervy fearfulness of the remnant of their successors. Kites were not designed to be great hunters, being relatively weak-footed compared to eagles or hawks, and they catch only small birds and mammals. They prefer to find carrion. Their niche is as scavengers. If they were to become established in more parts of the country they might find a benefit in the high animal mortality on the roads which could form a very positive contribution to their diet.

White-tailed Eagle

Haliaeetus albicilla

Sea Eagle
Erne (Orkney; Shetland)

This splendid bird, bigger and more powerful than the Golden Eagle, with the plaintive yelping cry, was known to the people of Britain over a thousand years ago as it no longer is to us. It appears in one of the most beautiful Anglo-Saxon poems, *The Seafarer,* adding the final touch of loneliness to a scene of rocks and savage seas where calling seabirds made the only company. These are the last lines of this section in James Fisher's translation:

> Storms there, the stacks thrashed, there answered them the tern
> With icy feathers; full oft the erne wailed round
> Spray feathered . . .

Bog Gled (East Lothian)
Duck Hawk; Snipe Hawk (South of Ireland)
Marsh Hawk; Moor Hawk; Moor Buzzard
Dun Pickle (Wiltshire)
Brown Hawk (Ireland)
Bald Buzzard (Essex)
White-headed Harpy
Puttock
Kite (Ireland)

Marsh Harrier

Circus aeruginosus

A weather prognostic quoted by the Reverend Swainson says that in Wiltshire it used to be said that Marsh Harriers alighted in considerable number on the downs before rain. It still rains in Wiltshire, but Marsh Harriers in numbers will not be seen. The *Atlas of Breeding Birds* was pleased to report that one pair of Marsh Harriers had bred in western Britain in 1973 and 1974. Any other Marsh Harriers seen there are in all probability birds of passage. There are a handful of sites where it is thought that the birds might possibly breed, but only in Suffolk do they regularly raise young.

Phragmites reedbeds are the site for the Marsh Harriers' large platform nest. The beautiful acrobatics of courtship are performed just above the level of the reeds, the great wings looking prodigiously large so close to ground level. Here their colours are seen at best advantage, the slate-blue, brown and black of the male, and the sombre brown of the female picked out by her bright yellow head. High in the air the colours vanish but the shapes are unmistakeable as the birds soar and glide, wings tilted upward, pinions outstretched, as large as a Buzzard but the wings with a straighter line to them. One name is Bog Gled, or glider of the bog. Despite its large size, the Marsh Harrier does not take particularly big prey, hunting mostly small or young mammals. They will also take birds including both duck and snipe, although these loom more largely in the minds of the humans who gave the names Duck Hawk and Snipe Hawk, than they do in the diet of the harrier.

Hen Harrier

Circus cyaneus

from male plumage:
Blue Hawk (East Lothian; Wicklow)
Blue Kite (Scotland)
Barcud-glas = blue hawk, *Bod-glas* = blue kite (Welsh)
Blue Sleeves; Blue Gled (Scotland)
Grey Buzzard (Hampshire)
White Hawk; White Kite (Donegal)
Miller
White Aboon Gled (Stirling)

from female plumage:
Ringtail (East Lothian)
Brown Gled (Scotland)
Brown Kite

various:
Faller
Katabella (Orkney)
Furze Kite; Vuzz Kite (Devon):Gorse Harrier (Sussex)
Moor Hawk
Dove Hawk
Seagull Hawk (Connemara)
Hen Driver
Hen Harrow
Flapper (Caithness)

Free now from all but illegal persecution, the Hen Harrier is increasing its breeding range quite vigorously. It favours well-grown heather moorland or brackeny hillsides and it has penetrated down from Scotland into some of the northern counties of England and Wales where the habitat is favourable. Turner (1544) makes the first record of the Hen Harrier in his list of birds, stating that 'It gets this name among our countrymen from butchering their fowls.' Willughby, over a century later, has two separate entries, confused by the dissimilar plumage into believing that the male and female were different species. The Ringtail, the larger, female bird is a warm brown in colour; displaying a white rump and barred tail in flight. The male (the Blue Gled or Blue Sleeves) is an altogether slimmer, smaller bird, pearl grey with the curved-back black wingtips. He too has a white rump though not as conspicuous as the Ringtail's.

Hen Harriers hunt low, usually gliding against the wind and searching the ground for small mammals such as voles, rats and rabbits. It will also take the young of moorland waders and small passerines. In connection with the Connemara name Seagull Hawk, Leslie Brown notes particularly that gulls, especially young Common Gulls which are common on northern moorlands, appear to be distasteful to these birds. It seems more likely that Harriers were so-called not because they preyed upon gulls but because the male with its pale grey appearance bears a resemblance to a gull.

Osprey
Pandion haliaetus

Fish Hawk (Scotland; Shetland)
Fishing Eagle (Northumberland)
Eagle Fisher (Scotland)
Mullet Hawk (Hampshire; Kent; Sussex)
Bald Buzzard
Pysg eryi = fish eagle; *Gwalch y werlgi* = sea hawk (Welsh)
Iolair uisg = water eagle (Gaelic)

The Osprey is one of the few birds which regularly makes the headlines. Public interest in this splendid bird may be measured by the fact that up to 1975 over half-a-million people had made their way to the rather out of the way public hides at Loch Garten and Loch of Lowes in the hope of chancing to see an Osprey from the public hides. Admittedly the Ospreys are a speciality, but it is not only at Loch Garten but in reserves all over Britain and Ireland that people are prepared to confine themselves in small and uncomfortable hides in order to see birds which are wild and free. It was not so long ago that we were just as energetically putting the animals behind bars and inside glass cases.

Up until quite recently the Osprey was relentlessly persecuted on the pretext that they depleted the stocks of trout and salmon in the Scottish lochs. While it is certainly true that Ospreys do take trout on occasion, they have probably never been about in large enough numbers to do any serious damage, nor are trout by any means an essential part of their diet. Though Ospreys will make spectacular plunges into the water, they much prefer to take surface basking fish and not to dip too far below the surface. They will catch pike, carp, bream, roach and perch, as well as small trout and salmon, and one of their particular favourites is the grey mullet; some Ospreys will fly to the sea in order to catch mullet in estuarine waters. They are in fact much more successful in catching surface swimming fish, so much so that a superstition grew up that the Osprey had a fabulous power which attracted the fish into the upper waters. An early literary allusion to this belief is to be found in George Peele's *The Battle of Alcazar* (1594):

> I will provide thee of a princely osprey,
> That, as he flieth over fish in pools,
> The fish shall turn their glistering bellies up,
> And thou shalt take thy liberal choice of all.

Michael Drayton, too, mentions it in his 'Song' of Lincolnshire where, in 1613, Ospreys were often seen:

> The Osprey oft here seene, though seldome here it breeds,
> Which over them the Fish no sooner doe espies,
> But (betwixt him and them, by an antipathy)
> Turning their bellies up, as though their death they saw,
> They at his pleasure lye, to stuffe his glutt'nous maw.
>
> *(Poly Olbion)*

Towards the end of the eighteenth century a pseudo-scientific explanation of the superstition was attempted:

> They say that when (the Osprey) hovers over the water, it possesses a power of alluring the fish towards the suface, by means of an oily substance contained in its body. So much is certain, that if a bait is touched with this oil, the fish bite greedily that it appears as if it were impossible to resist.

By a bizarre linguistic accident, at the end of the nineteenth century when the worst slaughter of Ospreys was being perpetrated, a hat decoration called an 'Osprey' consisting of a little plume of feathers, came into fashion. (They were actually not Osprey feathers, though just as unpleasantly, these soft plumes came from South American Little Egrets and were often torn from living birds which had been captured.) Perhaps the 'spray' of feathers became confused with 'osprey'. The word Osprey itself was mentioned in its Latin form *Ossifrage* by Pliny to denote a Lammergeier. Translated as Osprey it was used for the species *Pandion haliaetus* by Turner in 1544. This usage has continued through to the present day (though other writers have called the White-tailed Eagle by the name Osprey).

Merlin (Berkshire)
Van-winged Hawk (Hampshire)
Tree Falcon
Robin, Jack *male*
Riphook

Hobby
Falco subbuteo

The Hobby is one of our most beautiful falcons. In flight it can look like a large and languid swift, its wings long and scythe-shaped flickering before each strong, graceful beat. The name Hobby comes to us via the French *hobereau* derived from the Old French verb *hober,* meaning 'to stir'. You need to see a Hobby hunting to realize how appropriate this derivation is. Hobbies usually hunt in the early morning or just before dusk, quietly lounging in a tree for the better part of the daytime. Its preferred habitat consists of small woods, from which it is called the Tree Hawk. As a prelude to the hunt, a Hobby will fly about in an apparently casual fashion, behind the cover of some trees. Then with extreme suddenness and speed it will skim forward like the bolt from a bow into a flock of swallows or martins. If the eye has failed to follow it, a localized whirlwind of wheeling and screaming small birds marks the spot where the Hobby has aimed. Sometimes it will stir up swallows going to roost, obviously without serious intent, perhaps simply for the sensation, but a healthy Hobby can pick off one of these fast-flying birds, whose flight its own so much resembles, whenever it cares to do so. It will also eat large insects such as dragonflies, but during the breeding season the pair will feed themselves and their brood largely upon small birds. It is possibly because its diet consists of insects and insectivorous birds that the Hobby has not suffered so seriously from pesticides as most other birds of prey (though it does eat skylarks which are partly seed-eaters). The Hobby is a summer visitor, appearing and disappearing with the hirundine flocks. It breeds, not abundantly, but over a fairly wide range in southern England.

Both Hobby and Robin used to be common diminutive forms of the name Robert, and though Hobby came into the language from a quite different root, it attracted the familiar 'Robin' as a name. It is interesting that when Thomas Helton translated Cervantes into English in 1620 he interpreted the Spanish *alcotan* which means Hobby, as 'Robbin ruddock'. The passage from *Don Quixote* alludes to the lightness with which a Hobby comes to perch.

> Stepping a little back, she (Dulcinea) fetched a rise and clapping both her hands upon the ass's crupper, she lighted as swift as a hawk upon the pack saddle, and sat astride like a man. Then said Sancho: "By Saint Roque! our mistress is as light as a robin ruddock, and may teach the cunningest Cordovan or Mexicanian to ride on their genets."

The modern Penguin translation by J. M. Cohen simply uses the more general word 'falcon'. It is worth comment that neither the seventeenth century nor the twentieth century translator felt that the Hobby was a well enough known bird to be translated correctly in this context.

Another use of the name Robin for Hobby seems to be in the word robinet designating a slender kind of cannon, a half to one pounder culverin of the seventeenth century. Other culverins were also named after birds of prey; there were sakers, falcons and falconets and the firearm known as the musket was named after the male Sparrowhawk. The Hobby is smaller than both the Peregrine Falcon and the Kestrel which maybe why it acquired another familiar name Jack, which usually indicates smallness of size.

Peregrine Falcon

Falco peregrinus

from plumage colour:
Blue-backed Falcon (N England)
Blue Hawk (Mid-Scotland; Ireland)
Spotted Falcon

various:
Game Hawk (Scotland)
Duck Hawk (Gloucestershire; Sussex)
Hunting Hawk (Somerset; N England)
Stock Hawk (Shetland)
Faakin Hawk (Aberdeen)
Goshawk (Ireland)
Perry Hawk (Yorkshire)
Tiercel Gentle (falconry; Western Isles) *male*

Peregrines were the falcons of kings and nobles and were protected by royal decree in the Middle Ages. Today they are again under special protection, under Schedule I of the Protection of Birds Act and they appear to be slowly recovering from a nearly disastrous decline which reached its lowest point in 1963. At this time the total Peregrine population was down to 44% of what it had been before 1939, and only 16% of that small number were rearing young. Up to this point, the Peregrine had been one of the most successful birds of prey, possessed of superb hunting skills and able to adapt to conditions and different kinds of habitat that other large predators would not accept. (It has been known to nest and rear young on Salisbury Cathedral, though not during this century.) It is now generally accepted that it was the widespread use of organo-chlorine pesticides in agriculture which brought the great bird down. Peregrines are large birds and need to catch a lot of smaller ones to survive; many of these small birds were seed-eaters, and the pesticides they had consumed were accumulated by the Peregrine Falcons who ate them. The effects were horrific and so was the death toll, but now at least, there is a partial ban on these pesticides, and it is totally illegal to molest Peregrines or interfere with their nests in any way. The population seems now to be in the region of 54% of the pre-war figure though only 25% bring up young.

It is ironic that it should have been complaints from racing pigeon owners that the Peregrine population had increased out of all bearing that brought about the BTO (British Trust for Ornithology) survey which brought to light the Peregrine tragedy. But it is not untypical. Not only Peregrines, but countless other birds of prey, have been heedlessly persecuted by gamekeepers, farmers and sportsmen, quite outrageously and erroneously overestimating the damage to their interests done by these birds.

There can be no doubt that the Peregrine Falcon is one of the surest and most magnificently skilful of hunters. It often flies high, soaring and gliding on its powerful blue-grey wings, a distant arrow head in the sky. It nearly always catches its food on the wing, observing the prey from as high as possible. Then, with wings folded back, it plunges into a sky dive of tremendous speed and power to strike its subject a ferocious blow with a foot armed with a sharp hind claw. It is known both as the Duck Hawk and as the Game Hawk but it is by no means restricted to these species; the 1962 survey recorded 1240 different items of prey, including 117 species of birds from little passerines to large gulls and mallard, and even Tawny and Little Owls.

The name *Falco peregrinus* was given to the Peregrine by an early naturalist Albertus Magnus of Cologne (1206–1280). The rather unwieldly latinate adjective 'peregrinatory' is still in our modern vocabulary, meaning wandering, and it seems that the Peregrine Falcon was so called because out of the breeding season it would move about with the best food sources. In falconry the male Peregrine was called Tiercel (Tassel or Tercel) Gentle, because it was about a third, that is a 'tierce', smaller than the Falcon (female). It may have been called 'gentle' because of its disposition, though this seems an unlikely epithet for a hunting bird, though they do have a good temperament and respond gratifyingly to training. The origin of this word may possibly go back to the concept of 'gentilesse' of the Middle Ages which had a very complex meaning, but which could be summarized as nobility of character, a title very fitting for a bird carried only by the highest nobility, assumedly 'gentil'.

---

plumage names (male):
Blue Hawk (North Riding)
Small Blue Hawk (Stirling)
Jack

habitat names:
Stone Falcon (North Wales; Scotland)
Rock Falcon; Rock Kestrel (North of Tyne)
Stone Hawk (Cheshire; Yorkshire)

various:
Sparrow Hawk (Scotland)
Hobby (Shetland)
Hawk Kestrel (Shetland)
Maalin (Shetland)
Tweedler (Lancashire)

Merlin
Falco columbarius

The Merlin is smaller than the Peregrine Falcon, to which the name Blue Hawk is more commonly applied. The Merlin's normal method of hunting is to chase down its prey, usually pipits or larks. Sometimes it will begin the chase with a Peregrine-like 'stoop' from a height. Merlins are birds of northerly moorland, some are resident in Britain and Ireland, but there are also winter birds and birds of passage.

Amongst the Merlin's prey are many beetles and moths of the moorland but, as with the Goshawk, it is thought to be named after the largest prey it might conceivably take. The name Merlin is believed to come via the French *Emerillon* from the

Latin *Merula* = Blackbird, a bird fully as large as the Jack Merlin. The Blackbird is occasionally, but not usually, preyed upon by the Merlin. The scientific name for the Merlin gives it the specific *columbarius* which rates the size of capture a little higher even than the standard English name, to a dove or pigeon. Possibly too it might have been thought that the Merlin, a lady's falcon, should catch something fittingly ladylike such as a dove.

During the breeding season Merlins are quite fearless in defence of their nest, and will attack birds many times their size and strength, even herons, peregrines or owls. Near by to the nest there is usually to be found a stony eminence, boulder or post, which the Merlins use as a plucking post and which is usually surrounded by feathers and bones of carcasses which have been plucked and prepared there for the young Merlins to eat. This is sometimes given as the reason Merlins are known also as Stone Falcons and Stone Birds, but as they are creatures of stony moorland, these are just as likely to be habitat names.

Kestrel
Falco tinnunculus

Creshawk (Cornwall)
Cristel Hawk
Stand Hawk (West Riding)
Stannel; Stanchel
Stannel Hawk
Stonegall; Steingale

from its motionless hovering:
Windhover (South and West England)
Hoverhawk (Berkshire; Buckinghamshire)
Vanner Hawk (Sussex)
Wind Fanner (Surrey)
Wind Cuffer (Orkney)
Windsucker (Kent)
Wind Bivver (Sussex); Windbibber (Kent)
Cudyll y gwynt = wind hawk (Welsh)

from the red-brown plumage:
Red Hawk (Stirling; Lancashire)
Clamhan ruadh = red kite (Gaelic)

various:
Kite (Shropshire)
Keelie (Edinburgh)
Maalin (Shetland)
Sparrow Hawk (Ireland)
Blood Hawk (Oxfordshire)
Mouse Hawk; Mouse Falcon (Yorkshire; Orkney)
Field Hawk (Surrey)

The standard name for this, our most abundant and widespread falcon, came to us from the Normans. Kestrel comes from the Old French *crecele,* the modern version of which, *crecerelle* means a rattle. This is probably imitative of the birds' clear 'kee-kee-kee' cry. There were two Old English names which became eclipsed by Kestrel (probably because of the predominantly French usage of falconers) but these survive in the form of local names. One of them, Stannel, is also based on the cry, from the Old English *stangale* or 'stone-yeller'. One of the origins of this name is that in the West Riding and on the Yorkshire moors the Kestrel would perch on stones and boulders rather than on trees, and make its nest on ledges, cliffs and rocky outcrops. The Orkney name, Mouse Falcon or Moosie Hawk, has its Old English counterpart in *Mushafoc.* Kestrels do hunt and eat mice but it is the short-tailed vole which is of greatest significance in their diet, and research shows that good vole years are generally years of high Kestrel population and vice versa. Voles were very hard-hit by the drought of 1976 and it has been obvious that this year was a trying one for rural Kestrels. In towns, where there is quite a high Kestrel population, they prey mostly upon small birds, and in Ireland where there are no voles, a high number of woodmice contribute to the diet.

Whereas the Sparrowhawk is a bird of forest, the Kestrel prefers open land, and the present state of affairs in the British Isles tends to favour the Kestrel. It could today just as well be called Road Hawk as Field Hawk, as it is now a familiar sight poised hovering above motorway verges and roundabouts. The pattern of modern farming also suits it very well (so long as the pernicious organochlorines, so damaging to its metabolism, are absent). As one would expect there are a number of names which allude to the Kestrel's most distinctive behaviour, the superbly controlled fluttering hover, from which it maintains a steady vantage on the ground beneath. Nor are our eyes deceived in believing the bird holds itself entirely motionless in the air. A surveyor correspondent of BBC Radio's *Living World,* recorded how he fixed his theodolite on the beak of a hovering Kestrel and observed that it stayed in the same position varying only within one centimetre, for twenty-eight seconds, after which it flew off.

Red Grouse
Lagopus lagopus scoticus

plumage names:
Red Ptarmigan; Brown Ptarmigan
Red Game

habitat names:
Moor Bird; More Cock; More Hen (Yorkshire)
Moor fowl (N England)
Gor Cock; Gor Hen (Scotland)
Heath Cock; Heather Cock
Moor Game (Cheshire; Yorkshire)
Moor Poot; Moor Pout (Yorkshire) *immature*
Coileach-fraoch = heather cock (Gaelic)
Cearc-fraoch = heather hen (Gaelic)
Moss Hen (Yorkshire) *female*

young:
Cheeper

Until as late as 1952, the Red Grouse was classified as a separate species (*Lagopus scoticus*) and as such was accorded the distinction of being the only species of bird confined to Britain alone. However, it is now placed by most systematists under the wing of the Willow Grouse, as a dark race of this species, *Lagopus lagopus,* and given a third subspecies adjective *scoticus.* Unlike its relative of northern Europe, the Red Grouse never turns white in wintertime. It has rich red-brown plumage which blends well with the colours and shades of the open heather moors where it lives, and most of the local names are colour names or habitat names.

The name Grouse itself occurs as *Grows* (referring to the Red Grouse) in 1531 but its origins are obscure. As these birds are best known for the pleasure it affords people to shoot at them, it is not surprising that by the end of the eighteenth century the bird's name had become synonymous with the act and 'grouse' was used as a verb meaning to go grouse shooting. The usage of 'grouse' meaning 'to complain' seems to have come into being as army slang at the end of the nineteenth century and thence into wider currency. Maybe the complaints of the soldiers were ridiculed by likening them to the raucous 'kuk-kuk-kuk-kuk' calls of the Grouse – and quite likely were dealt with quite as summarily. The Reverend Swainson interprets the call of the Grouse as 'Go, go, go, go back, go-o back'.

The final 'go-o back' crescendos into a loud crow which may be one of the reasons that the Red Grouse has so many 'Crow' names. The repeated 'go's' deep and raucous in the male, rather higher in the female bird, might have given rise to the names Gor Cock and Gor Hen. MacGillivray in his *History of British Birds* (1837–52) reports on a different interpretation of the whole cry in the north:

> the Celts naturally imagining the moorcock to speak Gaelic, interpret it as signifying 'Co, co, co, co, mo-chlaidh, mo-chaidh'' '*ie* Who, who, who, who (goes there), my sword, my sword.

The calling is at its height during the spring courtship when the males indulge in (largely exhibition) fighting which goes on even after couples have paired off. The Red Grouse have only one mate and the young (like the young of Partridges) are known as Cheepers.

Ptarmigan

Lagopus mutus

White game
White Grouse
Grey Ptarmigan
Rock Grouse
White Partridge
Snow Chick
Snow Grouse
Cairn Bird

The Ptarmigan is a bird of the mountains. It lives on the high ranges from Spain to Scandinavia. It inhabits the high tops above the heather line and feeds off the sparse vegetation of crowberry and dwarf willow, lichens and mosses. The earliest known man-made record of a Ptarmigan is not a written one; it is an engraving on a piece of reindeer bone, from the Stone Age times, found at Isuritz in the Pyrenees. In the British Isles there are a number of Ptarmigan fossils from the Pleistocene period, including some from the place where the Forest of Dean now stands. Nowadays, Ptarmigan are confined to the north-west of Scotland.

The word Ptarmigan comes from the Gaelic *tarmachan*. Similar names, now obsolete, are Termagant and Termigant. The 'pt' beginning seems to have been brought in by Sir Robert Sibbald in his *Scotia Illustrata* (1684), in a false analogy with Greek. Willughby (1678) calls it White Game or White Partridge, but later ornithologists preferred the pseudo-classical 'Ptarmigan' and this became the standard name.

The Ptarmigan has three moults in all during a year, its most famous plumage being the winter white, which disguises its presence against the snow. In summer plumage the upper parts are mottled brown in the male, with white underneath; the female has a buffer mottle, nearly all over. Autumn plumage is greyer in the male, more brown in the female. Ptarmigan will run and freeze or hide, relying on their plumage to conceal them from predatory eagles or hill foxes, looking as T. A. Coward says like 'running stones'. A Ptarmigan which does not match its surroundings is inconveniently conspicuous, as pointed out by Tennyson:

The ptarmigan that whitens ere his hour
Woos his own end.

In fact, the male Ptarmigan tends not 'to whiten ere his hour', but to remain in his white guise longer than the female who in her browny breeding plumage will already be looking for a spot in which to lay her large clutch of purple-brown mottled eggs.

Black Grouse
Lyrurus tetrix

Black Game
Heath Fowl; Heath Bird
Heath Poult (Hampshire)
Killockdoe (Scotland)

names for the cock bird:
Black Cock
Heath Cock

names for the hen bird:
Birch Hen
Brown Hen
Grey Hen
Grigear
Hasel Hen; Hazel Grouse
Heath Hen

names for immature birds:
Moor Pout, Muir Pout (Scotland)

The Black Cock, the male Black Grouse, is an impressive figure. Considerably larger than the Red Grouse, he is black all over except for a white puff of under tail coverts and blotches of white on the shoulder and wing. He is also possessed of a beautiful, long, lyre-shaped tail. Black Grouse have Heath and Moor names which they share with the Red Grouse but the moorland they inhabit is less open than the habitat of the Red Grouse, and often dotted with a few trees, usually birch, and some scrub. The female is known as the Birch Hen (there is no corresponding cock name). The Black Grouse population is densest where forest and moorland meet. They also live in boggy areas and in young conifer plantations. Heather is

103

the most important single item in their diet but they will also eat conifer buds.

The hen Black Grouse, the Brown Hen or Grey Hen, is considerably smaller than the cock and mottled grey-brown in colour, with a blunt fork to her tail. She is also known as the Hasel Hen or Hazel Grouse in some places, a name now used as a standard title for a small woodland Grouse of Eurasian distribution (*Tetrastes bonasia*). In the early mornings in spring, cock and hen birds assemble, often in large numbers, at the 'lek' and the cocks display and fight. They posture and dance with drooping wings with the tail fanned and erect to show the white underfeathers to best effect, and they sing in a soft bubbling dove-like croon, all to win themselves a harem from the watching hen birds.

Capercaillie

Tetrao urogallus

Auer-calze (Scotland)
Capercailzie
Cock of the Wood (Ireland)
Cock of the Mountain
Wood Grouse; Great Grouse

The Capercaillie is known as the Great Grouse and for good reason. It is the biggest Grouse of Northern Europe, fully as large as a Turkey. (There has been considerable dispute over whether fossil remains found in Irish caves were those of early Turkeys or Capercaillies.) There are definitely identified Stone Age Capercaillies at other caves, indicating a taste for this game bird which continued until the end of the eighteenth century when the birds became extinct in both Britain and Ireland. The last indigenous Capercaillies in Scotland were shot in Aberdeenshire in 1785 and the last Irish birds were wiped out some time about 1790. The present Scottish population consists of the descendants of Capercaillies which were introduced from Sweden during the nineteenth century. The reintroduction has been successful and the Capercaillie has recolonised most of its former range, principally east-central Scotland where there is now a healthy community of Capercaillies, especially in the ancient woodland of the Caledonian forest.

The Capercaillie is very much a bird of the woods; Cock of the Woods is a well-used name. It feeds mainly on the shoots, needles, cones and seeds of Scots Pine, perching among the branches with considerable agility for an animal so large. (In summertime it also eats fruit and berries, and insects.) The Capercaillie makes a great clatter with its wings as it takes off from the branches but once in the air, the flight is strong and fast but not sustained, like that of most Grouse. At a distance, the cock bird looks predominantly grey, but at close range, subtleties of colour are revealed: the black tip to the tail, the brown wings with the white fleck, the black beard and the glossy, blue-green breast. It was probably these colours and the fact that the cock fans his tail in courtship display which led Giraldus Cambrensis to call Capercaillies by the name of *Pavones* or Peacocks in his *Topographia Hibernica* in 1185. 'Peacocks of the woods' he writes 'are here abundant' (*Pavones silvestres hic abundant*).

There are several versions of how the word Capercaillie came to be. The nineteenth-century ornithologist William Yarrell lends his support to the school which descends it from the Gaelic *Capull coille* meaning 'horse of the woods'; that is a 'large creature' of the woods. However, the adjective 'horse' when used to signify large size – as with Horsefly, Horse Mushroom, Horse Thistle (Spear Thistle), Horse Thrush (Mistle Thrush) – is generally used together with the noun it is qualifying, in which case *Capull coileach* 'Horse-cock' would seem the more likely candidate for this interpretation. *Cabhar Coille* 'Old Man of the Woods' and *Gabar Coille* 'Goat of the Woods' are two other possibilities, these two referring to the goat-beard chin feathers of the cock. No one as yet has had the final word.

Red-legged Partridge

Alectoris rufa

French Partridge
Frenchman
Green Partridge
Red Leg
Red Partridge

Partridge

Perdix perdix

variations of Partridge:
Patrick (West Riding; Lancashire)
Pertrick (Aberdeen)
Pairtrick (East Lothian)
Paitrick (Ayrshire)
Girgirick (Cornwall)
Partrig (Yorkshire)

various:
Brown Partridge; Common Partridge
Grey Bird (Suffolk); Grey Partridge (Sussex)
Mountain Partridge (Kent)
Stumpey (Sussex)
English Partridge

There are nowadays so many of the introduced species, the Red-legged Partridge in the South and East of England, that it has forced a qualifying adjective on to the native bird, previously known simply as 'Partridge' (still 'officially' the standard name). However to avoid confusion, one is safer using English Partridge, Grey Partridge or Common Partridge. The latter two names have anyway, a respectable history. Though Turner (1544) called this species just 'Pertrige', Willughby (1678) used the double Common Partridge and MacGillivray (1837–52) introduced Grey Partridge which is a commonly used name in Sussex. English Partridge has come up as a name because the Red-legged is commonly known as the Frenchman.

The name Partridge comes to us via French and Latin from the Greek *perdesthai* which means 'to make explosive noises'. This could well describe the loud, hoarse rasp of the Partridge's voice or the sound of the bird rocketing away in panic as someone approaches too near to its hiding place. Laurens Sargent makes the nice suggestion that in the Middle English *Pertriche* may be heard an echo of the pear tree in which the Christmas carol bird was situated, which seems plausible; but what the original words and associations were, is lost to us today. The *Perdix* of Greek mythology (and of the scientific name) was a sister of Daedalus, whose son, a youthful inventor, was turned into a Partridge when his uncle, in a fit of jealousy, tried to kill him by pushing him off the top of a tower. He flew to safety, but retained the shape of the bird, and thereafter avoided the heights, always keeping near to the ground and reminding men of his story by telling it over and over again in his hoarse voice.

In certain of its details, this story accords with the biological facts. Partridges are running birds rather than fliers, preferring to go only short distances on their short, whirring wings, though while in the air the flight is fast and strong. Robert Burns called them 'ye whirring paitrick brood'. The story is of course, full of rasping noises, the Partridge's voice repeating itself and also the voice of the saw which Perdix' son is credited with inventing and which was part of the cause of Daedalus' envy. The majority of the British local names are variations of the name Partridge. Others are descriptions of its colour and shape, though Grey and Brown scarcely do justice to the beautiful soft grey neck and brown-streaked back, and the chestnut hatched flanks – and Stumpy is more than a little unflattering to its neatly rounded lines and short tail. Other distinguishing marks are the orange-brown head and a horse-shoe shaped patch of dark chestnut on the lower breast, very conspicuous in the cock bird, less so in the hen. These details are only afforded at fairly close range; at a distance, the bird does look the brown-grey of its names, a very suitable guise for a bird of light arable soils which prefers to freeze against its background rather than fly for cover.

The Red-legged Partridge shares many of the behavioural characteristics of the English Partridge but it is more specific in its habitat, preferring well-drained chalky or sandy soils and places with a relatively low rainfall. It is a larger bird than the English Partridge and has strongly barred flanks, and a black eyestripe and a necklace of black, spilling out over its lower throat. The first recorded introduction of the Frenchman was in 1673 and this was followed by numerous other importations. The race introduced is *Alectoris rufa rufa,* a native of Southern France (hence Frenchman and French Partridge) and of Switzerland, the northern parts of Italy and Corsica. Suffolk (1790) was the first place where the birds managed to colonize successfully, but nowadays it is in fact a more successful breeding bird in its adopted territory than the English Partridge. Red-legged Partridges often make two nests and lay two clutches, the cock bringing up one brood, the female the other. It is ironic that this species imported on behalf of sporting interests is in some places so much regarded as 'poor sport' that determined efforts have been made (with, however, no great success) to eliminate the bird which was once coddled and encouraged.

Quail
Coturnix coturnix

from the call-notes:
Wet-my-feet; Weet-my-feet (East Lothian; North of Ireland)
Wet-my-lip (West Norfolk)
Quick-me-dick (Oxfordshire)
Wet Weather (Sussex)
But-for-but (Cheshire)

various:
Quailzie (Scotland)
Rine (Cornwall)
Sofliar = stubble hen (Welsh)
Throsher
Wandering Quail
Corncrake (Sussex)
Deadchick (Shetland)

The name Quail is an imitative name cognate with 'quack'. This association becomes clearer when it is seen that it comes, via the Old French *Quaille* (a form used also by Chaucer), from the Latin *Quaquila*. The Quail's voice also gave rise to a number of imitative names in Britain and Ireland, which incorporate the three sharp notes. Among these are But-for-but, Wet-my-lip, Wet-my-feet and Quick-me-Dick. The cock may make this call over a wide area, ranging up to forty kilometres or more; which may be what earned him the name Wandering Quail. Alternatively, this name could be associated with Quail migrations. The Quail population appears over history to have varied a great deal in its size; sometimes the migratory flocks are sparse, sometimes quite huge, like those described in Exodus which twice saved the Israelites from starvation: 'and it came to pass that at even, the quails came up and covered the camp' (Exodus xvi 13). J. H. Gurney (*Early Annals of Ornithology*) points out the the detail 'at even' is significant, for Quail like many migrants fly by night.

The Quail is the smallest of the European gamebirds and like a small brown and rounded Partridge in shape and looks. The British and Irish population is not large, though there are still fluctuations which in some years bring big numbers. In general the Quail favours chalk downland for its summer home. Cornfields and hayfields make a suitable habitat and give the Quail names like Corncrake and *Sofliar* which means stubble hen. It is probable that the Quails in Britain and Ireland never have been particularly numerous. There are relatively few historical records of them. Giraldus Cambrensis (1185) writes of Quail in Ireland and Sir Thomas Browne of Norfolk Quail. But considering that during the Middle Ages and later, people would eat almost any bird which was at all palatable, the Quail figures on very few banquet menus or household accounts. The Lestrange accounts have only two mentions of Quail during the period 1519–1578. Quails are summer visitors, small in size, and there would be a great amount of alternative food around at this season. These factors, however, did not stop the summertime slaughter of literally hundreds of Larks as recorded in these accounts. It is possible that one of the reasons that Quail was not widely eaten in earlier times, as it is today, was that, according to classical Greek writers, the flesh was made unwholesome through the birds' eating poisonous plants, in particular Hellebore.

The Quail is like the Partridge in its behaviour as well as looks, feeding in fields or rough pasture, on seeds and fruits, and running rather than flying when disturbed. The coloration and small size make it virtually indistinguishable from the land on which it lives and it will often 'freeze' as a defence technique, a habit noted by the sharp-eyed Chaucer who uses it as a simile at the end of *The Clerkes Tale:* 'And thou shalt make him couche as doth a quaille' (*couche* = crouch).

Pheasant
Phasianus colchicus

Black Pheasant *dark form*
Cock-up *male*
Ffeasant (Wales)
Ffesont (Cornwall)
Comet

It is common knowledge that the Pheasant is not a native bird, but its arrival in Britain was not a matter of a simple straightforward importation. The Romans kept Pheasants and it is likely that they first introduced the Pheasant to these islands, keeping them in pens for domestic use. A Pheasant has been definitely identified in the Roman excavations at Corbridge (*Corstopitum*). These birds were of the kind known as 'Old English' Pheasants (the race *Phasianus colchicus colchicus*) the cock of which has for its distinguishing feature a black neck. These Roman birds do not however seem to have gone feral, that is to have escaped into the wild and lived and bred independently of man. This is not altogether surprising. Conditions at the time of the Roman occupation may not have favoured their survival as they do today, and the birds themselves may not have been sufficiently acclimatised to have been able to live a feral existence. We know that the Canada Goose was imported into Britain during the reign of Charles II, yet there is no record of feral birds until 1840. (Though some may have gone unrecorded, it is unlikely that significant numbers would have passed notice.) It seems to have been only in the last thirty or so years that it has become a common goose.

Among some eleventh century documents belonging to Waltham Abbey in Essex, there is a bill of fare drawn up for the monastery, dated 1059, which makes special mention of the Pheasant. Another monastic record of thirty years later, assigned a number of Pheasants, along with other food items, to the monks of Rochester. So there were certainly living Pheasants in Britain before the Norman Conquest, though probably only in captivity. Towards the end of the eleventh century, when Norman lords and abbots were dispersing over England and Wales, more Pheasants were introduced. This time it was the race *Phasianus colchicus torquatus,* in which the cocks have a white ring of neck feathers and the lower back and rump are mostly green in colour. By the sixteenth century the descendants of these birds were well established in England (and by the nineteenth century in Wales). Many other introductions were made over the centuries (including representatives from several other Pheasant races). These birds interbred producing a plethora of different variants displaying between them characteristics of at least six different races. One of these, the melanistic mutant, a very dark bird, the cock dark blue and greeny-black, the hen a rich chocolate brown, has a name to itself, the Black Pheasant.

Another name, Comet, comes from the poaching vocabulary, and it is rather apt for the bird with the exotic long tail. Indeed the tail is so striking a feature that almost every bird with a tail of any length has among its local names a Pheasant compound. (The Long-tailed Duck is a Sea

Pheasant; the little Bearded Tit, a Reed Pheasant; the Pintail, a Pheasant Duck, and so on.) The word Pheasant itself and the scientific name *Phasianus*, and various European names such as the French *Faisan*, Swedish *Fasan*, Dutch *Fazant* and German *Fasan*, all come from the same Greek source: *Phasis*, the name of a river in Medea's country of Colchis (from which we get the *colchicus* of the scientific name) which is just south of the Caucasus on the Black Sea. Pliny particularly mentions this place as one where Pheasants were to be found.

Water Rail

Rallus aquaticus

from its quiet, stealthy run:
Velvet Runner
Brook Runner
Skitty (Somerset)
Grey Skit (Devon)
Skitty Coot; Skitty Cock (Devon; Cornwall)

various:
Bilcock
Brook Ouzel
Gutter Cock (Cornwall)
Rail (Suffolk)
Sharming (Norfolk)
Rat Hen (Yorkshire)
Grey Hen; Brown Hen
Darcock
Moorhen
Scarragrise = scared-in-the-grass (Lancashire)

Many of the names for the Water Rail describe the characteristic way it withdraws as soon as it becomes aware of observation. It runs quietly and swiftly over even the softest mud, its widely spaced toes spreading the weight, and its grey-brown colours blending with the background of mud and reeds. It scarcely parts the reeds with its slim light-footed passage, and it leaves no path behind it. This typical gait is beautifully captured in the name Velvet Runner (one of the names in the Willughby/Ray *Ornithology* 1678). A seventeenth century meaning of the word skit is 'to move lightly and rapidly'. (It comes from the Old

English *sceotan,* also the root of Scoter.) Skit survives as a dialect word in the West Country, where the Water Rail is Skitty, Grey Skit and Skitty Coot.

Watching at a distance, one easily accepts names like Grey Hen and Brown Hen for the Water Rail, but close up they are plainly inadequate. The separate colours of the soft, thick plumage are quite distinct, the rich brown back streaked black, the lavender-grey of the neck and breast, the red bill and zebra stripes of the flanks. (A number of birds with red bills are known as Bilcocks, including the Oystercatcher and the Moorhen as well as the Water Rail.) A close view is however a rare luxury, especially at breeding time. Breeding pairs were traced by the field-workers of the *Atlas of Breeding Birds* mainly by listening for the strange loud screams and grunts, known as 'sharming' (the same word as a local Norfolk name for the bird).

The Water Rail or Brook Ouzel is very much a denizen of reedy and watery places; as shown by its population map which follows the lines of reedy rivers and old canals. We get our name Rail from the Old French *Raale* and many other European languages use variations of this word (Dutch, *Wateral;* German, *Wasseralle;* Swedish, *Vattenrall;* and Modern French, *Râle d'eau*), but its ultimate origins are obscure.

Water Crake
Spotted Rail
Spotted Water Hen
Skitty, Spotted Skitty, Skitty Cock, Skitty Coot (Devon)

Spotted Crake
Porzana porzana

The Spotted Crake is a little bird, and its grey-brown, spotted plumage and secretive skulking habits make it difficult to discern as it makes its way alongside the reedbeds or through marshy land. It feeds on both animal and vegetable matter. In autumn the eye may be drawn to a little flurry of leaves which the bird throws about as it moves looking for food. The legs are long and angular like those of a Moorhen, but the body is so supple, stretching and bunching up as it searches for food, that it seems almost to move independently of its legs, in an elastic rocking movement.

Not a great deal is known about the Spotted Crake's distribution. Even *The Atlas of Breeding Birds* has only marked two sites of confirmed breeding, though there are probably many more, and it quotes John Buxton who believed that Spotted Crakes were not as rare as they were thought to be on the Norfolk Broads but were 'impossible little brutes to see'.

Corncrake
Crex crex

Creck, Cracker, Craker (North; Shropshire)
Bean Crake, Bean Cracker (S Pembroke)
Corn Drake (N Riding)
Grass Drake (W Riding)
Grass Quail (Cheshire)
Meadow Drake (Nottinghamshire); Meadow Crake
Land Hen; Land Drake (Shropshire)
Gorse Duck
Gallwell Drake
Gallinule Crake
Corn Scrack (Aberdeen)
Daker (Surrey)
Daker Hen (Westmorland)
Hay Crake (Yorkshire)
Land Rail
Corn Rake (Yorkshire)
Rape-scrape (West Country)

Though it may be found in fields of grain, nowadays the Corncrake habitat is more typically a grass meadow; but, sadly, whether you search for a Corn Scrack or a Hay Crake, a Grass Drake or a Meadow Drake, except in certain parts of Ireland and the Scottish islands, you will be lucky to find one. The mysterious 'crekking' of this reclusive little brown Land Rail which was once so familiar a sound of the night fields is now mostly silent. Yet it used to be one of the most evocative and characteristic sounds of a hay meadow on a warm summer night, and there are local names for the Corncrake all over Britain. In the 1880's

Corncrakes were heard regularly at Tooting, and on Streatham Common up to the turn of the century, though the decline probably dated from 1850.

It is a bird more frequently heard than seen. The name Crake is echoic of its rolled 'crreck' which comes first from the one hidden place, then from another, as the birds move and answer one another. Even John Clare, a most patient observer, was not entirely familiar with them:

> I believe the habits of the land rail or landrake . . . are little known in fact I know but little of them myself but that little is at your pleasure. Were is the school boy that has not heard that mysterious noise which comes with the spring in the grass and green corn I have followed it for hours and all to no purpose it seemd like a spirit that mokd my folly in running after it the noise it makes is a low craking very much like that of a Drake from whence I suppose it got the name of Landrake I never started it up when a boy but I have often seen it flye since about two years ago while I was walking in a neighbours homstead we heard one of these landrails in his wheat we hunted down the land and accidentily as it were we started it up it seemed to flye very awkard and its long legs hung down as if they were broken it was just at dewfall in the evening . . .

The main cause of the Corncrake's decline in population seems to be the increasingly widespread use of machines for farm work. These cannot be checked in time to spare nests and they progress too fast for the birds and their young to flee to safety. Also, machine mowing may take place earlier in the year, in June rather than late summer, a critical time for breeding Corncrakes.

Moorhen

Gallinula chloropus

habitat names:
Marsh Hen; Moat Hen; Moorcock; Mere Hen; Pond Hen
Morant (Shropshire)
Stank Hen; Stankie (from stank = a still pool) (East
    Lothian)
Water Hen; Water Rail

from its bob-tail:
Cuddy
Kitty Coot
Moor Coot

various:
Bilcock, Bilter (North Country)
Dabchick (Shropshire)
Nightbird (Sussex)
Skitty (Somerset)

The Moorhen is distrustful of large expanses of water; it is a creature of ponds and marshy banks, the reedy edges of lakes and reservoirs. It is the Stank Hen or Stankie of still and stagnant pools; the Mere Hen, the Marsh Hen and Water Hen. Whereas a Coot will swim to open water if threatened, a Moorhen will make a quick, tiptoeing retreat to discreet concealment in the waterside vegetation. It shares the name Skitty (or Kitty) Coot with the Water Rail, and for the same reasons.

Moorhens have the short pert tail typical of rails. One of its names is Cuddy, in Scotland a dialect name for a horse which has had its tail docked. During courtship and the elaborate preliminaries before mating, both cock and then Moorhen raise and flirt their tails displaying the soft puff of white feathers beneath. There are several ritual movements to be carried out during courtship and the matt-black bodies are put into expressively sexual shapes. Behaviour between mated pairs runs through extremes, at times intimate and gentle, at others unmercifully rough. Moorhens are territorial creatures, often faithful to a particular nesting place, which they will fight fiercely to defend. In his poem 'The Moorhen's Nest' John Clare describes some quiet moments as the brood is hatched on the platform nest:

And once again a couple from the brood
Seek their old birth place – and in safetys mood
Lodge there their flags and lay though danger comes
It dares and tries and cannot reach their homes
And so they hatch their eggs and sweetly dream
On their shelfed nests that bridge the gulphy stream.

Coot
Fulica atra

from the white frontal shield:
Bald Duck
Bel Poot (powt = fowl) (East Lothian)
Bell Kite (= bald coot) (Scotland generally)
Snythe; Smyth; Snaith (Orkney)
Bald Coot (Gloucestershire; Somerset; Sussex; Yorkshire)
Bald-faced Coot (Cheshire)
Bald Pate
Bald-headed Coot (Yorkshire)
White-faced Diver (Ireland)

various:
Black Diver (Ireland)
Black Hen (Shetland)
Water Crow (Dumfries)
Water Hen (Somerset)
Whistling Duck (Scotland)
Queet; Cute

Coots and Moorhens are often seen together on larger lakes and artificial waters, but whereas Moorhens are usually scattered severally along the margins, Coots tend to cluster in large groups further from the banks. They feed mainly on aquatic vegetation which they gather from the water bed, diving to a maximum of two metres or so to procure it, then rising to the surface to eat. The Coot dives constantly, has Diver names and, it is clear, gathers food effectively by this means. Its dives are however, awkwardly made, a jump and plunge marking its downward journey, while it surfaces in an ungainly tumble, sometimes head-first, sometimes tail foremost.

Many of the local names make reference to the white frontal plate which stands out on this otherwise charcoal black bird. The saying 'as bald as a coot' alludes to this featherless shield, and 'as

Moorhen

117

---

crazy as a coot' may also be connected with this feature. Michael Drayton in the sixteenth century writes of 'the brain-bald coot' suggesting, perhaps, that its brain suffers from inadequate protection. Coot craziness is used jocularly to describe odd and erratic activities, rather than genuine insanity, and this is possibly reinforced by the birds' own behaviour. They are squabblesome birds, apt to fly at one another in an apparently crazy fashion for no observable reason.

The Reverend Charles Swainson, and following him, H. Kirke Swann, state that the word Coot comes from the Welsh *cwta-iar* = bob tailed hen, but the *OED* is very firm in its opposition to this idea, proposing instead a derivation from the Dutch *Koet* which however, is of 'etymology unknown'. Swainson also draws attention to the celebration in Horsey, Norfolk, known as 'Coot custard fair' because of the sweets made from Coot eggs and the eggs of Black-headed Gulls which are sold there.

Oyster Catcher

Haematopus ostralegus

Oyster Plover
Oyster Picker (Somerset)
Mussel Cracker (N England); Mussel Picker (Ireland)

from the black and white of its plumage:
Sea Pie (Gloucestershire; Cornwall; Norfolk; Lancashire)
Sea Piet (Northumberland)
Sea Nanpie (Yorkshire)
Mere Pie (Suffolk)
Sea Pyot; Sea Pilot
Pienet; Pynot (Northumberland)
Shalder, Shelder (Shetland)
Sheldro (Orkney)
Skeldrake (Orkney)

various:
Olive (Essex)
Scolder (Orkney)
Chalder, Chaldrick (Orkney)
Tirma; Trillichan (Hebrides)
Krocket (Aberdeen)
Gilliebride (Scotland)
Dickie Bird (Norfolk)

Sea Pie used to be the most commonly used name for this sturdy black and white wader with the brilliant orange-red bill. Many of its local names are made up of variants of 'pied' and of 'sheld' which also has the meaning of parti-coloured (see Shelduck). The Sea Pie is mainly a coastal bird and many of its names are prefixed Sea-. It has been breeding in inland sites in Scotland for a considerable period but it is only in the last decade that gravel pits and a few other inland places have been colonized in England.

The name Oyster Catcher superseded Sea Pie as the standard term probably during the late eighteenth and early nineteenth century, after Mark Catesby in his *Natural History of Carolina* (1731) coined this name for the American species *Haematopus palliatus*. However, while the American Oyster Catcher may sometimes feed upon 'clams and coon-oysters', oysters are unlikely to feature at all in the diet of the European species. Mussel Picker and Mussel Cracker are more accurate British names; the fierce orange bill works as strongly and neatly as a pair of pincers, prising mussels and limpets off rocks and removing the food.

Lapwing
Vanellus vanellus

Lappie (Fife)
Lappin (Northumberland)
Lipwingle (Bedfordshire)
Lymptwigg (Exmoor)
Flopwing
Lappinch (Cheshire)

from the double note of the cry:
Peewit
Piewipe, Peweep (Norfolk)
Phillipene (Ireland)
Peesweep, Peeweep, Peesieweep (Scotland)
Weep, Wype (Northumberland)
Teufit (Cleveland)
Teuchit (Forfar)
Tewit (Lancashire)
Tuet (Westmorland; Lancashire; W Riding)
Chewit (Perth)
Tewet (Northumberland)

Lapwing

Tewhit, Teewheep (Kirkcudbright)
Tee Whip, Tee Whippo, Tee Wup (Orkney)
Tieves' Nacket (Shetland)

various:
Green Plover
Plover
Hornpie (Norfolk; E Suffolk)
Horneywink (Cornwall)
Cornwillen (Cornwall)
Old Maid (Worcestershire)
Wallock, Wallop, Wallopie, Wallopie Weep (Moray)
Scochad, Shouchad, Shuchad, Sochad (Caithness;
    Sutherland)

Lapwings have a wide distribution all over Britain and Ireland. You can find them picking their way over ploughed fields, sweeping over moorland or prodding about in estuary mud. All they require essentially are places with low vegetation or bare ground, where they may find insects to feed upon. The odd thing is that this striking looking bird, black and white with its green back and crested head, seems not at all out of place in any of the very different kinds of landscape which it inhabits.

The Lapwing has a distinctive, broad-winged flight, apparently flappy and unmanageable, but in fact beautifully controlled. One name for the bird, Flopwing, draws attention to this tumbling and wheeling and one might reasonably expect the word Lapwing to be a reference to this characteristic flight. However, it seems more likely that Flopwing is a comparatively modern rendition, and a perfectly valid one, of a name which originally meant something quite different. For the word Lapwing comes from the Old English *Hleapewince* which has the quite beautiful meaning of a 'leap with a waver in it' which conveys so well the tremulous power of the Lapwing's flight. The autumn and winter group flights are particularly 'hleapewince', a flock surging and turning, showing first the green-black upperside of the wide wing, then the brilliant white of the underside, moving together like a flickering chequerboard.

The haunting cry of the Lapwing has given rise

to a number of commonly used names: Peewit, Tewet and the Scots one which tries to capture the catch in the middle of the double note, Peesieweep. A Scots rhyme plays on the sobbing quality of the cry, and subtly allies this with another characteristic of behaviour, that of limping about in an opposite direction, crying loudly, if a nest is threatened:

> Pease weep, pease weep
> Harry my nest and gar me greet.

As the proverb in *The Compleat Collection of English Proverbs* has it: 'The lapwing cries most, farthest from her nest.' (John Ray 1670) This seems to have been something widely noticed from quite early times. Chaucer typifies the Lapwing as 'ful of trecherye' presumably for this habit of leading a false trail (*Parlement of Foules*), and in *The Comedy of Errors,* Shakespeare too points out that 'far from her nest, the lapwing cries away'.

The Peewit's distinctive cry finds a part in many old folk tales taking, it seems, almost arbitrarily good and bad roles, depending on the demands of the story. One tale has the Lapwing mocking Christ at the crucifixion, and condemned afterwards to live homeless, calling sorrowfully in its wanderings. In the south of Scotland there runs a story that the presence of a group of Covenanters was given away to raiding troopers by yelling Lapwings, but Yarrell quotes another tale in which the same action is placed in a good light. When the head of the ancient Lincolnshire family of Tyrwhitts (*sic*) fell wounded, no one would have known where to look for him had it not been for the Lapwing's alarm cry.

Another feature of Lapwing behaviour which became part of the common language in the early seventeenth century concerns the Lapwing chicks, who were thought to be specially precocious, running about as soon as hatched, sometimes with bits of shell still adhering. So people of brash and unconsidered behaviour were likened to 'lapwings with a shell upon their heads' by Ben Jonson. Similarly, Shakespeare in *Hamlet* has Horatio

Lapwing

observe, of the foolish and thoughtless young Osric, 'the lapwing runs with shell on his head.' In fact, the newly hatched youngsters are usually brooded for at least eight hours before they are encouraged to leave the nest, but if they are threatened with danger, they can run as soon as they are hatched. Since Lapwings and their eggs were much sought for food, it was the egg hunters who actually caused the phenomenon they observed by disturbing the nestlings.

Ringed Plover
Charadrius hiaticula

Ring Dotterel
Ringlestone
Ring-neck (Yorkshire)

from its haunts:
Sea Lark; Sand Lark (Northumberland)
Sandy Loo (Orkney)
Sand Tripper (County Down)
Sandy Laverock (Orkney; Shetland)
Stone Plover
Stonehatch; Stone Runner (Norfolk)
Shell-turner (Sussex)

various:
Dulwilly
Bull's Eye (Ireland)
Knot (Belfast)
Grundling (Lancashire)
Wideawake (Somerset)
Tullet, Tullot (Lancashire)

Little Ringed Plover
Charadrius dubius

A Ringed Plover with its back turned is scarcely distinguishable from the sand and mud background of the shoreline or estuary where it feeds and which as habitat-adjectives (Sand, Sea, Stone, etc) feature in a number of local names. Its identity is revealed when it moves, a characteristic little run of a few strides, then a couple of low bows as it stoops quickly to snatch up a small worm or crustacean. Face to face, the Ringed Plover is a very striking bird, the alternate black and white markings radiating out from the brown cap to the

complete ring which forms a necklace over its shoulder and under its breast. Head on, it has something of the appearance of a target which may account for the name Bull's Eye though, as it shares this name with both the Golden and Grey Plovers, it is more probable that this simply indicated a strikingly black and white portion of its plumage. On a typical pebbly beach where Ringed Plovers make their 'scrape' and lay their well-disguised eggs, a pair of Plover can vanish in a blink as you watch them, their plumage colours completely concealing them against the stony background.

The Ringed Plover is a swift runner and will often bolt rapidly for cover rather than fly; it is called Grundling (groundling) in Lancashire. It is an alert and nervous bird and has the habit, common to Plovers, of stretching its wings up above its back for a moment or two, when it will sometimes give its call from which the names Tullet and Dulwilly come, a low musical 'tooli-tooli'. The Ringed Plover is not a large bird. In fact a Blackbird is half as big again from beak to tail, but if length of wing is compared the Plover's is the longer. When in flight, these long, slim, pointed wings, carry the bird strongly and swiftly, with superb control in sharply angled wheels and turns.

Their near relative, the Little Ringed Plover, has similar markings, but it lacks the white wing bar and has a nun-like semicircle of white surrounding the brown cap. It is a comparative newcomer to the British Isles; the first records date from 1850. The first instance of breeding was at Tring in Hertfordshire in 1938 and the spread since then has been very substantial, reaching more than four hundred pairs over England by 1974.

The only alternative name for the Little Ringed Plover is Little Ringed Dotterel and this is a 'book-

Ringed Plover
Little Ringed Plover

name' rather than a local one, to be found in Gould's *Birds of Europe* (1832–1837). It seems, however, that Little Ringed Plover, introduced by Jenyns in 1835, was preferred and this was the name which came into general use.

Grey Plover
Pluvialis squatarola

from its haunts:
Sea Plover
Sea Cock (Waterford)
Sea Pigeon (Yorkshire)
Strand Plover (Cork)
Mud Plover
Rock Plover (Ireland)

various:
Whistling Plover
Bull Head; Bull-headed Plover (Suffolk)
Silver Plover (Cheshire; Yorkshire; Scotland)

Golden Plover
Pluvialis apricaria

from plumage colours:
Yellow Plover (East Lothian)
Grey Plover (Ireland)
Black-breasted Plover (Ireland)

various:
Whistling Plover (Norfolk; Scotland; Cheshire; Somerset)
Hill Plover (Scotland)
Plover (Surrey; Roxburgh)
Sheep's Guide (Cheshire)

Though these two species resemble each other strongly, the Golden Plover is far more of an inland bird than the Grey and is a resident breeding bird on high flat moorland areas. They are the Hill Plovers, in the fells known as the Sheep's Guide, whereas the Grey Plovers, the winter birds, are Strand Plovers and Sea Pigeon. In autumn and winter the numbers of Golden Plover are augmented by passage birds and winter migrants. In an early essay, George Orwell recollected the magical sound of a flock of migrant Golden Plover which he heard one twilight evening by the Thames at Westminster Bridge. In fact, both species are known as Whistling Plover but the whistles are different in character, that of the Golden Plover liquid fluting, the Grey Plover's shriller and more penetrating. In some places, the legend of the Seven Whistlers is associated with Golden Plovers (see Curlew) as it is also with other birds which make a distinctive whistling such as Redshank, Curlew and Geese.

Golden Plover are often to be found feeding in flocks with Lapwing in fields. There is an Aberdeenshire rhyme which says that the Golden Plover has advice for the ploughman to whom it calls

> Plough weel, shave [sow] weel, harrow weel.

In winter plumage both Golden and Grey Plover look greyish and they lose the conspicuous black underparts which extend from the cheeks almost to the tail in summer, bordered on the head and shoulders with a band of white. It is because of the location that one may be certain that Burns writes of a Golden Plover in winter time in the line:

> The deep-toned plover gray, wild whistling on the hill.

In breeding plumage the Golden Plover is resplendent in the golden-yellow and black mottle over its back and wings, while the Grey Plover, as one would expect from its name, takes on a silvery appearance with a grey-black mottle. When it flies, or raises its wings, in summer or winter plumage, the Grey Plover reveals a black 'armpit' (wing axillaries) which shows up clearly against the soft grey of the underside of the body.

Dotterel

Eudromias morinellus

An Tamadan Mointich = peat-bog fool (Gaelic)
Moor Dotterel (Yorkshire)
Dot Plover (Norfolk)
Spring Dotterel, Land Dotterel (Yorkshire)

various:
Stone Runner (Norfolk)
Wind (South of England)

'This dottrell is a lytell fonde byrde for it helpeth in manner to take itself stated a writer of 1526. The main obstacle to observing Dotterel is the inaccessibility of their haunts. They live on high, wild and remote mountain tops. Fowlers from early times have found that once the climb had been made, the birds, trustful and tame, were an easy catch. Accordingly they dubbed them stupid and simple-minded: that is 'dotterel' which comes from the same root as 'dote' and 'dotard' and the modern idiomatic 'dotty'.

Laurens Sargent, who was touched by the charm of these birds, felt that Dotterel were unfairly done by. (Even their scientific name *morinellus* means 'little fool'.)

> Personally, I have found few experiences among birds more engaging than sitting on a snow dappled Lapland fell and gazing at and stroking a dotterel as he brooded his mate's eggs, having eventually to lift him gently from them in order to admire them. But he was back on the nest before it could be photographed. That this parental boldness is not confined to one species or to one sex could be vouched for by any naturalist. I remember repeatedly lifting a hen mistle thrush from her nest high up in a tree in a country garden. She, like the dotterel, invariably returned to her eggs within a couple of seconds, as if she were on the end of a rubber cord. Stupidity? Would it be too trite to say that stupidity, like beauty, may be in the eye or the mind of the beholder?

(Pedigree, Word's from Nature)

Perhaps there is in human beings a failure to come to terms with the fact that we are predatory carnivores. Animals who do not resist slaughter we deride, in order to cover up a profound unease about killing a creature which is friendly towards us. This is very clear in our attitude to domestic and farm animals. We have tamed pigs, cattle and sheep for our own use and between them these three beasts provide for a considerable range of our material needs. Yet 'silly cow' is a common form of abuse. Sheep have become synonymous with excessive credulity and foolishness, and for the pig, so long the staple of domestic economy, we have nothing but insults. We have made our farm animals trusting and docile. Dotterel are naturally so; in both cases there is an underlying sense that they are not 'fair game' and we transpose our guilt, reviling not ourselves but the animals.

The Dotterel is now under Schedule I of the Protection of Birds Act, so it is strictly illegal to injure it or to interfere with its nest or eggs. Today there would not be many people outside the ranks of ornithology who would be familiar with the bird, whereas in the seventeenth century, Dotterel appeared quite frequently in literature. Michael Drayton calls it 'an apish bird'. This referred to a tradition recorded by the naturalist Conrad Gesner in his *Icones Animalum* (1660) and repeated over the centuries, that the Dotterel's 'Plover' habit of stretching out a wing or a leg, was an imitation of the fowlers as they drove the birds to the nets. For seventeenth century dramatists, Dotterel were handy metaphors for easy game, as in Beaumont and Fletcher's *Sea Voyage:*

See they stretch out their legs like dotterels

and Ben Jonson's fowl punning speech in *The Devil is an Ass:*

Bid him put off his hopes of straw, and leave
To spread his nets in view thus. Though they take
Master Fitz–dotterel, I am no such foul
Nor, fair one, tell him, will be had with stalking.

Turnstone
Arenaria interpres

Stanepecker (Shetland)
Tangle Picker (Norfolk)
Ebb Pecker (Shetland)

various:
Stone Raw (Armagh)
Sea Dotterel (Norfolk)
Hutan-y-mor = Sea Dotterel (Welsh)
Skirl Crake (East Lothian; Shetland)
Bracket (Lindisfarne)

It is not surprising that the Turnstone is also known as the Sea Dotterel, for the birds are quite similar in their small stocky shape, and both are tortoiseshell colours in summer, black and white in winter. The summer plumage comes on some time about the end of April, when the Turnstones which have wintered on the coasts of Britain and Ireland are beginning their migration to the breeding places on the Baltic. They do not breed in the British Isles, at the present time, but J. T. R. Sharrock (of *The Atlas of Breeding Birds*) has hazarded the opinion that given the pattern of colonization by certain northerly species (Fulmar, Godwit) Turnstones may soon be found nesting here.

Turnstones are very much birds of rocky or shingle shorelines, living up to their name by levering up stones with their small upturned bills for the succulent marine creatures which lie beneath; or pulling back the seaweed in a swift motion and pouncing on the titbits that dwell in its sheltered recesses. The name Turnstone is ubiquitous; the Dutch is *Steenloper,* German, *Steinwalzer,* Italian, *Volta pietre,* in Spain *Revuelve piedras,* and in France *Tourne-pierre interprete.* The *interprete* of the French echoes the Latin *interpres* of the scientific name, literally 'go-between' but in this case meaning a bird whose sharp 'skirling' cry gives a tell-tale warning to other birds of the approach of danger.

Snipe
Gallinago gallinago

Heather Bleater (Scotland; Ireland)
Bog Bleater (Ireland)
Gabhar Athair = She-goat of the Air (Celtic)
Gafr-wanwyn = Goat of the Spring (Welsh)
Ern Bleater
Horse Gowk, Horse Gawk (Orkney; Shetland)
Blutter; Blitter
Common Snipe
Whole Snipe (Somerset; Sussex)
Mire Snipe (Aberdeen)
Jill Snipe (Ireland)
Snippack; Snippick (Orkney; Shetland)
Full Snipe (Somerset)
Lady Snipe (Cheshire)

Jack Snipe
Lymnocryptes minimus

Jedcock; Jid; Juddock
Half Snipe (Norfolk)
Gaverhale (Devon)
Plover's Page (Orkney)
St Martin's Snipe

Burns called the Snipe 'the Blitter frae the boggie'. It is almost as if these birds form a living whole with the reeds and plants of the water's edge on marsh, moor and bog, so integrally do they fit with their surroundings. More than with most birds, pictures of Snipe usually fail to do them justice; they need to be seen in their wild places, appearing and vanishing as if by sorcery against the background of the reed bed, the beautiful stripey markings seeming to move like the reeds themselves. And the tremendously long bill (proportionately the longest of any European bird), which looks so oddly out of balance on the page, is in fact perfectly suited to feeding on the water margins, deeply probing the mud, its sensitive and flexible tip searching out worms and insects. It is from its bill that the Snipe derives not only many of its local names in the British Isles but all over Europe. The Old English *snite* and the Middle English *snype* (from the Old Norse *snipa*) are etymologically related to words like snuff, snub, snuffle, snout and one used in local names for a bill, neb.

Another Old English name which forms the base of the second main group of Snipe names is

129

Snipe
Jack Snipe

Haeferblaete, meaning 'goat bleater', still with us as the phonetically similar Heather Bleater and in 'air goat' and 'kid of the air' which retain the original meaning. The 'bleat' is descriptive of the quite extraordinary sound which the Snipe makes with the end wing primaries and outer tail feathers, a kind of fluting bleat in the wind as the bird drops in a steep descent from a special, high rapid flight. This is a courtship display flight but the birds may do it at any time during the year, though most regularly and often in spring and early summer. To some ears this wind music resembles the whinny of a horse, also giving rise to names, not only in Britain but also in Denmark (*Hingstefugl* = stallion bird) and Norway (*Himmerhest* = sky horse).

Several of the Snipe names are only comprehensible in relation to other names for the smaller Jack Snipe *Lymnocryptes minimus.* The Common Snipe is Jill to the other's Jack, and the Whole Snipe, or Full Snipe, to its Half Snipe. The latter would be wildfowlers' terms as are the collective nouns: a 'couple' for a pair of dead Snipe, a 'walk' for a group on the ground, and a 'wisp' for a party of Snipe in the air.

Woodcock
Scolopax rusticola

Cock
Great Snipe
Kyvellack (Cornish)
Longbill
Quis (Wiltshire)

Though by no means striking in its plumage, the Woodcock is one of the most beautiful of waders. Its back and wings are a dark brown mottle and the creamy-buff breast is crossed with dark bars. The bill is long with a sensitive probe at the tip like that of a Snipe, and the large eyes are well set back on the handsome, striped and barred head. The Woodcock is a forest dweller and this colouration enables it to lose itself against a background of dead leaves; literally to disappear before your eyes. A sitting bird and the nest can lie close at hand but unseen because of this camouflage. Unlike other

wood-dwellers, such as the Woodpigeon or Pheasant, which make a great clapping as they take off, a Woodcock can rise almost silently from the forest floor. The only time it shows itself openly is when the males make their evening display flights known as 'roding'. (Where this term originated is obscure.) Woodcock flight is normally rapid and darting, but during the roding the birds flap their wings in a slow rhythm. At the same time these normally quiet cocks fill the air with a deep repeated croaking growl. A roding Woodcock at dusk seems to fill the air with its wings and its sound. It is quite shocking, then, to see how tiny and pathetic the small figures are when shot. It seems somehow inconceivable that so much life could have been once commanded in such a tiny corpse.

Woodcock have been in the public eye since early times. There are no less than three Anglo-Saxon variants of its name *Wude-coco, Wudu-coc* and *Wudu-snite;* the last picking on the resemblance of colour and form to the Snipe. The *Coc* as in Cockerel and Cuckoo is imitative, echoing the 'kwark-kwark' roding call. Woodcock are fairly widespread over Britain and Ireland but it is not an abundant species. The numbers are considerably augmented during the winter months by migrant birds. The arrival of the visitors is the focus of weather and crop lore. If they come early, it is said to prognosticate good weather and a liberal harvest – especially if they stay into the following spring. (The return dates range between mid-March and early May.) On the other hand, if the hay has not been gathered by the time the Woodcock arrives, it spells ruin, particularly if you sowed your oats late (at Cuckoo time).

> Cuckoo oats and Woodcock hay
> Make a farmer run away.

There is a tradition that Woodcock arrive overnight, all together, on a change of wind to the easterly, some time near All Hallows. Several other migrants are said to 'pilot' the Woodcock flocks to their winter home (see Goldcrest; Short-eared

Owl). It used also to be thought that the months of absence were spent on the moon. (This theory continued to be promulgated until well into the eighteenth century, and by reasonably eminent people, though perceptive and intelligent men such as Sir Thomas Browne disbelieved it and supported the then rather off-beat idea of migration, put forward by Olaus Magnus in the sixteenth century.) Charles Morton in a tract in the *Harleian Miscellany* elaborates on moon migration, describing how the birds take two months to travel there and the same period to get back, spending three months in a lunar habitat. (There is a similar superstition about goose migration.) These ideas, far-fetched though they now seem, percolated through to the literary world; as in Pope:

> A bird of passage gone as soon as found
> Now in the moon perhaps, now underground.
> (*Epistle to Sir Richard Temple 1733*)

and Gay:

> He sung where woodcocks in the summer feed,
> And in what climates they renew their breed:
> Some think to northern coasts their flight they tend
> Or, to the moon in midnight hours ascend.
> (*The Shepherd's Week 1714*)

In common with several other birds who are easily trapped, Woodcocks were branded as stupid creatures. They were netted after being beaten from their hiding places or when making their low courting flights. Rumour grew that the Woodcock had no brain at all and the word became a synonym for slow-wittedness. The notion was current not only with the sporting and ornithological fraternity but had wide currency. Beaumont and Fletcher must have expected to be understood when they wrote in one of their comedies:

> Go like the Woodcock
> And Thrust your head into the noose
> (*The Loyal Subject 1618*)

and the title of a clever book of epigrams by H. Perot was entitled *Springes for Woodcocks*. Even

Willughby makes a comment in the *Ornithology* (1678):

> Among us in England this bird is infamous for its stupidity or folly so that a Woodcock is Proverbially used for a simple foolish person.

Curlew
Numenius arquata

call names:
Calloo
Courlie (Sussex)
Curlew-help (Lancashire)
Great Curlew; Full Curlew
Collier, Collier-jack (Cheshire)
Awp
Great Whaup (Orkney)
Stock Whaup (Shetland)
Whaup (North of England; Scotland; Shetland)

various:
Whitterick (East Lothian)
Whistling Duck (Somerset)
Seven Whistler (Sussex)
Guilbinn (Western Isles)
Gelvinak (Cornwall)
Marsh Hen (Suffolk)

The name Curlew is imitative but it is beyond the capabilities of most human throats to reproduce the haunting quality of this long drawn-out double note. The Sussex name Courlie (similar to the French *courlis*) with a strong accent on the first syllable holds something of the right sound. The Whaup group of names have an English tradition, deriving from the Anglo-Saxon *huilpe* (which resembles the modern Dutch *wulp*). The word whaup is also used for a Scottish goblin with a long beak, which it uses like a pair of tongs for the nocturnal carrying off of evil-doers. A whaup of this kind is referred to in Walter Scott's *Black Dwarf,* when one of the characters, Hobbie Elliot, exclaims 'To be sure they say there's a sort of worricows and langnebbit things about the land, but what need I care for them?' The fact that the Curlew's voice has a slightly human quality, like a lament, and that its long, down-curving bill is its most distinctive feature, probably led to this association.

133

Curlews, especially those on estuaries, will call at night while feeding, and birds which do this are often accorded a sinister significance. In the north of England, a flock of calling Curlews passing overhead and calling in their eerie, musical voices was said to presage a death, and such flights of the 'Seven Whistlers' were feared. Seven Whistlers is a name also accorded to the Curlew's close relative, the Whimbrel. The legend of the Seven Whistlers is not confined to Britain, nor is their identity restricted to a single species. In Portugal it is believed that Wigeon are the Whistlers and that they are the souls of unchristened babies. Golden Plover take the part in Lancashire, representing the souls of Jews who were doomed to wander forever, for having taken part in the crucifixion. In South Shropshire and Worcestershire it is said that six Whistlers search, calling for a lost one and when they reunite, the end of the world will come. Curlews are also associated with the Gabriel Hounds, a name also given to calling geese. Edward Armstrong argues that the Seven Whistlers and the Gabriel Hounds were both remnants of the 'Wild Hunt' belief, in which a weird company of hunters rides across the sky on the nights of the worst storms. In the Teutonic version of the legend, the god Odin often leads the throng and he is sometimes accompanied by Ravens. The spirits of the dead rise up and join the hunt and the hounds on earth also give tongue, in response to their ghostly counterparts.

The plumage of the adult Curlew is darker in summer than in winter, a streaky dark brown as opposed to paler brown and buff. This change is exaggerated in the Lincolnshire saying quoted by Willughby (1678) to 'black and white'.

Be she white or be she black
The curlew has tenpence on her back.

Another version has it that a Curlew 'lean or fat', 'carries twelvepence on her back'. And Curlews seem to have been popular eating birds far back into history. A table of permitted poulterers' prices issued by order of Edward I in 1275 states a price of

3d for a Curlew. Later in the time of Richard II (c 1384) the list was amended, the Curlews were up to 6d, and at the coronation feast of Henry VI Curlews were served along with a large selection of birds we should not now think of eating (Plover, Larks, Swan, Heron, Crane, Bittern). A taste for the bird may still linger in the Suffolk name Land Pheasant, though this could equally well be a plumage name which draws on the likeness in colouration between Curlews and hen Pheasants.

Titterel (Sussex; Dorset)
Chickerel (Dorset)
Winderal (Northumberland)

from its resemblance to the Curlew:
Curlew Jack (Yorkshire)
Curlew Knave (Cumberland)
Little Whaup (Scotland)
Curlew Knot (Spalding)
Peerie Whaup (Shetland)
Summer Whaup; Tang Whaup (Orkney; Shetland)
Half Curlew (Suffolk; Norfolk)
Whimbrel Curlew (Northumberland)

other names:
May Bird (Cornwall; Gloucestershire; East Anglia; Sussex)
May Curlew; May Whaap (Ireland)
May Fowl (Ireland)
Brame (Suffolk)
Corpse Hound
Chequer Bird

Whimbrel
Numenius phaeopus

The Whimbrel is a smaller bird than the Curlew and it has a much less pronounced bill. Otherwise it is quite similar, and has many names which relate it to the much more numerous and widespread Curlew, such as Little Whaup and Curlew Jack ('jack' signifying small size as in Jack Snipe). Whimbrel breed only in a few places in the north of Scotland and on the Northern islands, though they are known over most of the British Isles as passage migrants, which is why they are called Summer Whaup, May Bird and May Whaup.

In the Household Accounts of the old Norfolk family of Lestrange, from 1519–1578, forty species of bird appear as part of the domestic diet, among them Whimbrel, referred to as *Spowe, Spoe, Spooe* and *Spow,* which were eaten in November and December. The derivation of this group of names may be seen in the modern Icelandic name for Whimbrel: *Smaspov* = small curlew.

The title of The Seven Whistlers applied to the Whimbrel could be an allusion to its distinctive rippling call, not unlike the whimpering of hounds. Possibly Whimbrel is a diminutive form of 'whimmerel', whimmer being a Lowland Scots word for whimper. The Durham Household Book of 1530 calls it a Whimpernel so it seems very likely that the name Whimbrel is a diminutive and that it contains a reference to the voice, whether or not this has anything to do with the Seven Whistlers. Chickerel and Titterel are also attempts to reproduce the bird's strange call with the human voice.

Black-tailed Godwit

Limosa limosa

Red Godwit (Ireland)
Small Curlew
Jadreka Snipe
Shrieker (Norfolk)
Barker (Suffolk)
Whelp; Whelpmoor; Yarwhelp (Suffolk)

Bar-tailed Godwit

Limosa lapponica

Sea Woodcock (Shetland)
Godwin (Ireland)

from its sharp cry:
Yarwhelp; Yarwhip
Yardkeep
Shrieker (Norfolk; Shropshire)
Poor Willie (East Lothian)

various:
Stone Plover
Pick (Norfolk)
Prine (Essex)
Scammel (Blakeney)
Speethe (Lindisfarne)
Half Curlew (Norfolk); Half Whaup (Forfar)
Set Hammer (North of England)

These two species are not unlike Curlew and Whimbrel in general outline, but they are clearly recognisable from them because the long bill is straight or upward curved. They do however share names such as Half Curlew and Half Whaup with the Whimbrel, to which they are closest in size. It is interesting that while many of the 'half' names seem to have been coined by fowlers and fishermen, the half nearly always refers to the size of the bird and not to its potential cash value. In fact on most of the old accounts, the Whimbrel made a better price than the larger Curlew, and Sir Thomas Browne said of 'Godwyts' that they 'were accounted the daintiest dish in England and I think, for the bignesse, of the biggest price.'

The name Godwit may be traced back to the Old English god = good, plus wihte = creature, but opinions diverge on how this should be interpreted. Potter and Sargent suggest that as 'goodfellow' (godwihte) was also the name of Robin Goodfellow, or Puck, that Godwits might be considered birds of good omen. There are however no traces of superstitions or stories which would lend support to this idea. It is certain that, by the seventeenth century at least, if the birds augured anything it was a fine supper; nearly all the references to the Godwits were to their supreme tastiness.

Both species of Godwit are noisy birds, and several of the Yarwhelp and Whelp Curlew names have been passed on to them. The sounds they make are however different both from each other and from the Curlew. The Black-tailed Godwit, the Barker, has a harsh sharp yelp. The Bar-tailed Godwit's call has a certain similarity to the Lapwing's, though weaker and reedier. Unlike the Curlew, which is a very nervous and flighty bird, Godwits sit very tight on the nest and are called Scammel, an old word for limpet.

Green Sandpiper

Tringa ochropus

Black Sandpiper (Suffolk)
Drain Swallow (Yorkshire)
Martin Snipe (Norfolk)
Horse Gowk (Shetland)
Whistling Sandpiper

The Green Sandpiper is larger and darker-backed than the Common Sandpiper (hence Black Sandpiper) and without the white shoulder patch. It is a bird of passage over most of the British Isles, and spends the winter months in the south of England. The dark colour of its wings is tinged with olive green. Kirke Swann quotes Pennant as thinking that the standard name comes from the plumage, but it seems quite as possible that, like the Greenshank, it was so called because of its legs.

In flight, the Green Sandpiper shows the conspicuous white rump which gives it the name Martin Snipe. As in the case of the Storm Petrel's Martin-oil, this name is an allusion to the House Martin and its similarly conspicuous white rump. As it rises into the air it characteristically gives a clear whistling call, hence Whistling Sandpiper.

Common Sandpiper

Tringa hypoleucos

from its alarm cry:
Heather Peeper (Aberdeen)
Waterypleeps (Orkney)
Killieleepsie (East Lothian)
Kittie Needie (Kirkcudbright)
Willy Wicket (North of England)
Dickie-di-dee (Lancashire)
Tatler
Weet Weet

habitat names:
Sandie Laverock (North of England)
Sand Lark (Ireland; Scotland)
Sanny (Aberdeen)
Sand Snipe (Cheshire)
Shore Snipe (Perth)
Land Laverock (Scotland)
Water Junket; Water Laverock (Roxburgh)

various:
Summer Snipe

Skittery Deacon (Stirling)
Shad Bird (Shrewsbury)
Steenie Pouter (Orkney)

Sandpiper, the standard name for this bird, was originally (according to Willughby, 1678) a Yorkshire local name. The piper part of the name refers to the light fluting notes which the bird makes as it flies. Other names, Kittie Needie, Willy Wicket and Dickie-di-dee, repeated a few times, are closely imitative of the sound and rhythm. There is a large group of sand, shore and water names which are quite literal. The Sandpiper is a bird of the sandy or muddy margins of lakes and rivers where it wades in the shallows, picking up food in the form of larvae, worms and insects, in busy bobbing movements, the white patch of its shoulder and underparts contrasting with the warm brown tones of its back.

There are two possible associations for the names Sandy Laverock and Sand Lark. Laverock is an alternative name, and widely used, for the Lark, so the Sandpiper's piping could be thought to echo this sound. The Old English form of laverock contains the notion of betrayal, which might be an allusion to the way that a Sandpiper feigns injury, dragging itself convincingly along the ground away from the nest or young birds. This name is shared by the Ringed Plover, which is also expert at this ruse, while the Lark misleads would-be plunderers by alighting and making its way back to its nest by a devious and concealed route.

A commonly used name over England and Scotland is Summer Snipe. Sandpipers are not very Snipe-like in appearance, but Snipe, a common bird, is used as a kind of anchor name, and qualified by 'summer' to denote a wader of the water margins which is a summer migrant. In the reaches of the upper Severn, around Shrewsbury, Sandpipers were known as Shad Birds, because they arrived usually about the middle of April, about the same time as the shad came upstream and the shad fishing season began.

139

Redshank

Tringa totanus

Red Leg (Norfolk); Red Legs (Sussex)
Red-legged Snipe
Red-legged Horseman
Redshank Tattler

from its alarm cry:
Teuk (Essex)
Took; Tuke (Sussex)
Clee (Aberdeen)
Watery Pleeps (Orkney)
Warden of the Marshes
Watchdog of the Marshes
Whistling Plover (Cheshire)
Pellile (Aberdeen)

various:
Pool Snipe
Ebb Cock (Shetland)
Sandcock; Shake (Connemara)
Swat (North of England)

The Redshank seems not to have been much written about before the sixteenth century, where there are a number of references. Turner (1544) uses the name Redshank and there is no reason to suppose that the word, formed from two stout Old English components (*read* = red and *scanca* = leg-bone) should not have been in currency much earlier. Certainly, thirteen years earlier, the household of James V of Scotland purchased Redshanks and a number of other waders for the table. Red-legged Horseman, rather awkward for a local name, seems more likely to be an introduced 'book-name', a translation by Albin in his *Natural History of Birds* (1738) of the French *Chevalier à Pieds Rouges*.

The names which deal with the visual appearance of the redshank are few in comparison with those describing or imitating its beautiful clear-noted cry. Redshanks are birds of the marsh and of tidal estuaries and its voice seems particularly to fit in with bleak and remote places. Eric Parker in his *English Wildlife* catches some of the feel of it.

A cry half challenge, half lament, the very spirit of the estuary, of a life that chances and changes with wind and tide. . . No-one who has ever heard the redshank cry in the wind over the saltings will ever after think of those waste spaces of water and ooze and sunlight without that haunting voice 'tu-ee tu-ee', and the lovely curves of that swift and slanting flight.

Dusky Godwit; Dusky Redshank
Spotted Snipe
Black-headed Snipe
Courland Snipe; Cambridge Snipe

Spotted Redshank
Tringa erythropus

Greater Plover
Barker
Green-legged Long Shank
Green-legged Horseman

Greenshank
Tringa nebularia

Recognisably close relatives of the Redshank, these two species are far less common. The Greenshank nests in the north of Scotland but otherwise the birds we see over most of the rest of the British Isles are passage migrants (though Ireland and south and southwest England have wintering populations). Both these species are slightly taller than the Redshank and they are more sedate in their actions, compared with the Redshank's constant dipping as it probes the mud for food.

The Spotted Redshank has a long straight bill, giving a slightly Snipe-like impression about the head. Though a fairly rare visitor to many parts of the country, it is a very confiding bird, and will feed quite unconcerned on lakeside mud, though people may be approaching quite close to it. The Greenshank is one of the most elegant and graceful waders, always a pleasure to see on its regular passage visits, though it is nervous of human beings and has to be spied from a distance.

However, neither of these two attractive waders seem to have caught the popular attention. The alternative names are few and decidedly 'bookish' in character. They cannot be traced to particular

141

Spotted Redshank
Greenshank

localities, only to various works of ornithology published during the eighteenth and nineteenth centuries, and it is difficult to say which if any of the names were in common usage.

Knot
Calidris canutus

Gnat; Knat; Knet
Gnat Snap

plumage names:
Red Sandpiper (Ireland)
Black Sandpiper
Dun (Cheshire); Dunne (Belfast)
Griselled Sandpiper
Grey Plover, Silver Plover (Scotland)

various:
Male (Essex)
Howster
Sea Snipe (Dublin)
Spease (Lindisfarne)
Ebb Cock (Shetland)

Knot breed high within the Arctic circle and may winter as far south as New Zealand or Patagonia. Some of the less intrepid migrants spend the winter along the coasts of the British Isles where they may be seen in large flocks. They are highly gregarious birds and pack themselves together more closely than any other wader. T. A. Coward writes of an experience in Lancashire where he saw

> . . .for at least a mile, one continuous ribbon of birds varying in width from two or three feet to six or more yards. Where the 'Duns' . . . were thickest and the birds moved, all in one direction with their heads down, the impression given was of a slowly advancing grey carpet.

There is a tradition (mainly a literary one) that the name Knot came about because they were known as King Canute's birds. Willughby records that the old King was very fond of them. The earliest authority for this derivation seems to be Camden (1551–1623) who writes of '*Knotts, i. Canuti aves*'. Poets as well as ornithologists were

familiar with this association, Drayton in the Poly-
Olbion writes, 'The knot that called was Canute's
bird of old'. It seems however more than possible
that Camden (or possibly an even earlier source)
had written his *Canuti aves* as a vivid description of
the way the birds feed along the shoreline as if
daring the waves, rather than something to be
taken literally. It is generally thought nowadays
that the name Knot and other similar variants is
imitative of the bird's sharp alarm note which
Coward reports as a low 'knut, knut'.

Early migrants or immature birds may still be in
the rufous summer plumage when they reach our
shores: hence Red Sandpiper. The grey mottle of
its winter coat (the head and underparts turn silver
grey) which is the more commonly seen plumage
on our shores, give rise to colour adjectives such as
Griselled, Grey and Silver, often allied to 'anchor'
names belonging to other waders such as Snipe,
Sandpiper and Plover.

Brown Sandpiper
Little Sandpiper
Ox-bird
Purre
Stint
Wagtail (Sussex)

Little Stint
Calidris minuta

Temminck's Stint
Calidris temminckii

The word 'Stint' is not often used in everyday
speech except in certain idiomatic negative forms
as for instance when one works 'unstintingly' or in
'not stinting' materials, both these examples
having the sense of not being sparing. The phrase
'doing one's stint' means to do a certain minimum
amount of work. There is a sense of limited
measure in the word. Applied to birds, it seems to
have come into currency during the fifteenth
century and then it was applied to a number of
little waders, Dunlin and Sanderling especially, no
doubt because they seemed scanty little birds

143

alongside the much more substantial Curlews and Redshanks.

The bird we know as the Little Stint was not recorded in Britain until 1776, and Temminck's Stint seems not to have been observed until as late as 1832. However, both these waders are so diminutive in size (smaller than the House Sparrow), that they are clearly the best candidates for the old name of Stint and this has become their standard name.

From our point of view in Britain, these two species are spare not only in size but in number. We know them mainly as birds of passage on their long migration through from northern Scandinavia and Siberia, down to Africa. There have been a few records of Temminck's Stint, which has a slightly more southerly range, breeding in Britain.

Dunlin
Calidris alpina

Purre; Churre (Norfolk)
Peewee (Northamptonshire)
Ox Bird; Ox-eye (Essex; Kent; Sussex)
Stint (Northumberland)
Sea Lark (Cheshire; Gloucestershire; East Lothian; Northern Ireland)
Jack Plover (Yorkshire); Jack Snipe (Shetland)
Plover's Page (W Scotland)
Dorbie (Banffshire)
Pickerel (Scotland)
Sea Peek (Forfar)
Sea Mouse (Lancashire; Dumfries)
Sand Mouse (Westmorland)
Bundie (Orkney)
Ebb Sleeper; Ebb Cock (Shetland)
Sea Snipe (N England); Sand Snipe (Gloucestershire)
Sandy (Northumberland)

Dunlin are the most abundant small wader of our shores and they have a large number of names over a widespread range. Some Dunlin are resident, breeding on wet upland moors, but these are far outnumbered by the winter flocks which spend the cold months on seashore and estuary. Of all the 'sea' and 'sand' names, Sea Mouse is one particularly descriptive of the way these little grey-brown waders scuttle about searching out insects and worms. In summer plumage the back and wings are red-brown, and beneath, where the legs join the body, is a large black patch which is probably responsible for the name Ox-eye as applied to the Dunlin (see Ringed Plover, for the similar use of Bull's-eye). In winter, Dunlin often join up and feed with flocks of Golden Plover and in summer they frequent the same moorlands, which is why the Dunlin is known in west Scotland as Plover's Page. *The Atlas of Breeding Birds* records that their observers found the Golden Plover helpful in locating Dunlin pairs, for the Dunlin would join the Plover when they circled up in alarm at an intruder coming near to their nesting places. The song of a Dunlin is a trilling purr from which come the Norfolk names Purre and Churre.

---

from its haunts:
Sand Runner (East Yorkshire)
Sea Lark (Ireland)
Sand Lark
Ebb Cock (Shetland)

various:
Towilly; Curwillet (Cornwall)
Peep (Northumberland)
Ruddy Plover
Ox-eye (Essex; Kent)
Stint; Snent
Tweeky (Northumberland)

Sanderling
Calidris alba

A small proportion of Sanderling spend the winter here, but the great flocks which come to the sandy coastlines of the British Isles in May and September are birds of passage, on migration between the breeding grounds in the Arctic and the wintering places which may be as far as the southern parts of Africa, America and Australia. Some non-breeding birds may come over during the summer months, their breeding plumage red-brown on the face and breast, giving them the name of Ruddy Plover. They are highly active little waders. Sand Runner is one of the most aptly descriptive of

Sanderling names; they dash energetically about on the shore particularly at low tide (hence Ebb Cock) for pickings which include pieces of vegetable matter as well as marine worms and crustacea. They have two different cries, and names derived from both of them. On the beach they have a triple note which sounds not unlike 'cur-will-et' or 'to-will-y'. In flight they call something like 'twick-twick', which is rendered Peep and Tweeky.

Ruff
Reeve
Philomachus pugnax

Fighting Ruff (male)
Gambet
Oxen-and-Kine
Reeve (female)

The breeding Ruff is a decidedly exotic figure in his splendid long-feathered ruff and the two long ear tufts. The springtime congregation of these resplendent creatures and their prospective mates, the 'lek', is a highly ceremonial occasion. When displaying to a Reeve or to a rival male, he will bow forward so far that his beak touches the ground, erect his ruff into a magnificent circular frame and raise his ear tufts. The ruff feathers differ in colour from bird to bird; in some a rich brown, in others an ermine mottle of black and white, black, brown or white and combinations of each. The ear tufts sometimes match, sometimes not. Leg and bill colours are also variable, and, to quote Montagu (*Ornithological Dictionary*, 1802) 'neither the colour of the bill, nor the legs is to be depended upon'.

Though the name of this bird and the exaggerated collar popular in the sixteenth century are the same, the obvious conclusion that they are linked is not supported by etymology. Ruff, the item of clothing fashionable in the time of James I and Elizabeth I, entered the language some time about 1555 and is closely connected to a 'ruffle' group of words of Teutonic origin which implied wrinkling or folding. Ruff and Reeve are thought to be derived from the Old English *Gerofa* which meant commander, possibly associated with the ostentatiously aggressive show of the displaying Ruffs.

It would have been surprising if the language-loving Elizabethans had missed an opportunity for a play on words and ideas. A pamphlet of about 1586 which berated the extreme fashions of its time used for illustration a woodcut of a Ruff 'intangled and caught', intended as a caution against vanity. In a wider sense the history of the Ruff could be read as a cautionary tale for the twentieth century. For hundreds of years human beings have drained the fens and marshes where the Ruff breeds, and people have netted, shot, eaten and stuffed the birds and stolen their eggs for collections. Today the only regular breeding places are certain areas on the Ouse Washes, managed and preserved by conservation bodies. Here in the early 1970s there were up to 103 Ruffs at the leks, though only about twenty-one breeding Reeves. This is a far cry from the Lincolnshire of the eighteenth century when a single fowler could net no less than seventy-two Ruffs in a single morning, and a man might expect to take at least forty to fifty dozen between April and Michaelmas which, after being fattened, would fetch two shillings or half-a-crown as table birds.

Avocet
Recurvirostra avosetta

from the curved bill:
Cobbler's Awl; Cobbler's Awl Duck
Shoe Awl; Shoeing Horn
Scooping Avocet; Scooper
Awl-bird (Suffolk)
Crooked Bill

from the cry:
Yarwhelp (Norfolk)
Yelper (Lincolnshire)
Yaup (Norfolk)

various:
Butterflip
Clinker (Norfolk)
Picarini

147

The Avocet with its curved bill, long legs and distinctive black and white markings, is one of the most elegant of waders. The standard name is an English form of the Italian *avocetta* (Willughby calls it the 'Avosetta of the Italians'), which itself is from the Latin *avis* = bird. This is given the diminutive ending, characteristic of the Italian language, which indicates charm and grace rather than literal small size.

After an absence of about a century, Avocets have now been breeding regularly for fifteen years in Britain. They are on the edge of their range in Britain and are very specialized in their breeding habitat, requiring low muddy islands set in shallow brackish water. These conditions have been carefully maintained by the RSPB at the two reserves at Minsmere and Havergate in Suffolk, and their solicitude has been rewarded, for these reserves have become the two main strongholds for the Avocet in Britain. It is not surprising that the RSPB has taken the Avocet for its badge.

The long upcurved bill gives rise to a number of names, such as the simply descriptive Crooked Bill. Scooper and Scooping Avocet describe the side-to-side sweeping of the surface and shallows for food. The long, pointed bill also resembles the time-honoured tool of the cobbler, the awl, and several names make a play on this. The Middle English for awl was *eawl,* so perhaps it is not coincidence that the nearest pub to the Minsmere reserve is called the 'Eel's Foot'. Local people will tell you that the eel is a corruption of awl.

When disturbed, or if the nest or young are threatened, Avocets utter loud yelping cries and they share several names with other waders with piercing alarm calls, Yelper (also the Redshank), Yarwhelp (the Bar-tailed Godwit), and Yaup (more usually the Curlew).

Thick Knee (Norfolk)
Thick-kneed Bustard (Sussex)
Norfolk Plover (Norfolk)
Stone Plover; Whistling Plover
Land Curlew (Kent)
Clew (Surrey)
Cullew (Suffolk); Night Curlew (Sussex)
Night Hawk
Collier, Collier-jack (Cheshire)
Great Plover (Suffolk; Surrey; Sussex)
Little Bustard (Sussex)
Willie Reeve (Breckland)

Stone Curlew

Burhinus oedicnemus

The Stone Curlew is a strange beast. It is called after the Curlew because of the quiet 'cour-lie' call, 'a voice of the gloaming' as G. K. Yeates describes it. For him it was a bird of childhood and as such had a special place in his memory. Particularly evocative was the night singing:

> It begins with the witching hour when the sun is down but the light not yet quite gone, the hour when the older shrubs and juniper bushes seem to take on uncanny shapes of things that do not appear in the hard light of day. Then from one side of the valley the quiet *cour-lee* steals forth, to be taken up afar by another bird out upon its evening business. Then another, further off takes up the theme: then perhaps another quite close by. It is a restrained and eerie concert, and without it the valleys and downs would lose much of their charm.
>
> (*Bird Haunts in Southern England*)

Stony, open country, the Wolds, chalk downs and the Brecklands are the territory of the Stone Curlew. It leads a hidden fugitive existence, relying on the way its brown streaked plumage matches the stony ground to keep it from view, for it is an intensely shy bird. The names Night Plover and Night Hawk testify to the nocturnal habits of a bird which may often be heard singing well into the early hours of the morning. In the daytime it is extremely lethargic unless disturbed, as G. K. Yeates noted:

> By day the Stone Curlew is, like the night jar or

the owls and with equal reason, an inactive bird. Its large yellow eye bears eloquent testimony to its crepuscular and nocturnal way of life. If you see it by daylight, you will see a long-legged, brown-streaked plover, running rapidly over the skyline, or making for scanty juniper cover. You will not easily make it fly, unless the ground is very flat, for the Stone Curlew on the wing shows much white, and the bird believes in the maxim of out of sight, out of mind.

The eggs are laid in a 'scrape' on the stony ground and they too are well camouflaged. In fact, as T. A. Coward says 'from egg onward, the life of the Stone Curlew is spent in hiding itself from view.'

The chicks freeze or 'play dead' if approached. Young birds have an enlarged 'heel' (where the knee would seem to be on a human being) hence the Thick-knee names which are probably rather bookish titles translated from the scientific name *oedicnemus* meaning 'swollen shinned'.

There are only a few places in eastern and southern England where the Stone Curlew may be found. It is a summer migrant and Britain marks the northwestern edge of its range. Some of its territory, particularly that in the Norfolk Brecks has become unavailable to it as a breeding place over the last forty or so years because of the afforestation of regions previously uncultivated, and the Stone Curlew is today not only an elusive but a very rare bird.

Great Skua
Stercorarius skua

Bonxie (Orkney; Shetland)
Boatswain (Yorkshire)
Jager; Morrel Hen (Yorkshire)
Robber Bird; Tod Bird (Yorkshire)
Tom Harry (Cornwall; Scilly)
Wease-alley (Sussex)
Brown Gull; Black Gull (Tralee)
Tuliac
Sea Crow
Allan (Scotland)
Herdsman (Orkney)

The modern Icelandic name for this species is *Skumur,* from the same root as our Skua. It means dark or brown gull: a northern version of the names Brown Gull and Black Gull. In Orkney and Shetland the Great Skua is more commonly known as Bonxie, a name which comes from the Scandinavian, and makes a good sturdy name for a formidable bird. The Bonxie is a large, dark, heavily-built Skua. It spends most of its life at sea but comes to land in summer to breed on grassy moorland in northern Scotland and the islands. It is a powerful bird and more of a predator than the Arctic Skua, catching prey as large as Kittiwakes and Oystercatchers, and not above picking off the young of waders and Arctic Skuas. But a considerable proportion of the diet comes from pirating other birds and stealing their food. Despite their size, Bonxies are very quick and manoeuvrable. Their size enables them to harry large gulls and even Gannets as well as Kittiwakes and Terns. While prospecting for food, the Bonxie moves at an ambling cruise but it can leap into a high speed chase at instant notice. It has large broad wings, with a patch of white on both upper and lower surfaces, otherwise it is a dark brown–black all over.

The Bonxie adds fury to its attacks by accompanying them with harsh cries, a deep barking 'tuk-tuk-tuk' (which may be the origin of the name Tuliac), and a harsh down–slurred 'skee-ah' itself not unlike the name Skua. The Yorkshire name Jager is to be found (as Jaegar) in the standard North American names for the Arctic, Long-tailed and Pomarine Skuas. The Bonxie, the only Skua to have Jager as an alternative name in Britain, is known in America simply as Skua.

Bonxies used to be welcomed in the islands of Orkney and Shetland for they used to drive the White-tailed Eagles away from the lambing grounds, which is the rationale behind the name Herdsman. However, after the extinction of the Eagle in these islands, the Bonxie was severely persecuted both by the crofters for food and by egg collectors. The population declined to a dangerously low level during the nineteenth century but during the past few decades, under protection, there has been a vigorous increase in the numbers of this spendid and piratical seabird.

Arctic Skua
Stercorarius parasiticus

Arctic Bird; Arctic Gull
Shooi (Shetland)

from the mistaken notion that the parasitised birds are excreting rather than disgorging food which the Skua eats:
Dirt Bird (Scotland)
Skait Bird; Shite Scouter (Scotland)
Dung Bird; Dung Hunter
Dung Teaser (Berwickshire)
Dirty Allan; Dirty Aulin (Orkney)
Fasceddar; Feaser
Scoutie Aulin (Orkney; Shetland)
Chaser (Yorkshire)

various:
Man-of-War Bird
Labbe
Boatswain (N Scotland; Orkney)
Trumpie (Orkney)
Wagel (Cornwall)

The Arctic Skua is our rarest breeding seabird; the sites in Scotland and the islands are the southern-most breeding sites. As its standard name, and other names such as Arctic Bird and Arctic Gull would imply, this is a circumpolar species. It is attractive in appearance, with sharp-angled wings and long central tail feathers (though not as long as the elegant 'trailers' of the Long-tailed Skua). Arctic Skuas vary a great deal in their colouration from the dark phase birds which are sooty brown all over, to light phase ones which have creamy white neck, cheek and underparts.

The Arctic Skua is principally a pirate, certainly living up to its scientific name *parasiticus*. The flight of an Artic Skua resembles that of a hawk; it moves with graceful steady wingbeats and long glides. The British population feeds mainly at sea, victimizing Terns, Kittiwakes and Puffins. The Artic Skua is eager in chase, relentlessly shadowing every turn and twist of its chosen subject, until food is disgorged when the Skua will usually snatch it from the air as it falls. The whole manoeuvre takes place very rapidly and early observers, concluding that the pursued birds were excreting rather than disgorging, gave the Artic Skua all kinds of faeces names.

Arctic Skuas establish their nests on moorland in loosely grouped colonies and they watch over and protect them with exceptional vigilance. They will fiercely attack intruders or, as an alternative strategy, feign convincing injury. The alarm cry is a loud, mewing trumpet which may have given rise to the Trumpie name of Orkney, which with Shetland holds the majority of the British breeding population of the Arctic Skua.

Great Black-backed Gull

Larus marinus

plumage names:
Black Back
Black and White Gull; Black-backed Hannock (Yorkshire)
Swart Back (Orkney)
Swarbie (Orkney; Shetland)
Saddleback (Norfolk; Lancashire)
Greater Saddleback (Ireland)
Parson Gull, Parson Mew (Sussex; Galway)

others:
Cobb (Essex; Kent; N Devon; Wales; Galway)
Baagie, Baakie, Baugie (Orkney; Shetland)
Goose Gull (Ireland)
Gray Gull (Ireland)
Gull Maw (East Lothian)
Carrion Gull (Ireland)

young:
Wagell Gull (Yorkshire)

The largest and most powerful of our gulls, the Great Black-backed Gull, has a wingspan of over a metre. The upper wings are dark, nearly black. Swart, an Old English synonym for black, carries also the connotations of 'baleful' and 'malignant'. Swart Back has been a local name in the far north since as long ago as 1450, a fittingly descriptive name both for its physical appearance and of the maleficent pale-eyed stare. It prefers a flesh diet, 'either recent or ancient', as T. A. Coward puts it, 'a dead rat, dog or whale is alike acceptable to the Corpse-eater'. The Great Black-back also hunts live prey, and its formidable size and strength make it a fatal enemy to small seabirds, particularly Puffins and Shearwaters. The Irish call it the Goose Gull, probably out of deference to its size; it is actually larger than the Brent Goose or Barnacle Goose. It is a mostly maritime species, rarely coming in far from the sea and it has only a very few inland breeding sites. It is significant that all the counties which have local names for this bird have a stretch of coastline. The Cobb of the southern counties and parts of Ireland and Wales probably came to us across the sea from the Frisian *kobbe* some time during the sixteenth century, but little more than this is known. The Black-back has a particularly hoarse cry which the double 'a' and harsh consonants of Baakie and Baagie attempt to repeat.

Lesser Black-backed Gull

Larus fuscus

Gray Gull; Gray Cob
Blackback
Said Fool (Shetland)
Saith Fowl
Yellow-legged Gull
Coddy Moddy, Caudy Maudy (Northamptonshire)

The Gray Gull or Gray Cob is not only greyer than its 'great' relative, but more slightly built and generally smaller. It is almost always to be seen with yellow legs (in contradistinction to the Great Black-back's invariably pink legs) but the name Yellow-legged Gull which appears as late as 1828 in J. Fleming's *History of British Animals* seems like more of a naturalist's 'book name' than a popular one. Coddy Moddy refers to the Lesser Black-back's predations on shoals of young cod, described by Coward as 'frenzied raids . . . when the water is churned by the plunging and superficial dives of the excited birds, and the air rings with their cries'. Caudy Maudy is clearly a variant of this. Possibly the name Saith Fowl is a similar reference as *saithe* is an old Icelandic name for the fry of codfish (it is also an alternative name for the cod-relative colcy), and the rather quaint Said Fool looks like a scrambled form of this name. Though they have a number of fishy names and indeed do tend to fish more actively than either Herring or Great Black-backed Gulls, the Lesser Black-backs also eat shore invertebrates. They do a certain amount of scavenging, and may be seen inland with much greater frequency than their larger namesake.

Cat Gull (Kirkcudbright)
Laughing Gull (Belfast)
Silver Back; Silvery Gull (Ireland)
White Maa (Orkney; Shetland)
Willie Gow (East Lothian; Aberdeen)

Herring Gull
Larus argentatus

This fierce looking gull with the ominous laughing cackle is, as its standard name suggests, a predominantly sea bird which lives mainly upon sea fish. The densest populations of Herring Gulls are in areas with rocky cliffs but they are to be found along most coasts though they do not favour salt marshes, and sizeable breeding colonies are largely absent from the South Yorkshire coast down to the Thames estuary. With an expanding population (they are the second most populous gull in Britain and Ireland) they seem to be becoming more adaptable in their breeding sites, using shingle beaches and sand dunes, and there are now a few inland colonies.

Like other cliff-dwelling species, such as Pigeons and Kestrels, Herring Gulls too have discovered alternative nesting sites in buildings. It was in south coast seaside resorts that Herring Gulls were first noted making their nests upon buildings in the 1920s and the colonies are now quite sizeable despite the irritation of the human residents. The town colony at Dover is above 225 pairs. They are also becoming more flexible in their feeding habits, again making use of the facilities offered by man. Herring Gulls are now familiar figures at town refuse tips, especially during the winter months. They are expert scavengers, with a sharp eye for anything remotely edible.

The Herring Gull is an impressive bird; seen close to, it seems exceptionally large (it is in fact between a Lesser and Great Black-back in size, but these birds are less confident about being close to human beings). The grey mantle which gives it the names Silvery Gull and Silver Back is variable in colour and can be slatey dark. It is also called White Maa from the white of the head, breast and tail. It is a superb flier, ably using wind currents and eddies to achieve the desired effect: a stationary poise, perfectly controlled sailing, or elegant swoops. As well as its strange laughter, the Herring Gull has a plaintive mewing cry which has earned it the name Cat Gull in some parts of Scotland.

Common Gull
Larus canus

Mew, Sea Mew (Scotland)
Maa, Mar (Kirkcudbright)
Sea Maw, Sea Mall (Scotland)
Blue Maa (Shetland)
Small Maa (Shetland)
White Maa (Orkney)

various:
Winter Mew; Mew; Winter Gull
Gow (Aberdeen)
Cob, Sea Cobb (Kent; Essex; Suffolk; Norfolk)
Annet (Northumberland)
Coddy Moddy
Winter Bonnet
Barley Bird (S Devon)
Seed Bird (Roxburgh; Teviotdale)
Green-billed Gull

Turner (1544) calls this gull simply the 'Se-cob or See gell'. Modern dictionary definitions also say that as well as being a generic term, Sea Gull refers specifically to the Common Gull. It is, however, not a very common gull, even in Northern

Scotland and the North of Ireland where it is most abundant. Willughby (1678) called it the Common Sea-mall and Pennant (1776) the Common Gull. In this case, it would seem that the word 'common' refers not to the frequency of occurence but is used in the Middle English sense of having no distinguishing features.

This is not to say that the Common Gull is dull. On the contrary, it is one of the most attractive of the gull family in appearance. It is a nicely proportioned bird, smaller than a Lesser Black-back, slightly larger than the Black-headed. The blue grey back and the white of the head, breast and underparts account for the Blue Maa and White Maa names. The Common Gull has a greeny-yellow bill, smaller than the cruel wedge of the Herring Gull but still a practical instrument of some power, and used in pursuit of a variety of food. As well as small marine and land creatures and insects, and dead fish and garbage, the Common Gull includes seeds in its diet, hence the name Seed Bird. It may have acquired the name Barley Bird in Devon on two counts. It is a winter visitor, arriving about the time for the sowing of the barley, and it will also follow the plough eating the seed. A winter visitor to most coasts, the Common Gull also has 'winter' names. It tends not to come inland very much, though at Tring, one of the most inland of waterways, it is usually possible to find one or two Common Gulls in a winter drift of several thousand Black-headed Gulls.

---

plumage:
Black Cap, Black Head
Brown-headed Gull
Hooded Crow, Hooded Mew (Orkney; East Lothian)
Masked Gull
Pigeon Gull (Yorkshire)
Patch
White Crow

Black-headed Gull

Larus ridibundus

leg colour:
Redshank Gull (Ireland)
Red-legged Gull (Ireland)
Red-legged Pigeon Mew (Norfolk)

feeding and habitat names:
Mire Crow
Sea Crow (Cheshire; Yorkshire)
Puit Gull; Peewit Gull
Carr Swallow (East Yorkshire)
Tumbler (Yorkshire)
Tumbling Gull
Sprat Mew

local names:
Potterton Hen (Aberdeen) from Potterton loch, now
    dried up
Scoulton Pie, Scoulton Peewit (Norfolk) from Scoulton
    mere, Norfolk
Collochan Gull (Kirkcudbright) from the loch of that
    name.

various:
Bakie (Shetland)
Crocker; Cob
Pine, Pine Maw (Antrim)
Maddrick Gull (Cornwall)
Pick Sea; Pictarn; Pickmire (Roxburgh)
Pickie Burnet (Roxburgh)
Rittock (Orkney)

As a child I found the arrival of 'seagulls' on the park lakes, an event of annual significance, a sure indication that winter was on the way. Children today are much more likely to see gulls all the year round. The Black-headed Gull is the most widely distributed gull, quantities of them living and breeding inland, many of whom will have lived all their lives with not so much as a glimpse of the sea. Actually, the Black-headed has always been the most landlubberly of all our gulls, but now their larger numbers make them more conspicuous. This gull has more than trebled its population over the last forty years; a dramatic revival for a bird which was facing extinction in Britain during the nineteenth century.

There are a number of old names which testify to the Black-headed Gull's diversity of habitat; it is for instance Pickmire and Picktarn, as well as Picksea. It is both Carr Swallow (carr = pool or fen) and Sea Crow. It seems also to have been called Peewit or Puit Gull, because it feeds in the same field, estuary and moorland habitats as the Lapwing and arrives and departs at the same time. (There is also some food parasitism between the two species, the Black-headeds forcing Lapwings, better adapted as field feeders, into giving up their food.) In 1771 gulls were a comparatively rare sight in Selborne but at the end of the hard winter of that year, Gilbert White observes in his journal:

It seems probable that the gulls which I saw were the pewit-gulls, or black caps, the *larus ridibundus* Linn: They haunt, it seems, inland pools, & sometimes breed in them.

He seems quite familiar with several names quite naturally varying them in his writing. Six years later he writes a terse almost Haiku-like entry:

Sea-gulls, winter mews, haunt the fallow. Beetles flie.

Smaller than the other common gulls, the Black-headed is compact in form with a slim, startlingly red bill and legs, with an archer's bow of white traced along the front of the extended wings. Pigeon Mew seems at first an odd name, but there is a certain resemblance in general deportment between the two species; they have also a watchful eye, squabblesome gregariousness, and plentiful opportunism in common. During the summer months, the chocolate brown hoods give the birds a quaintly nun-like aspect. Black-headed Gulls use a kind of drifting, wavering flight while generally prospecting for food. But they can also fly fast, tumbling, twisting and banking steeply when they are catching flying insects, which may have given rise to the Tumbler and Tumbling Gull names.

Kittiwake
Rissa tridactyla

from the cry:
Kittick, Kishiefaik, Kittiwaako (Orkney)
Keltie (Aberdeen)
Kittie (East Coast; Banffshire)
Sea Kittie (Norfolk; Suffolk)
Waeg
Kittiake

various:
Cackreen
Annet
Craa Maa (Shetland)
Petrel (Flamborough Head)

immature:
Tarrock

No person who has visited a seabird colony will have any doubt about how the Kittiwake got its name. The high pitched 'kitti-kitti-wake' calls, with the haunting rise in the last note, echo from the cliffs. It is only during courtship and nesting time that the birds 'kittiwake'; for the rest of the year they are mostly silent except for an occasional 'kit'.

Before their first moult, the young Kittiwakes are known as Tarrocks. The 'w' of black across the wings and back and the black bar on the tail distinguishes them from the adult birds where the only black is at the tips of the wings, as if they had been dipped in ink. The steady beat of these black tips is usually the first thing to catch the eye as a group of Kittiwakes beats its way over the waves in a graceful, buoyant flight. Unlike other gulls, a Kittiwake spends most of its time at sea, coming to land only as far as the coastal cliffs during the summer breeding time. Kittiwakes are also gentlest in appearance of all gulls, and it may be this, combined with their plaintive calling that lies behind a belief that the souls of dead children go into Kittiwakes.

Stern; Starn (Norfolk)
Carr-swallow (Cambridgeshire)
Carr Crow
Clover-footed Gull; Cloven-footed Gull
Blue Darr; Blue Daw (Norfolk)
Scare Crow
Black Kip (Sussex)

Black Tern
Chlidonias niger

The Black Tern used to be a more common bird in Britain than it is now, breeding regularly in south and southeast England. Today only a few pairs breed irregularly in East Anglia, but as spring and autumn migrants, Black Terns are fairly regular. They are marsh terns and favour inland waters more than the mainly maritime group the sea terns; hence Carr Swallow (a carr being a word, which goes back to the Middle Ages, for a pool or fen). Black Terns often stop off for several days feeding in inland lakes or reservoirs during migration. They feed upon flies and water insects as well as fish, darting and fluttering as they fly, and banking steeply in the characteristically fast sure-winged tern flight. Black Terns, however, rarely dive directly into the water; they simply skim an insect or fish from the surface or just below.

The Tern and Stern names come from the Old Norse and have been in use in Britain at least since Anglo-Saxon times.

Darr (Norfolk)
Starn (Norfolk)
Tarnie
Pictarnie (East Lothian; Fife)
Tarret; Tarrock; Taring (Shetland)
Piccatarrie (Shetland)
Speikintares (Ross-shire)

from the cry:
Pirre (N Ireland)
Skirr (Lambay Island)
Great Purl (Norfolk)
Kirrmew
Scraye
Sparling, Spurling (Lancashire)
Dippurl (Norfolk)

Common Tern
Sterna hirundo

161

Common Tern

from the flight and long fork of the tail:
Sea Swallow (General)
Shear Tail (Orkney)

various:
Gull Teaser (South Devon)
Picket-a (Orkney)
Miret (Cornwall)
Clett
Kip
Great Tern
Rittock, Rippock
Kingfisher (Lough Neagh)
Willie Fisher
Pease Crow

Arctic Tern
Sterna paradisaea

Tarrock (Shetland)
Sparling (Lancashire)
Rittock; Ritto (Orkney)
Pickieterno (Orkney)
Skirr (Ireland)
Sea Swallow (Ireland)
Tarry (Northumberland)

These Sea Swallows with their long pointed wings and forked tails must be the most beautiful and graceful of all sea birds. More slender than gulls, they are immensely supple and adroit in flight, characteristically coming suddenly out of an easy up-wind beat over the sea with a rapid twist to dive obliquely into the water after a small fish or marine insect. On their 'hunting' flights, terns carry their heads low, closely scanning the water beneath, and they often poise with wings raised and the tail fanned, before half closing their wings and making the dive.

Although the Common Tern is the more widespread of these two species and has a wider selection of local names (including ones from East Anglia and South-East England), the Arctic Tern is actually more numerous. Found mostly in Scotland, the Arctic Tern, a circumpolar species, achieves greater numbers in more northerly parts. The Common Tern is a bird of temperate regions, widely distributed over Europe, Asia and North America. In Britain and Ireland the species overlap;

in the northernmost parts, the tern colonies are composed mostly of Arctic Terns, in the South, of Common Terns, and in between there are mixed colonies, usually with the Common Tern predominating. The two species are very similar in appearance, hence the ornithologists' vernacular name Comic Tern. Only an extra greyishness, shorter legs and a slightly more silvery wing (and in summer, redder beak) distinguish the Arctic Tern. The harsh calls are also alike, and as well as the name Sea Swallow 'voice' names such as Skirr and Sparling are shared.

The skirring and attacking calls are at their most insistent when the birds have eggs or young chicks. Both species nest in large numbers and groups of adults will tackle any kind of intruder first with cries of anger, then with diving attacks. Two or three terns can make a great enough disturbance to drive off a wandering sheep or shift a cow away from a nest.

---

from the cry:
Skirr (Ireland)
Small Purl (Norfolk)
Sparling (West Lancashire)
Chit Perl

various:
Richel Bird
Little Darr (Norfolk)
Shrimp Catcher (Norfolk)
Fairy Bird (Galway)
Sea Swallow (General)
Dip Ears (Norfolk)
Little Pickie (Forfar)
Hooded Tern

young:
Sea Mice

Little Tern
Sterna albifrons

Well named the Fairy Bird in Galway, the Little Tern is a bewitching bird. Much smaller than other terns, it has taken many of the local tern names with a diminutive prefix, such as Chit Perl, Little Pickie, Little Darr. It is active and darting in its flight and hovers more than its larger relatives, holding itself in barely fluttering poise before shooting into a close-winged dive which often takes it well under the water. Reappearing immediately, it mounts the air again with just a few strong wing beats, as often as not gulping a fish as it goes. (This submersion tactic is possibly why it is called Dip Ears in Norfolk.)

The Little Tern does not actually look any more conspicuously 'hooded' than any other sea tern, all of which have black caps, though it is different in that it has a horizontal band of white on its forehead. Though not a common bird, it is well distributed over most of the coastline of the British Isles. The breeding colonies of Little Terns are smaller than those of other species, usually under twenty-five pairs, but they are no less fierce in defending their nests and young, despite their small size and number. In West Lancashire, the baby Little Terns are known as Sea Mice.

Sandwich Tern

Sterna sandvicensis

The Tern (Farne Islands)
Boatswain
Crocker Kip (Sussex)
Surf Tern
Screecher (Kent)

The Sandwich Tern, the largest and most impressive of the terns, was, according to P. J. Selby, called simply The Tern in the Farne Islands; all other species being referred to as Sea Swallows. It is found in Britain as a breeding bird and as a bird of passage on its way to winter in West Africa. The Sandwich Tern has a heavy build and a long wing span and a bluntly forked tail. The black feathers of the nape and neck are long and make a crest at the back of the head, raised formidably when the bird is excited. The Tern is dubbed Sandwich, according to John Latham (in his *General Synopsis of Birds* 1781–90), because some boys from the town of Sandwich told him about the birds there. They may perhaps be seen there occasionally today, offshore fishing or passing through, but the only breeding colony in Kent now is at Dungeness. The Sandwich Tern is noisier than most other terns and often calls attention to itself with its strident, high, harsh double note which earned it the name Screecher. The name Boatswain is more usually applied to the Arctic Skua.

Razorbill
Alca torda

Alk; Auk (North of England)
Falk; Faik (Hebrides)
Bawkie (Orkney)

from its call:
Murre (Cornwall)
Marrot (East Lothian; Aberdeen)

various:
Gurfel
Hellejay; Helligog (Shetland)
Puffin (Antrim; Sussex)
Scout (Scotland)
Sea Blackbird (Pembroke)
Sea Craa (Shetland)
Sea Crow (Orkney)

The *Alca* of the scientific name for the Razorbill, like the Auk, Alk, Falk group of names, comes from the Icelandic word for the bird: *Alka*. These names are probably imitative of the harsh growling calls which sound something like 'arrc–arrc'. The auk group of seabirds look a little like small Penguins (in fact, the word Penguin was originally applied to the Great Auk) but auks are able to fly. Typically they are stocky in build, black or very dark brown in colour and, being fish feeders, very vigorous divers.

Unless you are well out at sea, the only time you are likely to see Razorbills is when they come in to coastal cliffs to breed between the months of March and July. The Razorbill pairs each choose a ledge or crevice on which to lay their single egg. Razorbills are usually to be seen in amongst Guillemot colonies but they tend to choose more private spots than this species, and are in general

165

less gregarious. They are distributed over a wider area than Guillemots but are not as numerous.

A Razorbill can be easily distinguished from other Auks, by its extraordinary wedge-shaped bill. 'Bill' and 'beak' are often used interchangeably but they are not quite synonymous. Bill comes from the Old English *bile* and is related to the word for a flat sword of the Anglo-Saxons, which is very suitable for the flat bills of Razorbills and Puffins (and in the horizontal plane, for ducks).

Razorbill as a name seems to have been first written about in the ornithologies of the seventeenth century. Sir Thomas Browne, the Norfolk naturalist, was among the first to record its presence in 1662, and Razorbill was also included in Christopher Merrett's list of 1666. Willughby (1678) writes of 'The bird called Razorbill in the West of England, Auk in the North, Murre in Cornwall.'

It is possible to see a visual similarity between one mandible of the Razorbill's bill and a cutthroat razor. On the other hand, there might be another, auditory explanation. The word razor has its origins in the Latin *radere,* to scrape and the voice of the Razorbill resembles a grating or scraping noise. Auk, as we have seen, may be an imitative name from the same sound. Murre is also an imitative name; it echoes another part of the Razorbill's call, a kind of 'urrr–urrr', deep toned, with a couple of seconds space between each grunt. So the three names mentioned by Willughby (which retain the same geographical distribution except that the 'name of the west' Razorbill, has become the standard term) seem all to be the representations of the Razorbills distinctive, if unmusical, voice.

Guillem, Gwylog (Welsh)
Willock (Norfolk; Orkney)
Willy (Norfolk); Will (Sussex)
Foolish Guillemot
Wil-duck (Suffolk)

Guillemot
Uria aalge

from the call:
Murre, Murse (Cornwall; Devon; Cork)
Marrot, Morrot (Firth of Forth)
Muir-eun (Horn Head, Donegal)
Meere (Gloucestershire)

various:
Eligny (Pembrokeshire)
Spratter (Hampshire)
Quet (Aberdeen)
Auk (Orkney)
Scout (Yorkshire; Forfar; Orkney)
Skuttock, Skiddaw (East Lothian)
Kiddaw (Cornwall)
Maggie (Forfar)
Tarrock
Tinkershire, Tinkershue
Lavy; Lamy (Hebrides)
Sea Hen (Durham; Northumberland; East Lothian)
Strany
Frowl (Scotland)
Eun a chrubian = the crouching bird (Gaelic)

bridled form:
Bridled Guillemot
Bridled Marrot (W Scotland)
Ring-eyed Scout (W Scotland)
Ringed Guillemot (Yorkshire)
Silver-eyed Scout (W Scotland)

William Yarrell was among the first to use the name Guillemot for this species. He points out that this name is derived from the French, strictly speaking from the Breton *Gwelan*. Yarrell believes this name and the Norfolk name Willock to be imitative of the cry of the young Guillemot. At the time Yarrell wrote his *British Birds* in 1843, a name still in local use was the more popular one:

> In England the commonest [name] is the onomatopoetic 'Murre', from the murmuring noise of the assembled multitudes at their breeding haunts.

The 'mot' ending of Guillemot may have an imitative quality in common with the name Murre. Mot, originally 'Moette', had a Germanic origin and corresponds to the Old English 'meaw', the word which gave us Sea-mew for the gulls. There is good reason for thinking that the 'Guille' part of the name is related to the words which gave us Gull. The Low Breton *gwela* means 'to weep' and *gwelan*, 'the wailer', is the Gull. The Welsh have *gwae* meaning 'woe'; Gull in Welsh is *Gwylan* and an alternative Welsh name for Guillemot is *Gwylog*. The French made *Goëland* out of the Breton *gwelan* and, possibly for emphasis, they added their other word for Gull, *Mouette,* which finally shook down to Guillemot or 'wailing mew'. Guillemot breeding colonies consist of huge concentrations of birds (70,000 have been recorded at Westray, 25,000 at Marwick Head, in Orkney) and they are extremely noisy, so it is not surprising that the voice features so heavily in the names.

Yarrell also suggests that the name Scout may be a reference to the short cut-tail of the Guillemot, but it is perhaps more likely that this and the related names Kiddaw, Skuttock and Skiddaw derive from the word 'skite', a variant of 'shite'. By the end of the breeding season, the guano-covered ledges of the Guillemot colony's cliffs are messy and unpleasant smelling, a feature more likely to impress itself upon people out to catch the birds or plunder the eggs than a physical detail such as tail length. Like other birds which are easy game for the trapper, the Guillemot is epitomized as a stupid bird, the Suffolk 'Silly as a Willock' corresponding to the French *'Bête comme un guillemot'*.

There are two races of Guillemot which breed on British and Irish coasts. The one which occupies the more southerly niche (*Uris aage albionis*) has a chocolate brown summer plumage, the northerly birds (*Uria aalge aalge*) are distinctly blacker. There is also a variation in plumage which can occur in both races, but gets commoner as you go north. This is the 'bridle'. Bridled birds have a narrow but distinct white line around the eye, running back towards the nape. This earns them a number of special names such as Ring-eyed Scout and Bridled Marrot.

---

from their affectionate behaviour:
Sea Turtle; Greenland Turtle
Greenland Dove (Orkney)
Sea Pigeon (Ireland)
Sea Dovie (Forfar)
Diving Pigeon (Farne Islands)
Rock Dove (Ireland)
Doveky (whalers' name)
Turtle Dove (Lindisfarne)
Turtur (Bass Rock)
Turtle (Northumberland)

various:
Tystie (Orkney; Shetland)
Taister; Toyste; Tinkershere
Puffinet (Lindisfarne)
Scraber (East Lothian; Hebrides)
Spotted Guillemot

Black Guillemot
Cepphus grylle

The Black Guillemot or Tystie is similar in shape to the Guillemot but smaller, and in summer it is all black except for a brilliant white patch on the wing. It also has very bright red legs and feet. Unlike the cliff breeding Guillemots and Razorbills, the Tystie ignores craggy coastlines in springtime, choosing instead rocky or boulder strewn shores to bring up its young. The Tystie pair generally select a cavity beneath a boulder or a crevice or hole as the site to lay, usually, two eggs. The eggs may be some distance from the sea and the Tystie is much better at scrambling about over the rocks than other auks. A parent Tystie makes a splendid and dramatic picture standing sentinel on a rock near to its nesting spot, the bright legs gleaming, its white marks brilliant against the black.

The name Tystie, from the Old Norse *Teiste,* is generally used in Orkney and Shetland. Dove and Pigeon words figure in a large number of local names. It is difficult to see anything either in appearance or in the voice which might give rise to this connection. The association seems to lie in the gentle and affectionate behaviour of Tysties. The Turtle Dove in particular is a symbol of tenderness and fidelity and it lends itself to at least five names for the Tystie. Of all seabirds, Tysties are among the most charming. Not only are mated pairs affectionate and solicitous, the same spirit stretches to larger congregations. Before they split off into separate pairs, a pre-breeding flock will gather offshore. Dr Frazer Darling watched one such flock in Ross and Cromarty:

> [They] are extremely playful birds and a pleasure to watch. . . . The constant exercise of the voice is a characteristic of the springtime flocks of tysties. They have one small, plaintive and high-pitched call which may be represented by the syllable "peeeee". Within a large flock of sixty or seventy, which may cover five acres of sea, small groups come together for play and within these again it is possible to pick out pairs which keep close. Play is of a varied kind and very infectious. One bird may make a shallow dive and swim along just below the surface by the active use of the wings. The pattern of the white markings on the wings, the black body and the brilliant red feet moving under the rippled water is striking to the observer and it is probably visible to the immediate members of the group. Most of them will join in the fun, rising again in two or three seconds to stand up in the water and vibrate their wings rapidly. Then one will chase another until the first bird drops suddenly to the water and dives with a splash. The second bird is carried forward a yard or two before it can stop and make a similar dive. Both birds come to the top again near together and the little run is over. One day the peregrine falcon flashed through the flock when four birds were playing in the air. The sudden drop to the sea of all four birds was no longer that of play. They fell like stones and those on the sea dived.

(Bird Flocks and the Breeding Cycle)

from its broad, coloured bill:
Bottlenose (Wales)
Guldenhead (Wales)
Parrot-billed Willy (Sussex)
Bill (Galway)
Sea Parrot (Norfolk)
Coulter Neb (Farne Islands)

familiar names:
Tommy; Tom Noddy (Farne Islands)
Willy (Sussex)
Tammie Norie (Orkney; Shetland)

place names:
Bass Cock (Scotland)
Ailsa Cock, Ailsa Parrot (Scotland; Antrim)
Flamborough Head Pilot (Yorkshire)

various:
Pipe, Pope (Cornwall)
Scout (Farne Islands)
Willock (Kent)
Bouger; Bulker (Hebrides)
Mullet (Scarborough)
Helegug (Wales)
Marrot; Cockandy (Fife)
Coliaheen = old woman (Galway)
Pal (Wales)
Lunda; Lunda Bouger; Lundi (Faeroes)

The Puffin is a most appealing little bird. Both its appearance and behaviour win it friends far outside the coterie of ornithological enthusiasts. It is the emblem for the first paperback imprint of children's books, and those children who read 'Puffins' came to care also for the bird itself. When an appeal went out to save a stretch of Puffin coastline in northeast England, they responded vigorously and enough money was raised to purchase the land and make it into a reserve. Puffins sometimes get blown inland by gales and when they do they always attract attention. The Puffin who walked down the Strand in 1935 and stopped the traffic is almost a legend. While a number of interesting and exotic species pass though the Nature Reserve at Tring they are usually, at best, accorded a dutiful small paragraph in the local press. However, when a Puffin was found in a Buckinghamshire field last summer, it made headlines and a front page picture. Nor does the attraction of this species seem to be restricted to our own times. The sixteenth century ornithologist John Kay (who founded Caius College, Cambridge) cared for a Puffin in his house for eight months. He reported that it 'bit with right good will' and when hungry begged for food with a little cry of 'pupin, pupin', though it was soon satisfied.

In 1662, John Ray and Francis Willughby observed the Puffins on Bardsey Island (now also under consideration as a Nature Reserve). Ray notes that he heard there of the superstition that Puffins were incapable of flight over land. Another old tradition associated with these birds was that, like the Barnacle Goose and the Scoter, it was classified as a 'bird-fish' and eaten during Lent. John Kay, who lived in Norfolk, was among several who commented on this dispensation.

Many of the Puffin names refer specifically to the big brightly coloured beak. Sea Parrot and Guldenhead are obvious examples. Coulter Neb is another; neb (which we find in a number of duck names) is a northern word for 'bill'; a coulter is the iron blade fixed in front of a ploughshare which cuts through the soil and is roughly triangular in shape. The familiar Orkney and Shetland name Tammie Norie used to be used for a person who was shy in their habits and perhaps a little solemn in appearance as the Puffin is—

> Tammie Norie o' the Bass
> Canna kiss a bonny lass.

Puffins do not actually breed on Bass Rock ('the Bass') since they need grassy slopes in which they can excavate their burrows, but they are found very near by and have the name Bass Cock. They are also called Ailsa Parrot after Ailsa Craig. In the case of Lundy Island, however, we seem to have a case where the place has been named after the bird rather than the more usual way around. *Lunde* is the Icelandic and Norwegian name for the Puffin. This survives in the Faeroese names Lunda, Lundi and Lunda Bouger.

Cushat (Northamptonshire)
Wood Dove (Scotland)
Bush Dove
Craig Doo (Northumberland)
Hill Pigeon (Cheshire)
Burrow Pigeon (Yorkshire)
Blue Pouter (Suffolk)
Sand Pigeon (Cheshire)
Scotch Cushat; Scotch Queest (Cheshire)
Stoggie (Yorkshire)

Stock Dove
Columba oenas

The Stock Dove is a bird of open woods, farmland and parkland. Smaller than the Woodpigeon (with whom it shares the name Cushat), without the white patches on neck and wings, and much less common, the Stock Dove has a loud gruff double 'coo', with the accent on the second note. It is possible that the name Stock may come from the way the birds sometimes nest in the 'stocks' or tall stumps of trees. (It is also said that it derives from a mistaken belief that it was from this 'stock' that our domestic pigeons were descended.) They will also nest in old rabbit burrows, and in holes in rocks; hence Burrow Pigeon and Craig Doo (doo = dove). Pouter is a pigeon fancier's name usually given to a breed of domestic pigeon which is able to 'pout' or greatly inflate its crop.

Blue Dove (North Riding)
Sea Pigeon (Ireland)
Rock Pigeon (Ireland; Scotland)
Rock Doo (Shetland)
Sod (Forfar)
Doo (N Scotland)
Wild Pigeon (Shetland)
Cliff Pigeon (Yorkshire)

Rock Dove and Feral Pigeon
Columba livia

Wild Rock Doves are birds of the coasts and islands of the North of Scotland and Ireland. They are the ancestors of domestic pigeons, and there is a large population of hybrid birds and tame birds which have reverted to the wild. The birds which live in towns are descended from dovecote birds which have gone feral. They differ quite widely in

173

plumage; Derek Goodwin made an analysis of the variations and distinguished seven different colour forms. The most numerous form (possibly about fifty per cent of the population) he called the 'blue chequer', basically a bluish bird like the wild Rock Dove but with the closed wing spotted with black. The 'blue' feral pigeon (estimated at ten per cent) is the nearest in colour to the wild Rock Dove, unspotted wing coverts, two black wingbars and with white on the rump and underwing – but feral birds tend to have a looser shape, thicker beaks and larger wattles.

Except in some northern cities, where the Collared Dove has formed a stronghold, the Feral Pigeon is the principal urban dove, roosting and nesting upon ledges of high buildings, as its wild relative does upon rock ledges and crevices in caves. They pick about for food, mostly spillage or rubbish littering the town, with extraordinary perspicacity. They court their mates with inflated breasts, bows and bubbling coos and draggling tails, while commuter crowds dash back and forth around them.

The pigeon has a long association with man. The ancient Egyptians used homing pigeons to carry messages as the British army did during the last war. They seem to have lost their fear of man and man's machines and will feed boldly along roads, scarcely perturbed by the monster container lorries roaring by them. Once, I saw a pigeon walking on a drag race track in Northamptonshire apparently unconcerned by the eight-litre engines whose banshee power deafened the spectators a quarter of a mile away. It held up two races while the marshalls twice waited for it to cross and recross the track.

Woodpigeon
Columba palumbus

from its call:
Too-zoo (Gloucestershire)
Cooscot (Craven; Teesdale)
Cushat (Berkshire; Buckinghamshire; Craven;
   Westmorland)
Cruchet (North)
Cusha (Roxburgh)
Dow, Doo (Norfolk; Suffolk)
Cooshat (Yorkshire)
Timmer Doo (Scotland)
Cushie, Cushie Doo (Scotland)

from the plaintiveness of the voice:
Queest, Quest, Quist (West Midlands)
Quice, Quease (Shropshire; Gloucestershire)
Wood Quest (Dorset; Ireland)
Quisty (Suffolk)
Queece (Cheshire)

various:
Ring Dove (General)
Culver (Dorset)
Clatter Dove (Yorkshire)

The Woodpigeon is the most numerous and widespread of all the dove family in the British Isles. Originally a relatively scarce bird of deciduous woodland, its increase over the past two hundred years has gone with improved farming methods and the growing of winter fodder crops. They eat not only grain and wild seeds, but leaves, roots and some animal matter such as worms, snails and insects. Unfortunately, the good turn the Woodpigeon does the farmer by eating weed wildflowers and insect pests, is more than exceeded by its appetite for grain and seedlings. The pigeons clearly prefer the fat, full seeds, whether wild or agricultural, so when they turn to the delicately beautiful family of grasses, the 'bents', whose seeds are infinitesimal, it has been a bad year. Thus:

> When the pigeons go a benting
> Then the farmers lie lamenting.

There is a story from the North Riding of Yorkshire that says that at one time the Peewit used to nest in trees, and the Dove on the ground, but

175

they changed places. Nowadays, Woodpigeons make their nests in woods or even in isolated trees by suburban roadsides, or in shrubs or tall heather. The nest itself is no work of art, twigs laid roughly one against the other. The light can be seen through it from beneath and so too can the eggs. These are usually laid in pairs as the smug Wren rhyme says:

> Coo-coo-coo,
> It's as much as a pigeon can do
> To bring up two
> But the little wren can maintain ten
> And keep them all like gentlemen.

The word pigeon is of Norman origin, from the Latin *pipio,* a young cheeping bird. It was only at the beginning of this century that Woodpigeon has been adopted as the standard name for a bird still known in many places as the Ring Dove. Turner (1544), Merrett (1666), Sibbald (1684) and Pennant (1776) called it Ring or Ringed Dove and Willughby (1678), Ring Pigeon. The ring referred to is the clasp of white feathers on the bird's neck. Woodpigeon was often given as an alternative name and may in fact have been a spoken rather than a written name, but it was used also for the Stock Dove.

Dove, which comes from the Old English *dufan* meaning 'to dive', is an old fashioned past tense of 'dive'. The name refers to the way in which pigeons dive in the air in their swooping courtship flights. Another English name of long-standing is Cushat from the Old English *cuscote* which alludes to the speed of the bird's flight ('cu' imitative of the call, and *sceotan* = 'to move rapidly like an arrow from a bow'). There is yet another name of long standing, Culver from the Old English *culfre*. This name has found its way in into the names of wildflowers: Culverkeys is a local name for Cowslips, Bluebells, Columbines and the 'key' fruits of Ash. The Bluebell is also known simply as Culvers. It is possible that these plants were so named because Woodpigeons were seen eating the fruits and seeds, but there may also be a religious element in the naming. The Ashkeys and the flowerheads of Cowslips bear some re-semblance to a bunch of keys, which is the badge of Saint Peter who kept the keys of heaven. Since the Dove (Culver) is the symbol of the Holy Spirit, Culverkeys may be a living reminder of the keys of heaven, an earthly reflection in much the same way as so many plants were named after Our Lady: (Our) Lady's Smock, Lady's Slipper, Lady's Bedstraw and probably as many as a dozen others.

The cooing of the Ring Dove could be said to have a sad and plaintive quality to it, and there are a number of names thought to come from the Latin *questus* = to lament: Quest, Queece, Quice and so on. 'Thee bist a queer quist' is a Wiltshire saying, implying half-wittedness. This sense was also found in pigeon in the sixteenth century when a 'pigeon' was a person easily duped or swindled, especially in gaming. The American 'stool pigeon' has the same kind of meaning, referring meta-phorically to someone employed (again usually in gambling) as a decoy. In its literal meaning, a pigeon used to be fastened to a stool as a decoy for birds of prey. A gentler usage of the word pigeon, for a sweetheart, comes no doubt from the softly wooing song.

Turtle Dove
Streptopelia turtur

Wrekin Dove (Shropshire)
Troet (Cornwall)
Turtle
Turtur (Wales)
Summer Dove (Surrey)
Wood Dove (Sussex)

The soft but sustained purr of the Turtle Dove gave it its name at least as far back as Pliny in the first century. It is a beautiful gentle sound, evocative for poets of the sweetest and strongest of emotions. For the poets of *The Song of Solomon*, it was the sound of the promise of spring

> For lo, the winter is past, the rain is over and
> gone; The flowers appear on the earth; the time

of the singing of birds is come, and the voice of the turtle is heard in our land.

Chaucer saw the Turtle Dove as a loving bird, 'The wedded turtel with hir herte trewe', and for him it was the symbol of utmost fidelity, faithful in its love even after death.

The voice of the Turtle is heard more in the fields of England and eastern Wales than any other part of the British Isles. Its most important food plant is the delicate looking, smoky leaved Fumitory, a wildflower of arable fields, and there is a correspondence between the distribution of the Turtle Dove and that of Fumitory. The plant too has long been associated with rich cultivated lands, as the poet of the *Stockholm Medical Manuscript* wrote in about 1400:

> Fumiter is erbe, I say
> That springyth in April and in May
> In feld, in town, in yerd and gate
> There land is fat and good in state.

And such areas are attractive to the Turtle Dove which also likes grain and other weed-wildflower seeds. The local names for Fumitory are Birds on the Bush (Somerset)and Dicky Birds (Dorset) and these may have something to do with the Turtle Dove.

Collared Dove
Streptopelia decaocto

I hope that the days when there was a true regional response to a bird, in the form of a local name, have not passed with the introduction of standard checklists and the standardized names of field guides. The Collared Dove, it seems to me, calls out for recognition which establishes its new position as an urban resident, a form of record which is not found simply in books, but is part of the language of the people who see it on their chimney pots and around their factories, and who are themselves plagued by its insistent voice, repeating the montonous trisyllabic 'cuh-*cóo*-cuk'.

This species has a spectacular history. The first official record of Collared Doves breeding in

Britain was only in 1955; now the *Atlas of Breeding Birds* reckons its numbers at something between 15,000 and 25,000 breeding pairs. There are localized populations, some now quite dense, in the towns and suburbs of the Midlands and Northern counties and parts of Scotland. Birmingham, Sheffield, Leeds and Manchester have large numbers of Collared Doves, though they are not strong in number around London. These 'City Doves' have very quickly made themselves at home in their industrial environment to the extent that they were noted by Eric Simms including soft pieces of wire in the construction of their nests.

Gawky, Gawk (Dorset)
Geck (Cornwall)
Gog, Gok (Cornwall)
Gowk (Yorkshire; Scotland)
Hobby (Norfolk)
Welsh Ambassador

Cuckoo
Cuculus canorus

The Cuckoo is a migratory bird. It is also distinctive in its looks and flight, in its habits and its song. All these things combine to make the Cuckoo a focus for a huge amount of folklore and literary allusion. There are traditional dates for the arrival of the Cuckoo from the South of France (21 March) all the way across Europe, to Norway on 14 April. In England it is due in Sussex on 14 April, Cheshire 15 April, Worcestershire 20 April, Yorkshire 21 April. Why is it looked for with such eagerness and expectancy? The Cuckoo arrives with the spring and is seen as the bringer of spring. Its significance is further marked by the way in which it gives its name to other springtime sights. Lady's Smock (*Cardamine pratensis*) is also Cuckoo Flower and so is Ragged Robin (*Lychnis flos-cuculi*, *flos-cuculi* = flower of the cuckoo). Lords and Ladies *(Arum maculatum)* is Cuckoo Pint – cuckoo's pintle or penis, because of the largeness and shape of the spadix, an allusion to the Cuckoo's supposed promiscuity. Then there is 'cuckoo spit' the lump

179

of froth which encloses the young froghopper bug.

The importance of the arrival of spring and the season of new fresh life is reflected in these old Cuckoo names. There are many pieces of lore, too, about what to do on 'cuckoo day'. You can turn your money over so you won't be short of it, or, (if you're in Somerset or Northamptonshire) so you may have a wish, a reasonable one anyway, granted. If you count the number of 'cuckoos' the bird utters, you may discover: how many years will pass before you marry; the number of children you will have – or, if neither of these is relevant, the number of years before you die. There are many other cuckoo day beliefs; most of them have to do with fecundity and increase, as does springtime itself. By association there are a number of farming rhymes which feature Cuckoos, this one is from Norfolk:

> If the cuckoo lights on a bare bough,
> Keep your hay and sell your cow
> But if he comes on the blooming may
> Keep your cow and sell your hay.

When life was more precarious and the rural economy and people's existence were more directly related to the seasons, the coming of spring was vitally important. Even today, in our civilized world, we look out for the first Cuckoo in spring, with unabated eagerness, and every year *The Times* prints its first-Cuckoo letters. Everything bursts into life on the day of the Cuckoo as an anonymous poet noted some time about 1225 in one of our best-loved early poems:

> Summer is icumen in
> Llude sing cuccu
> Spryngeth sed and bloweth mede
> And groweth the wude nu.

It was not only the Cuckoo's arrival that was watched carefully (and accurately) by people centuries ago. One old rhyme, of which there are numerous versions, describes the sequence of its behaviour – right down to the change of song which could have two interpretations. The male changes from 'cuckoo' to a stuttery 'cuck-cuck-coo' which seems to be most noticeable in midsummer and later in the season the female begins her 'bubbling' call.

> In April come he will
> In May he sings all day
> In June he changes tune
> In July he prepares to fly
> In August go he must.

But where did he go in August? There were stories that the Cuckoo (like the Swallow) spent the winter months hibernating in the stumps of trees. Another belief, more commonly held in the north of England (Durham, Yorkshire, Cambridgeshire and Derbyshire), was that the Cuckoo changed into a hawk from August to April. This is not so far-fetched as it seems. Though more slow and heavy in flight, a Cuckoo looks quite similar to a hawk in wing shape. And why shouldn't a bird so extraordinary as to raise its young in another bird's nest, be capable of changing its guise again, later in life?

It is clear from early poetry that people were not deceived about the kind of behaviour to expect from a Cuckoo. In *The Parlement of Foules* the Merlin addresses the Cuckoo as

> Thou mordrer of the heysugge on the braunche
> That broghte thee forth, thou rewtheless glotoun

The notion of the Cuckoos spending the day in song, while other birds reared their babies, led to another discreditable association, that of 'cuckold'. It was the cuckold who like the Hedge Sparrow, kept up the home, while the Cuckoo-lover romped with his wife. There is however, something much more jocular about the word 'cuckold' than that of 'adulterer'; it is a word of Elizabethan wordplay and of the comedy of manners.

> The cuckoo then on every tree
> Mocks married men, for thus sings he
>
> 'Cuckoo'.
> *Love's Labour's Lost*

181

In 'cuckold' there was certainly the suggestion that the husband must have been pretty dull-witted and silly to have been hoodwinked in the first place. Perhaps there is a sense of this bantering derision in the more modern, idiomatic usage of cuckoo to mean 'soft in the head'. In many places still, the word gowk is used colloquially to mean a simpleton. The adjective is gawky, which may shed a little light on its derivation, for the young Cuckoo just out of the nest and learning to fly is ridiculously inept, many of its attempts ending in crash-landings. However, after only a few weeks that same gawky bird will be flying a journey of over a thousand miles to Africa.

Barn Owl
Tyto alba

Church owl (Craven; N England)

from the pure white of the under plumage and the light tawny yellow of the upper parts:
White Hoolet
White Owl
Silver Owl (Forfar)
Yellow Owl
Cailleach-oidhche Gheal = white old woman of the night (Gaelic)

from its voice:
Screech Owl (General)
Scritch Owl
Hissing Owl (Yorkshire)
Roarer (Borders)
Screaming Owl (Yorkshire)

familiar names:
Billy Wix, Billy Wise (Norfolk)
Jenny Howlet (North Riding)
Jenny Owl (Northumberland)
Madge Howlet (Norfolk)
Moggy (Sussex)
Padge; Pudge, Pudge Owl (Leicestershire)

various:
Woolert, Oolert, Owlerd (Shropshire)
Hoolet (Lowlands)

Hullart (Cheshire)
Cherubim
Hobby Owl (Northamptonshire)
Gill Howter (Norfolk; Cheshire)
Berthuan (Cornwall)
Gillihowlet (Scotland)
Gil-hooter (Cheshire)
Ullat (Yorkshire)
Ullet (Cheshire)

immature:
Gilly Owlets (Shropshire)

All over the world owls are held to be creatures of magic and superstition and as the Barn Owl is perhaps the most distinctive as well as one of the most widespread owls, it has naturally attracted a great deal of special attention. Its appearance and its behaviour are of precisely the kind to give rise to elemental fears. The Barn Owl, like most owls, is a creature of the night and for this reason associated with the powers of darkness. Witches were believed to depend greatly upon the owl-kind, hardly a charm or potion would be effective without an owl, or portion of an owl, in the ingredients.

Strange powers are often attributed to birds who in some way or another resemble human beings. The face of the Barn Owl, flat and pale, bears this similarity much more than the faces of other birds and its weird unearthly shriek has enough strangeness in it to unsettle even a sophisticated modern ear. Other attributes heighten the total effect, its ghostly whiteness and the huge soundlessness of its wingbeats. Today the Barn Owl is on the decline in Great Britain to the extent that it has been placed under the special protection of Schedule I of the Protection of Birds Act. It is now generally recognised that the Barn Owl is a species beneficial to mankind, a fact pointed out by a great advocate for Barn Owls, Charles Waterton, over a century ago. Even so, Barn Owls are still regularly trapped and shot. The superstitions of centuries take a long while to die out.

183

Inhabiting ruins, it was by association believed to bring ruin, and from this it was an easy step to the Barn Owl's becoming in a more general way a creature of doom and death. Shakespeare often made use of owl symbolism, readily available and immediately understood by his audience. The witches in *Macbeth* naturally include an 'owlets wing' (Act IV i) in their poisonous brew, and at the hour of his murder, King Henry tells Richard of Gloucester 'The owl shriek'd at thy birth, an evil sign'. This is fairly straightforward imagery, but in *Julius Caesar* Shakespeare contrives a double effect when, among other foreboding events which precede Caesar's death, Casca reports:

> . . . yesterday the bird of night did sit
> Even at noon-day, upon the market place,
> Hooting and shrieking.

Here, the owl, originally picked out as an ominous symbol because it was a bird of night, is made more sinister appearing by day, and its somewhat clichéd imagery refreshed.

This kind of play on meaning could only be effective with a bird which was very familiar and the review of the names for the Barn Owl shows that it was not only a symbolic byword, but was well-known in its physical presence to folk all over Britain. It was called by its colours White, Silver and Yellow Owl, and its 'voice' names recognise not only its wild scream (as in Scritch Owl and Screaming Owl), but precisely recorded its other noises as in Hissing Owl and Roarer. A range of everyday names were also accorded to the Barn Owl such as Billy, Jenny and Madge, signifying perhaps an uneasy familiarity, as in the way the devil was called Old Nick.

The owl, like most birds of ancient symbolism could be capricious in its powers. The evil owl could also assume a benign influence. Until fairly recently, it was a widespread custom all over Europe to nail an owl, or part of an owl, to a barn door to avert the evil eye. And as a counterpart to the evil charms of the witches, the owl was used in herbal medicine. In Yorkshire, owl broth was believed to be a cure for whooping cough and it was also thought all over England that owls' eggs, charred and powdered, would improve the eyesight, both clearly instances of sympathetic magic, where treating oneself with a bird which possesses certain features imparts the power to oneself (or brings about its discharge). There are two aspects of sympathy in these cures. In the first, the hooting owl is believed capable of removing the hoot-like whooping of a coughing child, in the second, the owl's keen eyesight is transferred to the person taking the potion.

Little Owl
Athene noctua

also from its size:
Little Grey Owl
Little Night Owl
Little Spotted Owl (Somerset)

'foreign' names:
Belgian Owl (Sussex)
Dutch Owl (Sussex)
French Owl (Sussex)
Indian Owl (Sussex)
Little Dutch Owl (Somerset)
Spanish Owl (Somerset)

various:
Sparrow Owl
Lilford Owl (Northamptonshire)

Little Owls were first introduced to Britain by the Yorkshire naturalist Charles Waterton in 1842 and several other enthusiasts, notably Lord Lilford, also tried to establish the species by bringing over Little Owls from Holland. By the end of the century, breeding was established in a few English counties and subsequently exploded over the rest of the country and parts of Wales and southern Scotland. The Little Owl is unusual among the owls in being almost completely diurnal and it is nowadays by no means an unusual sight to see Little Owls flying back and forth over fields in search of the small mammals and insects which make up their diet. It might on occasion pick off a Sparrow, but it is much more likely that its name Sparrow Owl refers to its own diminutive size than to its prey.

In Greek mythology, the Little Owl was the bird sacred to Pallas Athene, the goddess of wisdom, and it is from this that we derive the idea of the 'wise old owl' though nowadays, other owls, the Tawny in particular, share this reputation: Athens, the city devoted to Pallas Athene, held the Little Owl in great reverence, to the extent that the expression 'to bring owls to Athens' meant much the same as 'to carry coals to Newcastle'. The goddess Athene stood for calmness and moderation and often appears in direct opposition to the god of revelry and ecstasy, Dionysus. As a result, the owls, already figuring in strange recipes, took on another association, through classical literature, being supposed to cure drunkenness, alcoholism, madness and epilepsy. Salted owl was taken as a remedy for gout (which was believed to be brought on by over-indulgence in alcohol).

Tawny Owl
Strix aluco

also from its colour:
Tawny Hooting Owl (Shropshire)
Brown Owl; Brown Ivey Owl; Brown Ullert; Brown Hoolet
Golden Owl; Grey Owl

from its hooting cry:
Ullet; Hoolet
Jenny Hoolet; Jinny Yewlet
Billy Hooter, Gilly Hooter (Shropshire)
Hollering Owl (Somerset; Sussex)
Screech Owl (Sussex)
Hill Hooter (Cheshire)

from its day-time haunts:
Wood Owl
Ivy Owl
Wood Ullat
Beech Owl

various:
Ferny Hoolet
Cailleach oidhche = old woman of the night (Gaelic)

The Tawny is the most abundant owl in England, Wales and Scotland. (There are no Tawny Owls in Ireland.) It is the owl which makes the traditional 'tu-whit, tu-whoo' of fairy tales, though usually the 'tu-whit', the commonest cry, is heard on its own, as Shakespeare noted in *Love's Labour's Lost:*

> And nightly sings the staring owl
> > Tu whit.

The 'woo-oo' is a courting song made mostly during the breeding season. (It has not, as far as I know, any etymological connection with the verb 'to woo'.) The word Owl itself goes back to the *ūle* of Anglo-Saxon times, and has similar counterparts all over Europe (French, *Hibou;* German, *Eule;* Danish, *Ugle;* Dutch, *Uil;* Latin, *Ulula)* all derived from some ancient root meaning 'to howl'.

Many of the beliefs and superstitions which seem to have originated with other owl species are accorded also to the Tawny in Britain. It is nearly always attributed with wisdom, even if of a whimsical kind as with 'Wol' in A. A. Milne's Pooh stories. An altogether tougher line is taken with the characterisation of 'Old Brown' in Beatrix Potter's *Squirrel Nutkin.* The details of this story, as one would expect from a sensitive storyteller, who was also an accomplished naturalist, are true to life. 'Old B' is no fubsy figment of a fireside imagination; the other animals (excluding Nutkin) know to treat him with deference.

Long Ears (Berkshire)
Horn Coot
Horned Owl (Somerset)
Hornie Hoolet (Scotland)
Cat Owl
Long-horned Ullat (Yorkshire)
Tufted Owl (Sussex)

Long-eared Owl

Asio otus

Short-eared Owl

Asio flammeus

Hawk Owl
Mouse Hawk
Moss Owl = Mouse Owl (Yorkshire)

from its plumage:
Brown Yogle (Shetland)
Grey Yogle (Shetland)
Red Owl (Dartmoor)
Grey Hullet (Lancashire)

various:
Fern Owl (Ireland)
Moor Owl; Marsh Owl; March Owl
Woodcock Owl (Norfolk; Kent; Suffolk; Berkshire)
Sea Owl (Kent)
Cat Ool (Shetland)
Day Owl
Pilot Owl (Suffolk)

Both the rather heavy-tongued standard names for these owls were coined by Thomas Pennant (1776), an enthusiastic naturalist and correspondent of Gilbert White, if perhaps not an inspired giver of names. The first written record of the Long-eared Owl in Britain was probably in Turner's ornithology (1544) where it is called the Hornoul. Later it figures again in Willughby as Horn-owl and this volume also included the Short-eared Owl under the same name, but both these were superseded by the more prosaically exact names of Pennant.

The dislike of the Athenians for the Long-eared Owl (which suffered considerably from the Little Owl cult) probably gave rise to the superstition that it is so stupid that if someone walks round and round it as it sits in its daytime doze, it will turn its head following the movement until it wrings its own neck. The Athenians used its name *Otus* synonymously with 'simpleton' as a term of derision.

Both Long and Short-eared species share the name Cat Owl on account of the cat-like look the 'ear tufts' give them, but although they are quite closely related, they have very different habitats and behavioural characteristics. The Long-eared Owl is a tree nester, living in scattered pockets of woodland all over Britain and Ireland. It is a night feeder and hunts small birds to a larger extent than most other owls. The Short-eared Owl is slightly bigger and usually hunts by day. It feeds predominantly on small mammals, in particular the Short-tailed Vole, though it also takes the mice which gave it the names Mouse Hawk and Mouse Owl. It prefers the more open country of fens, marshes, rough grazing, moorland and sand dunes, and has habitat names of Moor, Marsh and Sea Owl. Such terrain is largely treeless and as one would expect, the Short-eared Owl nests and roosts on the ground. There are no Short-eared Owls known to breed in Ireland, and the resident population, which is not large, is situated mainly in northerly and coastal regions of the rest of Britain. Winter migrants and birds of passage arrive on the East coast in the autumn with the Woodcock, with which, along with several other migrants, it is associated, hence Woodcock Owl and Pilot Owl.

Long-eared Owl
Short-eared Owl

Nightjar
Caprimulgus europaeus

from the churring call:
Night Churr (Cornwall)
Eve Churr (Hampshire)
Evejar (Surrey)
Wheel Bird (Stirling)
Spinner (Wexford); Jenny Spinner (Cheshire)
Razor Grinder (Norfolk)
Scissors Grinder (Norfolk; Suffolk)
Jar Owl
Screech Hawk (Berkshire; Buckinghamshire)
Heath-Jar (Surrey); Heave-jar

from its nocturnal habits and hawk-like silhouette:
Night Hawk (Norfolk; Hampshire; Cornwall; Shropshire; Lancashire)
Night Crow (Northamptonshire; Cornwall)
Night Swallow (Devon; Surrey)
Dor Hawk (Cornwall; East Suffolk)
Moth Hawk (Forfar)
Gnat Hawk (Hampshire)
Moth Owl (Cheshire)
Fern Hawk (Gloucestershire)

189

Nightjar

from the belief that it takes milk during the night:
Goat Sucker (Somerset; Surrey; Sussex)
Goat Chaffer (Scotland)
Goat Owl (Shropshire; East Lothian)
Puck Bird (Sussex)
Puckeridge (Hampshire; Surrey; Sussex)

various:
Fern Owl (Gloucestershire)
Lich Fowl (Cheshire)
Gabble Ratchet; Gabble Ratch (Yorkshire)
Flying Toad (Lancashire)

The strange churring voice of the Nightjar has many times been recorded. It is a quite astonishing sound, a rapid succession of notes all at the same pitch with a down-toned slur interrupting at intervals. Analysed, the song has been found to contain some 1900 notes per minute. But not even the finest recording nor the closest song-study can startle one like the real sound of the bird on a heath at evening time.

Ideally, the Nightjar likes dry, sandy heaths with scattered trees and copses. It remains silent as dusk falls, the time when the last light is fading and the land familiar and bright by day, takes on a dark soft-edged eeriness. The best Nightjar nights are warm and windless; silent, except for the rustling of trees and a low hum of insects. The song breaks on the air with extraordinary sonority. It is directionless, seeming to come from one place, then from another (an impression enhanced by the way the birds call to each other and fly about from one singing place to another). The flight is silent, they sing only when perched on some suitable branch. Any sound you make, even along a path, echoes and crashes through the stillness between 'churrs' – and sometimes the Nightjar will come to investigate. Against the dim sky, the hawk-like shape can be made out, the noiseless wings tilted upwards as the bird wheels round, often accompanied by the smaller forms of pipistrelle bats, like tiny footmen. Occasionally, a courting Nightjar will 'clap' its wings in a sharp report. Then, as the night blacks out every visible object, it will be gone, suddenly, leaving you lost in the darkness.

It is no wonder that the Nightjar was thought to be associated with another weird spirit of the dark, Puck, who troubled folk travelling home, or stole into their yards at night to make mischief. Among his other misdeeds he may

Skim milk, and sometimes labour in the quern
And bootless make the breathless housewife churn
(*Midsummer Night's Dream* II i)

The Nightjar, too, is said to steal milk, sucking it from the udder. One of its names is Puckeridge and it is also said to cause an infection in cows called 'puck'. In fact, the Nightjar is innocent of all these accusations; the only reason its large gaping beak might be seen near a goat yard would be the insects to be found there. The Goatsucker superstition is an ancient one, dating back to Aristotle, and possibly before. The Latin *Caprimulgus*, literally 'goat-sucker', comes originally from the Greek. The bird is also said to poison the goats that it milks, like some bird-vampire. Nor do the sinister associations end there. Almost every night-bird superstition that there is seems, in some time or place, to have been attached to the Nightjar. Like the Tawny Owl, it is known as the Corpse Bird or Lich (corpse) Fowl. It is also given the title Gabble Ratchet, a name for the Gabriel Hounds of the Wild Hunt. In Nidderdale in Yorkshire, there is a tradition that the souls of dead unbaptised children go into Nightjars.

The Nightjar's looks serve only to increase the frightening impression given by its behaviour. At rest, it looks almost reptile-like, stretched out along the bough of a tree or crouched quietly on the ground, hidden by its beautiful marbled grey-brown plumage. Or it may be secreted within the bracken (hence Fern Owl). It will stay very still, until a person or animal comes right up close to it, then fly out, as if from nowhere, which gives it another element of shock and surprise in its repertoire. Wordsworth was obviously impressed by the Nightjar (through he was mistaken about its singing on the wing).

Nightjar

> The burring dor hawk round and round is wheeling
> That solitary bird
> Is all that can be heard
> In silence deeper far than deepest noon.

The Nightjar was called Dor Hawk because it feeds on Dors or Dor Beetles (*Geotrupes stercorarius*), the black beetle which flies after sunset. The Nightjar is entirely an insect eater, catching its prey on the wing like a Swift, and it is named after other crepuscular insects which make up its diet, such as Moth Hawk, Moth Owl and Gnat Hawk. Night Swallow is in the same genre.

The voice, as one might expect, engendered a considerable group of names. The 'jar', which forms part of several names besides the standard name, is not, I think, to be taken in the usual sense of 'a harsh and discordant sound or shock' but more that of a definition of the late seventeenth century: 'a quivering or grating sound'; though even this is to my ear, too harsh for the song's deep vibratory purr. Razor Grinder and Scissors Grinder also seem too strident but Jenny Spinner catches the evenness of pitch and rhythmicality, as George Meredith must have thought when he wrote this marvellous Nightjar couplet:

> Lone on the fir branch his rattle notes unvaried
> Brooding o'er the gloom spins the brown eve-jar.

Swift
Apus apus

from its cry:
Screecher (Hampshire)
Screamer; Squealer (Sussex)
Jack Squealer (Shropshire)
Screech Martin
Shriek Owl
Screek (Gloucester)

'devil' names:
Devil (Berkshire)
Deviling (East Anglia; Lancashire; Westmorland)
Devil Bird (West Riding)
Swing Devil (Northumberland)
Skeer Devil (Devon; Somerset)
Devil's Screecher (Devon)

Devil Shrieker (Craven)
Devil Squeaker (Yorkshire)
Devil Swallow (Yorkshire)
Devil's Bitch (Yorkshire)
Devil Screamer (Hampshire; Yorkshire)
Devilton, Diverton (Suffolk)

various:
Black Martin (Hampshire; Scotland)
Brown Swallow (Renfrewshire)
Black Swift (Kirkcudbright)
Cran Swallow, Crane Swallow (East Lothian)
Harley, (Forfar)
Bucharet
Whip (West Riding)
Hawk Swallow
Tile Swallow (Yorkshire)

In moments, the arrival of a flock of Swifts can change a demure summer sky into something furious and wild. The fierce strength and agility of these black sky-racers has made its impression on earlier generations; they are called Devil Birds in places all over England. The name Swift, like the adjective, comes from the Old English *swifan* = moving fast.

In a superb poem Ted Hughes matches his Swifts observed with a syntax as quick and full of verve. It is an apotheosis of Swifts; Hughes' own savage talent finding exact expression in the Devil Screamers. Here are just a few lines from a poem which should be read in full:

> They've made it again,
> Which means the globe's still working, the Creation's
> Still waking refreshed, our summer's
> Still still to come –
>
> And here they are, here they are again
> Erupting across yard stones
> Shrapnel-scatter terror. Frog-gapers,
> Speedway goggles, international mobsters –
>
> A bolas of three or four wire screams
> Jockeying across each other
> On their switchback wheel of death
> They swat past, hard fletched,

Veer on the hard air, toss up over the roof,
And are gone again.

Now that the air above our towns is cleaner and has more insects flying there, Swifts too, have moved in towards city centres, though wheeling high up, they often escape the eye. The ear is soon alerted to them in places which have old buildings or other suitable nesting places, where they will rocket along town streets in low-flying shrill-screaming courtship. They nest inside the eaves or on the rafters of buildings, usually finding access beneath the eaves or through a crack in the structure. Unfortunately most new buildings lack facilities for Swifts and this severely reduces the number of possible nesting sites. In Amsterdam, where there has been a great deal of roof renovation, it has been made illegal to re-roof unless access for Swifts is retained.

Swifts spend most of their lives in the air. It is thought, though as yet not conclusively proved, that they roost on the wing; they come down to earth only to breed. Their short legs are too slight for walking, though they can grip on to surfaces such as walls and rock faces with their sharply clawed feet, and with a great deal of effort crawl about if grounded. Aristotle called them 'footless' and this has survived in their scientific name *Apus* (*a* = without, *pous* = foot). Heraldry caught on to this by designating a martlet as a mark of cadency for the fourth son, who being four down the line would be unlikely to inherit land. The Reverend Swainson gives us a neat quotation on the subject of these unfortunates: 'the bird that lacketh feet wherewith to settle upon land, and they lacking land whereon to set their feet. . . .'

Swifts resemble hirundines in their feeding habits and are often to be seen flying with Swallows and Martins, but they are not closely related. In the scientific classification, Swifts have not only their own 'family', but their own 'order'; (to which no other British bird belongs) though this has not prevented everyday observers giving them Martin and Swallow names.

Dipper (Shropshire)
Fisher (Yorkshire)

Kingfisher
Alcedo atthis

Frederick William Faber, in a poem about the river Cherwell, writes of the sharp streak of colour which marks the shy Kingfisher's straight and undeviating flight:

> There came
> Swift as a meteor's shining flame
> A kingfisher from out the brake
> And almost seemed to leave a wake
> Of brilliant hues behind.

Poems like this which are true to the real beauty of the bird are hard to find, though there are countless references to the Halycon bird of mythology and, along with them, imported scraps of lore and legend.

The Greeks held that the body of a Kingfisher, when dried and hung up, would ward off Zeus' lightning. Giraldus Cambrensis in his *Topographia Hibernica* (1185) was one of the first British writers to comment on the remarkable properties of Kingfishers, but oddly it was the moth rather than lightning which was allayed.

> . . . these little birds . . . if they are put among
> clothes and other articles, . . . preserve them
> from the moth and give them a pleasant odour.
> What is still more wonderful − if, when dead
> they are hung up by their beaks in a dry
> situation, they change their plumage as though
> the vital spark still survived and vegetated
> through some mysterious remains of its energy.

Another naturalist of the Middle Ages, Albertus Magnus, or Albertus of Cologne, who wrote a good deal about birds in his twenty-six volume work *De Animalis*, also remarked on this 'dead moult'. It seems possible that the idea of the 'vital spark' which survives death could be an echo of the Kingfisher tradition from ancient Greece.

Alcyone, a manifestation of the moon goddess, was worshipped by the seafaring Aeolians and she gave them protection from storms. (In one version

195

of the legend she is the daughter of Aeolus, god of the winds.) Alcyone was alternately the goddess of Life-in-Death at the winter solstice and of Death-in-Life at the summer solstice, and it was she who, at the end of the great lunar year, sent for Zeus who was then to die and to be reborn.

In its way it seems that the legend retells history – giving it the point of view of Zeus worshippers. Late in the second millenium BC the Aeolians were subordinated to the Acheans, and they were forced to worship Zeus. In the legend, Zeus defies Alcyone's power over the wind and waves and sends a thunderbolt to destroy a ship which holds her husband, Ceyx. Alcyone, mad with grief, plunges into the sea and both she and her husband are turned into Kingfishers.

Just as Alcyone could protect sailors from rough weather, the Halcyon bird was credited with the power of calming storms. It was also said that there were seven days before the winter solstice, and seven days after, in which time the Halcyon brooded her eggs in a nest made of fish bones which floated on the ocean. During this time there was complete calm. It is from this that the 'Halcyon days' of Shakespeare and the poets derive. There are details in this story which bear relation to fact. The Mediterranean is usually calm about the time of the solstice. The nest of the Kingfisher, though it is made in a deep hole in a riverbank not on the ocean, is indeed composed of fish bones.

There is another tradition which is found in several places in Europe and which probably rises out of Alcyone's legendary control of the winds. Mentioned by several English writers (including Sir Thomas Browne, who discredited it as 'not made out by reason or experience') the tale was that a Kingfisher, when hung up, would always turn its beak to whatever direction the wind blew. On the Loire, *Vire-vent* or 'turn-in-the-wind' is a local name for the Kingfisher. Shakespeare made use of the belief in a passage in *King Lear* when Kent is raging against sycophants like Oswald, Regan's steward, who

Renege, affirm and turn their halcyon beaks
With every gale and vary of their masters.

Like the Nightingale, another bird much loved by poets, the Kingfisher has a deficiency of local names. Turner recorded the Kynges Fissher and this seems to have been then, and since, the standard name. It was 'Kynges' because it was thought to be the chief or king of fishers. Possibly its beautiful irridescent plumage enhanced the image of Kingliness in the sense that its garb was fit for a king. What local names there are, are self-explanatory, the Yorkshire one simply drops the 'king', and Dipper indicates that the bird dives into the water after fish.

The fishing is usually done from an overhanging perch, but where there are no such perches, the Kingfisher will make a series of short hovering flights over the water, watching for the fish beneath. A perch is usually preferred though, and this has given rise to an ornithological variant of the 'fisherman's tall story' — many an angler will relate how he has been favoured by a Kingfisher perching on the tip of his rod.

Wood Sprite (Norfolk; Gloucestershire)
Sprite (Suffolk)
Wood Spack (Norfolk; Suffolk)
Wood Pie (Somerset)
Wood Knacker (Hampshire)
Wood Hack (Lincolnshire)
Woodwale; Woodwall (Somerset)
Hew Hole (Somerset)
Pick-a-tree (North)
Nicker Pecker; Nickle (Nottinghamshire)
Awl-bird; Wood-awl; Hood-awl (Cornwall)
Whetile (Essex; Hertfordshire)
Whitwall; Whittle (Somerset)
High Hoe (Shropshire)

from the laughing cry:
Laughing Bird (Shropshire)
Laughing Betsey (Gloucester)
Yaffle (General)

Green Woodpecker
Picus viridis

Green Woodpecker	Yaffler (Hereford)
	Wood Yaffle (Suffolk)
	Yaffingale (Wiltshire; Hampshire)
	Yappingale (Somerset)
	Hefful; Heffalk (Yorkshire)
	Hecco
	Eccle (Oxfordshire)
	Jack Eikle (Worcestershire)
	Icwell (Northamptonshire)
	Eaqual, Ecall (Shropshire)
	Yuckel (Gloucestershire); Yockel (Shropshire)
	Stock-eikle (Staffordshire)

as rainbringer:
Rain-bird (Sussex)
Rain-fowl (Northumberland)
Rain-pie; Storm Cock (Shropshire)
Weather Cock
Wet Bird, Wet-wet (Somerset)

various:
Bee-bird
Coit (Cornwall)
Green Peek (Lincolnshire)
Kazek (Cornwall)
Green Ile (Gloucestershire)
Popinjay
Snapper
Jar Peg (Northamptonshire)

Great Spotted Woodpecker
Dendrocopos major

Pied Woodpecker (Surrey)
Woodwall (Hampshire)
Wood Pie (Staffordshire; Hampshire)
Black and White Woodpecker (Norfolk)
French Pie (Leicestershire)
Witwall (Gloucestershire; Surrey)
Magpie-ile (Gloucestershire)
Eckle, Hickwall (Gloucestershire)

Lesser Spotted Woodpecker
Dendrocopos minor

Barred Woodpecker (General)
Little Wood Pie (Hampshire)
Wood Tapper (Shropshire)
Tapperer, Tabberer (Leicestershire)
French Pie; French Magpie (Gloucestershire)
Hickwall (Gloucestershire)
Crank Bird (Gloucestershire)
Lesser Galley Bird (Sussex)

There are several species of Woodpecker to be found over Europe and Asia and the considerable folklore attached to these birds tends to be shared among the various species. Of the three kinds of Woodpecker to be found in Britain (Ireland has no Woodpeckers at all) the largest variety of names, and the most folklore, is attached to the Green Woodpecker. This is a very eye-catching bird with its green plumage, bright yellow rump and red head. It used also, certainly, to be the most abundant species (although with changing conditions, it now seems likely that it is exceeded in numbers by the Great Spotted).

Many of the numerous Green Woodpecker names are related to each other and derive distantly from the Old English name *Hyghwhele*. Some names have subsequently been affected by other literal associations but kept the basic sound of the original, such as Hewhole or High Hoe or Wood Awl. John of Guildford's poem *The Owl and the Nightingale* refers to the Woodpecker as *Wudewale* as does Chaucer in *The Romaunt of the Rose* (1369). This too appears to have a sub-family of names in Whitwall, Whetil and Whittle. It is possible that Yaffle may be a remote descendant of *Hyghwhele* and by the end of the eighteenth century this was a name in wide use, and the word was being used as a verb meaning 'to make a sound like a Woodpecker' or 'to bark'. This name also has its augmented variations, as in Yaffingale and Yappingale; Yaffle added to *gale,* meaning singer (see Nightingale). The Hewel in stanza 68 of Andrew Marvell's *Appleton House* has a clear relationship with the Old English name:

> But most the Hewel's wonders are,
> Who here has the Holt-flesters [forester] care.
> He walks still upright from the Root,
> Meas'ring the Timber with his Foot;
> And all the way, to keep it clean
> Doth from the Bark the Wood-moths glean.
>
> He, with his beak, examines well
> Which fit to stand and which to fell.

As well as 'gleaning' moths in the way that Marvell

describes, the Green Woodpecker feeds upon ground insects, and notably upon ants. It will dismantle ant hills, prod its enquiring beak into the ground, and root out the little creatures, gathering them up with its long sticky tongue. It was probably actions of this kind which drew the woodpecker into association with other bird 'diggers' of creation myths. It later became the bird of the plough and of fertility.

Nearly all woodpecker legends strongly link the bird with water, which is another main theme of the names. In Britain, it is known as Rain Bird, Rain Fowl and Rain Pie. In France it is called *Pic de la pluie* and *Pleu-pleu* (the latter imitative of the cry as well as associated with rain – *pluie*). The German is *Giessvogel*, Austrian *Gissvogel* (*Giss* = torrent) and the Danish *Regnkrake* (another name which allies 'rain' and the cry or 'crake').

In one version of the Genesis, when God had finished making the earth, he ordered the birds to dig out hollows with their beaks where the seas, rivers and lakes were to be. The woodpecker alone refused this office and in retribution God condemned her, as she had refused to peck earth, to ever after peck wood, and as she did so to cry 'plui–plui' for the rain because she was also forbidden to drink from the lakes and streams as other birds did. A German story tells how the woodpecker refused to dig a well as God commanded because he would spoil his beautiful plumage. So he was forbidden ever to drink from pond or pool and must call instead for rain (in this case 'geit-geit' or 'giess-giess') climbing upwards to receive the drops.

There are several folk-rhymes about Woodpeckers and rain or storms. This French couplet connects the downpour with the Woodpecker's cry:

Lorsque le pivert crie
Il annonce la pluie.

Another couplet, this one Italian, indicates that it is when the Woodpecker pecks that rain or tempest follows:

Quand el picozz picozza
O che l'e vent, o che l'e gozza.

In England, John Aubrey wrote in the early eighteenth century that the Woodpecker had been greatly esteemed 'by the Druides for divination' and added that, 'To this day the country people doe divine of raine by their cry.'

The oak being the tree sacred to the Druids, it is likely that a bird much associated with the oak should also be attributed special powers. (The tree of Zeus was also the oak, the 'thunder tree'.) The Woodpecker is connected with a sacred grove in both Greek and Roman legends. As well as helping the wolf to feed Romulus and Remus, the Woodpecker aided the wolf in the defence of certain sacred trees. A Roman coin survives depicting two Woodpeckers perched in a sacred fig tree, the wolf feeding the foundling twins beneath. A Woodpecker's drumming is a thundery kind of noise and this probably served to reinforce rain-making beliefs which might have widened into more generalized powers of divination (there is written and pictorial evidence of a Woodpecker oracle in the Apennines) but which now survive only in rain-forecasting superstitions.

A common thread in the many stories and legends about the Woodpecker is that at some time the bird went contrary to a god's commands. It seems possible that there was in early times a Woodpecker cult and that when this was super-seded by other religions, the Woodpecker was vilified and relegated to a minor role. In Aristophanes' *Birds,* Euripides has a passage in his speech which may support this:

Zeus won't in a hurry the sceptre restore to the
    woodpecker tapping the oak,
In times prehistoric 'tis easily proved, by evidence
    weighty and ample,
That Birds and not Gods were the rulers of men,
    and the lords of the world.

Edward Armstrong, in a brilliant essay tracing the different threads of the Woodpecker legends back through history, and assembling all the clues as to what they might signify, surmises that a Woodpecker cult arose during Neolithic times, when there was still widespread oak forest, but when men were beginning to practise rudimentary cultivation using a hoe and later the plough. In these early days of arable farming, rain would assume a role of great importance, and the Woodpecker bringing it would also bring fertility. The bright green colour, the shade of new growth and its 'excavating' activities linked with those of the plough, would reinforce this notion.

It seems that Christianity as well as the worshippers of Zeus felt a need to put the Woodpecker in its place. There is a story from North Wales (which corresponds closely to a Norse legend) which describes how Christ one day requested food and water from an old woman (in the Norse version, a baker). She refused Him and was turned into a Woodpecker. A variant of this tale has the Owl as protagonist and this is what Ophelia had in her wandering mind when she cried:

'They say the Owl was a Baker's daughter'.

It is probable that the Great Spotted Woodpecker and the Lesser Spotted Woodpecker also shared the general Woodpecker lore, though, being (in the past) less in evidence, they would have assumed a minor role. The Lesser Spotted is a shy and elusive bird and not very numerous and it is only comparatively recently that the Great Spotted has increased its British range and numbers. Both birds are called French Pie, French in this case denoting an alien, and distinguishing these birds from the main or 'stock' species the Green Woodpecker (called Stock Eikle). Most of the names for Spotted Woodpeckers are descriptive. Both have 'Pie' names for their black and white plumage with its red flourishes (the female Lesser being the only Woodpecker with no red at all). The Lesser Spotted has more of a striped effect on its wings and back than the Great (which has white patches) and it is also known as the Barred Woodpecker. It is a tiny bird, about the same size as a Hedge Sparrow and has a correspondingly softer 'drum' which is possibly why it has 'Tapper' rather than 'Pecker' names. It is said to have been given the name Crank Bird on account of its flat, creaky 'keek-keek' call notes.

Wryneck
Jynx torquilla

Writhe Neck
Twister
Snake Bird (Gloucestershire; Somerset; Hampshire)
Barley Snake-bird (Hampshire)

from its arrival at about the same time as the Cuckoo:
Cuckoo's Mate (Hampshire; Shropshire; East Anglia;
   Gloucestershire; Somerset; Surrey; Sussex)
Cuckoo's Footman; Cuckoo's Fool (Gloucestershire)
Cuckoo's Messenger; Cuckoo's Marrow (Midlands)
Cuckoo's Leader (Norfolk)
Cuckoo Waker (Somerset)
Gwas-y-gog = Cuckoo's Knave (Welsh)

various:
Long Tongue; Tongue Bird (Somerset)
Rinding Bird; Rine Bird (Surrey)
Rind Bird; Peel Bird (Sussex)
Slab (N England)
Pee Bird (Surrey)
Weet Bird (Hampshire)
Peet Bird (Somerset)
Mackerel Bird (Channel Islands)
Dinnick (Devon)
Barley Bird (Hampshire)
Emmet Hunter (Somerset)
Emmet (Surrey)
Summer Bird (Northumberland)
Turkey Bird (Suffolk)

The earliest written reference to the Wryneck is William Turner (1544) who lists it as *Inyx* and *Torquilla*, names which now form the two parts of the scientific name. Merrett (1666) and Willughby (1678) use the name Wryneck which like Writhe Neck is descriptive of the odd way this bird can swivel its head around so that the bill points over its back. Both 'writhe' and 'wry' come from the Old English *wrigian* meaning 'to turn'. The Wryneck performs this snake-like contortion when threatened, and accompanies it with a violent hissing, also raising the feathers of its crown into a crest, in an endeavour to frighten away the foe. There are names to cover every one of these actions; Wryneck itself, or Twister, for the head movement; Snake Bird for the turn and for the hiss. There is also Hisser and, for the way the feathers of the head and neck are puffed-out, Turkey Bird. It was clearly a bird whose movements were much observed. Its talent for turning itself back to front was given a literal application in witchcraft. In order to bring about the return of a faithless lover, a Wryneck was caught and attached to a wheel which was revolved. Rather on the principle of sympathetic magic several elements of 'turning' are employed to effect a return. The Wryneck or Inyx could also be used against an enemy, so the phrase 'to put a jinx' on somebody, came about.

The Wryneck is a summer visitor, hence Summer Bird and probably also the Barley Bird names. (Barley Bird is used for two other summer migrants, the Nightingale and the Yellow Wagtail, but also crops up for the Grey Wagtail, Greenfinch, Siskin, Common Gull, Wheatear – and it is difficult to see anything but the most contrived of common factors for this range of species.) There is a rhyme about the way the Cuckoo and the Nightingale-Barley-Bird arrive in close succession (see Nightingale), and the Wryneck who can be expected about the same date has a number of Cuckoo epithets. The names don't quite agree on whether the Wryneck should arrive before or after, for it is the Cuckoo's Messenger and the Cuckoo's Leader (presumably going before), the Cuckoo's Mate or Marrow, that is companion, using 'marrow' in the same way as the rhyme about the Martin and the Swallow (see Swallow) and the Cuckoo's Knave, who might perhaps be following after. Gilbert White reports in his *Journal* that in the Spring of 1771: 'Wryneck pipes about in orchards. The first spring-bird of passage.' (April 9). The 'Cuckow' was not reported until 26 April for 1771, but three years later the *Journal* marks a reverse trend with 'Cuckoo cries' on 22 April and three days later 'Wryneck returns & pipes', so it appears that some years it 'leads' and in others accompanies or follows. The piping notes also have their counterparts in local names. The clear 'qui-qui-qui' calls are rendered variously as Pee (Bird), Peet and Weet.

The Wryneck is strange in its appearance. Taxonomically, it belongs with the Woodpeckers and it feeds in trees picking small insects off the trunk and branches with its sticky tongue. (It is called Long Tongue and Tongue Bird.) It is also, like the Green Woodpecker, partial to ants, hence Emmet and Emmet Hunter (Emmet being an old word for ant). The Wryneck's beak is, however, much less stout than those of other Woodpeckers and its brown marbled plumage which conceals it so beautifully against the bark of a tree is more like that of a Nightjar than the dramatically coloured Woodpeckers. Dinnock may be (like Dunnock) a reference to this browny-grey colour. Rine or Rind, which nowadays refers only to the skin or peel of fruits, used to mean primarily the bark of a tree, so the Rind Bird would be a bird whose plumage matched the bark.

Laverock, Lavrock (Scotland)
Learock (Lancashire)
Lerruck (Orkney)
Sky Laverock (Northamptonshire)
Rising Lark (Northamptonshire)
Field Lark (Surrey)
Short-heeled Lark (Scotland)
Lintwhite (Suffolk)
Melhuez (Cornwall)
Lady Hen (Shetland)
Sky-flapper (Somerset)
Ground Lark

Skylark
Alauda arvensis

Shore Lark
Eremophilia alpestris

Horned Lark
Sea Lark (Yorkshire)
Snowbird, Snowflake (Lancashire)

Woodlark
Lullula arborea

Skylark
Shore Lark

The Skylark is one of our most merry and eloquent songbirds, and also one which is widespread and abundant, and it has inspired a corresponding abundance of poetry. As with that other much written-of bird, the Nightingale, Skylark poetry is almost entirely about the song; but in general it is more realistic than that of the Nightingale, probably because the Skylark is a much more familiar bird and does not have to contend with a legendary bird, as the Nightingale does with the Philomel.

Several 'lark' words and sayings have sprung from our observations of Lark behaviour. 'To sing like a lark' dates at least from the early seventeenth century. The gaiety of the song gave rise to the usage of a 'lark' as synonymous with a frolic, now old-fashioned, but introduced about the beginning of the nineteenth century. Considering that from earliest times Larks have given us so much pleasure, we have treated them ignominiously. The pretty French part-song *Alouette, gentille Alouette* goes on to describe in great detail how the bird is to be plucked. Enormous numbers of Larks were killed and eaten. A proverb quoted by John Ray in his *Collection of English Proverbs* said that 'One leg of a Lark is worth the whole body of a Kite,' and at a later date the 'land where Larks fall ready roasted' was equivalent to a 'land of milk and honey'. Larks, like other singing birds were prized as cage birds and it was not so long ago that caged larks were cruelly blinded on the basis of a barbarous superstition that Larks sang better with their eyes put out.

It is not a creditable history. Yet there was another side. Many of our greatest poets not only loved the Lark but fiercely opposed the whole practice of caging birds, preferring to hear them as they flew free. There were others, too, who were happy just to listen to the birds. A Norfolk saying advises that if one wants to hear what the Lark says, one should lie down on one's back in a field and listen; a recommendation probably followed by Norfolk sweethearts on the hot still summer days when nothing stirs but the seductive trilling of the Lark far above.

The French *Alouette*, like our old name Laverock, seems to contain a musical trill in its sound, and the English phrase 'up with the Lark' has a nice counterpart in the French *Qui se leve comme l'Alouette, chantera comme elle.*

The fifteenth century poet William Dunbar paints a glorious image of early morning Larks in Spring:

> Through beamis red, gleaming, as ruby sparks,
> The skyes rang for the shouting of larks.

On the subject of early rising, again, an old Scots Lark rhyme poses the options:

> Larike, larike lee
> Who'll gang up to heaven wi'me
> No the lout that lies in his bed
> No the doolfu' that dreeps his head.

There is little that is doleful about Skylark verse. For better or worse, the poets are affected by the blithe song and seem drawn to reproduce it. The airy, rhythmical *Ode* by Shelley is probably the best known single Skylark poem, but there are many others devoted to this bird. Gerard Manley Hopkins' Lark is perhaps straining a little as it 'pelts music', a 'rash, fresh, re-winded new skeined score'. A. E. Housman's Skylark with its 'rubbed and round Pebbles of sound' is a calmer, more reflective bird. But taken as a whole, George Meredith's 'Lark Ascending' has surely the most perfectly balanced and descriptive imagery which has ever been written about a Skylark, suggesting the way that the song seems to widen and spread from its high origins, filling the air with the delicate but energetic progression of notes.

> He rises and begins to round
> He drops the silver chain of sound

Of many links without a break
In chirrup, whistle, slur and shake
All intervolved and spreading wide
Like water dimples down a tide
Where ripple ripple overcurls
And eddy into eddy whirls . . .

The Skylark is a bird of open places, of heaths and commons and will even sing in cities over an area of waste ground where it can find a spot to nest undisturbed. Its shyer cousin the Woodlark is a considerably rarer bird, only to be found in a few south and southwest counties where it frequents the outskirts of woods and hillsides of birch and oak. Its voice has warmer tones than that of the Skylark but the song is not so varied. Contradictory as it seems, both Skylark and Woodlark are also called Groundlarks. This they are in the sense that they feed upon the ground, running in rapid movements, rather than hopping. They also nest on the ground as described so exactly in John Clare's 'Lark's Nest' (in this case a Skylark).

Behind a clod how snug the nest
Is in a Horse's footing fixed
Of twitch and stubbles roughly dressed
With roots and horsehair intermixed.

The Woodlark is slightly smaller than the Skylark but they are similarly streaky-brown in colouration, with buff to white underparts. The Skylark has white outer feathers in its tail which show when it flies off and which it displays in courtship. These give it the name Lintie White, which it shares with the Linnet which also has this tail marking. Both Woodlarks and Skylarks have on their head a little clump of feathers which erects into a crest.

The name Laverock derives from the Old English *laferce* or *lawerce*, literally 'treason worker' which might well refer to the Lark's habit of misleadingly dropping down into an area some distance away from the nest and then, well-concealed by the summer herbage, running swiftly to its young. It is not to be relied upon to behave straightforwardly if an intruder approaches near the nest, when it will try to deceive you into believing that it is injured and lay a limping false trail away from the nesting place.

The Shore Lark, a winter visitor to eastern England, has a splendidly diabolic double crest which has given it the name Horned Lark. In winter plumage, however, its horns are absent and the striking black moustache and breastplate are masked by yellow and brown and only wear down to the more conspicuous courting dress later in the season, by which time the birds are back to the breeding grounds in Arctic Europe. In its winter quarters, it keeps to the seashore and to stubble fields near the sea, feeding off insects, crustacea and seeds, which is why it is Sea Lark and Shore Lark. It seems not to have been observed in Britain before the 1830s and this short period, together with the Shore Lark's sombre winter dress and its restricted distribution, have probably been limiting factors on the number of names for it.

Barn Swallow
Chimney Swallow (Northumberland; Sussex)
House Swallow
Red-fronted Swallow
Swallie (Lincolnshire)
Tsi-kuk (Cornish)

Swallow
Hirundo rustica

The saying 'one swallow doesn't make a summer' has its counterpart in several European languages, and it is interesting that this rather negative admonition has in fact an extremely positive value. For, perhaps more than any other birds, Swallows do mean summer. Nor is it simply in modern times that we watch eagerly for the first birds to come, flying in from the sea like tired aerial spiders on their flickering wings. There are old Greek songs which welcome the Swallow, and a black-figured Greek vase in the Vatican collection depicts a man and two boys watching for the first Swallow, with words coming from their mouths like modern-day captions. The first boy says 'Look there's a swallow', the man 'By Herakles, so there is', the other boy, his arm raised in a gesture of greeting, says 'There she goes, spring has come'.

The Swallow's flower or Swallow-wort is the Celandine, but this is not the little Lesser Celandine (*Ranunculus ficaria*), itself a bright herald of spring, but the Greater Celandine (*Chelidonium majus*) a member of the poppy family, introduced to Britain probably well over a thousand years ago. *Chelidonium* comes from *chelidon* the Greek word for Swallow. (At the end of the sixteenth century, the plant was also known as *Hirundinarium major* from the Latin for Swallow which also figures in the modern scientific name for the bird.) The connection between the bird and the plant is first recorded in classical times. It is mentioned in Pliny, and also in Dioscorides, both writing in the first century, that Greater Celandines were an efficacious remedy for unclouding filmy eyes. Mrs Grieve quotes a number of medical usages for the plant which contains several alkaloids, including its employment in milk to remove spots on the cornea. It was Pliny who drew a connection between the time of the plants' flowering and the arrival of the Swallow in Europe. However, Pliny was largely an anthologist, spending much more of his time compiling books than observing the things that went into them. It is said that he could not even spare half an hour to go for a walk. His contemporary, the herbalist Dioscorides, applied his attention to a narrower sphere, dealing only with plants which he considered medically important, but he brought to them a great deal of personal investigation. It was from him that the English herbalist Gerard got his information on the Greater Celandine.

> The juice of the herbe is good to sharpen the sight, for it cleanseth and consumeth away slimie things that cleave about the ball of the eye, and hinder the sight . . . as Dioscorides teacheth.

In a similar tradition to the Swallow-wort, the old Greek writings also describe the Swallow stone, a small stone which like the herb was an eye cure. It was said to be found inside Swallows' nests and to cure blindness. The Swallows were also credited with having discovered the curative powers of the Celandine.

It was also believed that Swallows themselves could be of medical use. A broth made of crushed Swallow might cure both epilepsy and stammering, both applications of sympathetic magic. The Swallow, whose own cry sounds high and stuttery and in flight quivers and flutters, could remove these conditions from human beings. In general Swallows are well thought of as birds of good omen. To have them nesting on one's property is thought to bring good fortune. In some versions of the legend of the bringing of fire to the earth, it was the Swallow who carried it to man, burning its head and chest, red as it did so (see Robin). It is supposed to be a sign of good weather to see Swallows soaring high up in the sky. However, if Swallows desert their nesting places, it is bad luck on the house, and if they fly low, a sign also of bad weather or ill omen. (There seems more than a germ of truth in this, as Swallows will come down low to catch the great hatches of insects which abound in humid or thundery weather.) And if one should fly so low as to skim beneath a domestic animal such as a cow or a goat, this too bodes ill. 'Swallows are unlucky birds to kill', as Dryden says in *The Hind and the Panther,* because they are specially favoured by the Almighty.

There are several versions of the rhyme –

The robin and the wren
Are God Almighty's cock and hen.
The martin and the swallow
Are God Almighty's birds to hollow [hallow].

or

The martin and the swallow
Are the two nest birds that follow

or

Are God Almighty's mate and marrow

In some versions the Martin is paired with the Swallow, in others the Swift is the favoured bird.

The notion that Swallows hibernated at the bottom of pools, current in sixteenth and seventeenth century ornithology, has penetrated through to today, principally through Gilbert White who was an affectionate admirer of Swallows and observed them closely. He gave the idea considerable attention, drawing together the behaviour he observed, the way autumn flocks of Swallows drop down to the roost in the reedy edges of lakes, and their subsequent abrupt disappearance, and he decided that it was probable that they hibernated. He does not, however, ever profess to having found one in this state or to have personally seen them in hibernation, unlike many of the more imaginative 'observers'. It is interesting that over two centuries earlier, Olaus Magnus in his *History of the Northern Nations* actually sweeps aside the correct solution of migration in order to promulgate the hibernation theory, which he then supports with some very strange and imaginative observations.

> Although the writers of many natural things have recorded that the Swallows change their stations, going, when winter cometh, into hotter countries; yet, in the northern waters, fishermen oftentimes by chance draw up in their nets an abundance of Swallows, hanging together like a conglomerated mass. . . . In the beginning of autumn, they assemble together among the reeds; where, allowing themselves to sink into the water, they join bill to bill, wing to wing, and foot to foot.

One can't help being immensely curious about what it was the northern fishermen drew up in their nets.

from its living in and around houses:
Eaves Swallow; Easin Swallow (Craven)
Window Swallow (Northumberland)
Window Martin

various:
Swallow (Roxburgh; West Riding)
Martin Swallow (East Lothian)
Martlet
River Swallow (Yorkshire)
Black Martin (Northumberland)
Marthin Penbwi (Welsh)

House Martin
Delichon urbica

from its sandbank nests:
Bank Martin (Sussex)
Bank Swallow (Craven)
Pit Martin (Yorkshire)
Sand Swallow; River Swallow
Sandy Swallow (Stirling; Roxburgh)
Sand Backie (Forfar)
Bitter Bank (Roxburgh)
Bitterie (Roxburgh)

various:
Shore Bird
Witchuk (Orkney)

Sand Martin
Riparia riparia

Elsewhere in Europe the House Martin is known generally as House Swallow, or Window Swallow (French, *Hirondelle de fenêtre;* Dutch, *Huiszwaluw;* Swedish, *Hussvala* etc). Perhaps we in Britain felt an affection for this attractive little migrant which makes itself at home in such close proximity to us, and reflected this in our choice of the familiar name Martin. We seem to have taken the name in the first place from the French name for that other fork-tailed migrant the Swift, which was called variously *Martinet, Martinette, Martnet* and *Martlet.* William Turner in 1544 calls the House Martin by the names 'Rok martinette' and 'Chirche martinette', and just over a century later, both Merrett

213

(1667) and Willughby (1678) are using the name
Martin. Shakespeare in the early seventeenth
century called them Martlets. The way that
Martins build their neat mud-nests on the outsides
of buildings and masonry seems to have made a
particular impression on him. He may also have
been trading on the belief that it was lucky to have
Swallows and Martins nest on your home when he
led Banquo to point out the Martins' nests on
Macbeth's castle to Duncan, using the image to
create an ironic pathos, for both men are soon to
meet untimely deaths.

> This guest of summer
> The temple haunting martlet, doth approve
> By his loved mansionry, that the heaven's breath
> Smells wooingly here: no jutty, frieze
> Buttress nor coign of vantage, but this bird
> Hath made his pendant bed and procreant cradle.
> Where they most breed and haunt, I have observed
> The air is delicate.

Caroline Spurgeon, that indomitable Shakes-
pearian scholar, in a search to identify the proto-
type for Macbeth's castle, visited Kenilworth and
Warwick, which it is likely Shakespeare
would have known well – but no Martins had
graced the walls, nor had ever done so it seemed.
She then approached Berkeley Castle to which
passing reference is made in *Richard II* and found,
after some initial discouragements, that none other
than Edward Jenner, the doctor and ornithologist
(see Introduction), had remarked in a *Notebook* of
June 1787 that he had been examining the Martins'
nests on the castle. This together with other details,
confirmed her impression that Berkeley had
indeed provided the outlines of Macbeth's castle.

The name Sand Martin was used fairly early, by
Merrett and Willughby, to distinguish this
browny, bank-nesting species from the Martin of
caves and houses, which was commonly known
just as Martin. (The double name House Martin
seems to have come into use quite a lot later,
possibly with Montagu who, in 1813, gives it as a

provincial name.) Most of the Sand Martin's names are quite literal, referring to the way it digs out its own burrow for a nest in a bank of sand, 'biting' itself out a home for its young as in the names Bitter Bank (= biter bank) and Bitterie. Where natural sand faces are not to be found, colonies of Sand Martins will often 'borrow' a man-made pit or quarry and in general people are very well disposed towards the little creatures, the workmen leaving the pit, cutting, trench or sand face as undisturbed as possible apart from inspecting the welfare of the birds, until the young have flown. Perhaps it might be seen almost as a good omen to have Sand Martins nesting in the construction site or pit. Clare wrote of Sand Martins in disused workings and continues, in a more than usually Wordsworthian vein, to write of a 'lone seclusion and a hermit joy' when he sees the Sand Martins burrowing against . . .

> the desolate face
> Of rude waste landscapes far away from men
> Where frequent quarrys give thee dwelling place
> With strangest taste and labour undeterred
> Drilling small holes along the quarrys side . . .

Corbie Craw (Scotland)
Corbie (N England; Scotland)
Croupy Craw (N England)
Fiach (Ireland)
Marburan (Cornwall)
Ralph

Raven
Corvus corax

The Raven is a mighty bird. It is not just that it is the biggest of the *Corvidae* or that it is one of the most powerful beasts of mythology and antiquity. Its very presence commands deference, and acquaintance increases one's admiration for it. R. M. Lockley, an ornithologist of insight and imagination, and not given to fancy, lived on the Welsh island of Skokholm, an island just big enough for a pair of Ravens.

When I see our ravens I have a feeling, almost, that this island is not mine, but theirs. They have been here from time immemorial. They are, so to speak, indestructible, for they are believed to pair for life, and when one of the pair dies, a young bird immediately steps in to fill the gap. The ravens have been there through all the gaps in the occupation of the island by man, and will probably continue long after man has finished with Skokholm. Such continuity compels respect; you must admire the dogged persistence of the raven in clinging to its native crags, in lording it over all the other birds of the island, for it can mob and drive away every other bird and will rarely suffer a mobbing itself. It is certainly one of the most intelligent . . . among birds.

The word Raven has remained virtually unchanged since Anglo-Saxon times when it was *Hrafn*. The Norse god Odin was also the *Hrafnagud*, the Raven God, for he had two Ravens who used to fly all over the world and returned to perch one on each of his shoulders and whisper to him everything that was happening. The Norsemen had great esteem for the Raven, a bird who was ominously familiar to their armies, feeding on the carrion of the battlefields. This forbidding looking bird, so closely associated with death, took on an ominous character and, later, abstracted from the scene of death, was credited with powers of prediction. Of all birds, Macaulay wrote, the Raven was believed by the St Kildans to be 'the most prophetical'. In Ireland predictions were made by the different calls of the Ravens. The most famous of the Norse standards, the *Landeyda* or land ravager, bore the image of the Raven, and it was believed that when they marched to victory the standard soared and the Raven stood erect, but when they were due for defeat, the Raven drooped its wings and dropped its head. Perhaps in same way that the threat of 'Boney' outlived the Napoleonic wars, so wayward children in the West Riding of Yorkshire were told that the 'black Raven' would come to fetch them.

As with that other powerful bird of legend, the Diver, it is impossible to understand the importance of the Raven unless the British traditions are seen in a wider context. The Raven was an important symbol in early cultures all over the northern hemisphere. There are Basque myths which tell that the Raven is the spirit of prehistoric caves and Edward Armstrong believes that there is a strong case for thinking the totem bird of the 'Birdman' painting at Lascaux to be a Raven. From Genesis, we are familiar with the Raven as one of the birds which Noah sent out during the flood which went 'forth and fro, until the waters were dried up from off the earth.'

Not only in Europe, but in Asia and North America there are numerous myths which connect the Raven with water, storms and rain. In one story the Voguls associate the Raven with Divers in the making of the world. While the Divers toil under the waters bringing up mud to make the earth, the Raven is commissioned to fly around, returning at progressively longer intervals to report on the increasing size of the growing earth (much as Noah's Raven flies 'forth and fro'). Armstrong directs our attention to the similar motifs in these myths and argues that it is likely that they derived originally from a single origin, probably Babylonian. One of the most fascinating details is that Babylonian cosmology originated at Eridu, a seaport on the Persian Gulf, where silt piled up very rapidly, so it is quite conceivable that its people might imagine the creation of the world as a piling together of mud on a huge scale.

The Biblical account of the deluge was, then, possibly derived from Babylonian sources, but it seems that these earlier legends were less anthropomorphic than the Old Testament story and that primitive cultures tended to think in terms of animal gods, or animals who represented gods, rather than creating gods in their own image. If the Raven had actually been considered a god, or the close associate of a god, then many of the contradictions and ambivalences in Judaism towards Ravens would be explicable in terms of a new order vilifying, or subordinating, the old. So in some places in the Bible – as in the flood, or in the feeding of Elijah – the Raven plays a helpful but relatively minor role, while in others it can be a symbol of desolation (Isaiah xxxiv. 11) or uncleanliness (Lev. i. 15).

In some contexts however, the Ravens keep their pagan character. Some stories say that the souls of the unbaptised go into Ravens. In Denmark the appearance of a Raven foretells the death of a pastor, and in Languedoc wicked priests became Ravens when they died. Sometimes we find an echo of the bird's former powers when the Raven seems not just to foretell doom, but actually to bring it. In Marlowe's *Jew of Malta* we find

> The sad presaging raven, that tolls
> The sick man's passport in her hollow beak
> And in the shadow of the silent night
> Doth shake contagion from her sable wing.

This is a bird which holds real terror, unlike that of Edgar Allan Poe, whose Raven is much more the villainous character of a present day horror film. However, though predominantly ominous, the Raven in folklore as in the Bible, is sometimes seen as a power for good. A Celtic myth tells that King Arthur may return in the form of a Raven, and in Wales it is said that blind people who are kind to Ravens will regain their sight. This latter seems to be another example of sympathetic magic, based on the observation that Ravens devouring their prey will take the eyes, as well as viscera and other soft parts, first. The poem 'The Twa Corbies' makes special mention of this detail; they say one to another:

> Ye'll sit on his white haus-bane
> And I'll pike out his bonny blue een:
> Wi'ae lock o'his gowden hair
> We'll theek our nest when it grows bare.

Matthew Lewis in his 'Ballad of Bill Jones' offers a kind of Russian roulette chance of good or bad

> To see one raven is lucky, 'tis true,
> But it's certain misfortune to light upon two
> And meeting with three is the devil.

Carrion Crow
Corvus corone corone

Car Crow (Yorkshire)
Carner Crow; Carener Crow (Norfolk)
Flesh Crow (Yorkshire)
Gor Crow (Oxfordshire; Yorkshire)
Ger Crow (Craven)
Ket Crow (North Country)
Midden Craw
Corbie Crow (North Country)
Corbie (East Lothian)
Craw (Aberdeen)

from its black beak:
Black Neb (Westmorland)
Blackbill

various:
Land Daw (Northamptonshire)
Daup (York)
Doup (Lancashire)
Dob; Doupe (Westmorland; North Riding)
Hoddy Fraw; Huddy Craw (South Scotland)
Bran (Cornwall)
Raven Crow (Yorkshire)
Black Crow (Nottinghamshire)

When Saint Cuthbert lived alone in the Farne Islands, Crows (it is not specified whether Carrion or Hooded) were among his bird companions and it seems he regarded them with affection, despite their pagan reputation. A Saxon tradition deemed that to see a crow on your left was a portent of disaster, but, as with so many of this crow tribe, they are capricious with their powers. In Wales it is said, that to see one crow is unlucky; to see two, good fortune.

The word crow, Old English *crawe*, comes from the bird's cry as does the verb 'to crow'. Turner (1544) calls it simply 'crouu', but by 1589 at least it carried the adjective 'carren' (carrion). There seems to be little that attracts a Carrion Crow more than a nice corpse (though it will also take eggs and fledgelings and frogs, toads and some vegetable matter) and it is this feature of its diet which has generated most local names for it. The Anglo-Saxon *gor* (carrion) gives us Ger Crow; Ket is a North Country word for carrion and Midden means dung or filth.

About the same size as a Rook, the Carrion Crow is an impressive figure. Raven-black all over, and like the Raven, called Bran, it has a brooding dark presence which gives the name Black Crow a double meaning. Unlike the Rook it is usually a solitary bird. Typically it sits still, slightly hump-backed in a tree, closely observant of everything that happens around it. Even the powerful curved beak is black and it is probable that it was the crow's skill in prising open possible food sources that gave us our 'crowbar', just as the Romans had their *corvus*, a beaked piece of iron hinged to the masts of ships which was used as a grappling hook.

If one looks at local flower names, it seems as if the word 'crow' used in conjunction with another name carries sinister overtones; the fritillary, the Death Bell is also Crow-cup; Shepherd's Needle is both the Devil's Darning Needle and Crow Needle. It also appears sometimes to indicate a coarse quality as in Crow Garlic, another name for which is Crow Onion. Crowberry, the standard name for *Empetrum nigrum*, is also applied to the Cowberry, neither of them is particularly delicious (but the name is also used in Morayshire for the tasty Bilberry). The Crow is particularly associated with the buttercup family (*Ranunculaceae*). There is of course the generally used name Water Crowfoot, but also Crowflower (Meadow Buttercup), Crow Toe (Creeping Buttercup), Crow Bells (Bulbous Buttercup) and Crow Claws (Corn Buttercup). It may be that these plants were not regarded kindly by country folk; they contain an acrid juice and some species can be injurious if eaten by grazing animals. (The juice of the celery-leaved Buttercup, *Ranunculus sceleratus*, was used by beggars to produce impressive looking skin blisters.) However, I can offer no explanation as to why the Bluebell (*Endymion non-scriptus*) should have attracted no less than ten 'Crow' names, nor why several species of orchid likewise share several 'Crow' epithets.

Hoodie, Hoddie (Perth; Moray)
Dun Crow; Dunbilly (Craven)
Grey-backed Crow (Hampshire)
Grey Crow (General)
Blue-backed Crow (Ireland)
Greyback (North Country) Grey Crow (Orkney)

place names:
Royston Crow (General)
Royston Dick (Midlands)
Kentish Crow; Kentishman
Danish Crow; Denman (Norfolk)
Norway Crow; Northern Crow (Norfolk; Craven)
Harry Dutchman; Dutch Crow (Yorkshire)
Isle of Wight Crow
Market Jew Crow (Cornwall)

various:
Cawdy Mawdy (North Country)
Corbie (Perth)
Craa (Shetland)
Moor Crow (Yorkshire)
Scald Crow (Ireland)
Praheen Cark; Hen Crow (Ireland)
Bunting Crow (Ireland)
Winter Crow
Carrion Crow

Hooded Crow
Corvus corone cornix

It was only recently decided that the Hooded Crow, for the purpose of taxonomy, was not a separate and closely related species to the Carrion Crow, but that these two kinds of crow were different forms of one species, the European Crow. Accordingly, the Hoodie, *Corvus cornix* as was, became *Corvus corone cornix* to the scientific world. It is believed that during the last Ice Age, populations of the European Crow were separated and began to develop in different ways. The Hooded Crow has a grey mantle and underparts

221

and its voice is not so loud or so clear as that of its relative. The diet of the two is very similar, but Hooded Crows are much more sociable than the solitary Carrion Crows. Breeding habits also are similar and where the species overlap they will interbreed, producing oddly marked but fertile hybrids. The Hooded Crow is the bird of Ireland and the North-West of Scotland; the Carrion Crow of England, Wales and the remainder of Scotland.

The Hoodie is known in England and the more southerly parts of Scotland mainly as a winter visitor, which was probably why Turner introduced the bird as the Winter Crow. Willughby and Ray in the seventeenth century use the name Royston Crow. The first record of the name Hooded Crow is in Thomas Pennant, more than two centuries later. Pennant also records a ceremony carried out by Scottish herdsmen in which offerings are made to, amongst others, the Hooded Crow and the Eagle, by which they hope to induce them to spare their flocks. Most of the folklore is from the north and west. The Irish hero, Cú Chulainn, had a 'Scald Crow' on his shoulder when he died. One of the most unattractive characters in Scottish folklore is a terrible old hag called Cailleach who feasts upon the bodies of men and who may reappear at any time in the form of a Hooded Crow or a Raven. Cailleach had a fertility aspect in that she was said to possess a cow which gave huge quantities of milk. Armstrong, who links together all these aspects of folklore, also points out that in the Faeroes ...

... an unmarried girl used to go out on Candlemas morning and throw three objects in quick succession at a hooded crow, a stone, a bone and a piece of turf. If the bird flew to the sea the girl expected her future husband to come over it; if it alighted on a house or farm she would marry a man from that family, but if it remained where it was she would know that her fate would be to remain a spinster. As hooded crows are wary birds the girl would have to be a very bad shot not gain reassurance.

Cra (Westmorland)
Craw (N Riding; Lancashire)
Croaker
Crow
Scotch Craa
Brandre (Cornwall)
Barefaced Crow

immature:
Percher; Brancher

Rook
Corvus frugilegus

Rooks may be seen almost as the clowns of the crow family. They look a little eccentric, compared to the svelte and glossy crows. The bare-white beak patch which gives it the name Barefaced Crow softens the fierce corvid appearance and the rather uneven, ragged appearance of the plumage adds to this effect. Rooks are sociable in temperament and generally feed in groups, and at dusk they return to a communal roost. Before they settle for the night they sweep *en masse* through the evening skies in a noisy pre-roost display. James Thomson describes the end of the day for Rooks in the 'Winter' poem of *The Seasons*:

> Retiring from the downs, where all day long
> They picked their scanty fare, a blackening train
> Of clamorous rooks thick urge their weary flight,
> And seek the closing shelter of the grove,

Rooks also nest in communal groups, where a wide range of behaviour may be observed, as recorded by Gilbert White in his *Journal* for 1775.

> March 10. Rooks are very much engaged in the business of nidification: but they do not roost on their nest-trees 'til some eggs are lain. Rooks are continually fighting & pulling each other's nests to pieces: these proceedings are inconsistent with living in such close community. And yet if a pair offers to build on a single tree, the nest is plundered and demolished at once.

> March 18. . . . As soon as rooks have finished their nests, & before they lay, the cocks begin to feed the hens, who receive their bounty with a fondling tremulous voice & fluttering wings &

in 1771; he saw 'an ordinary fellow carrying a cage

> all the little blandishments that are expressed by the young while in a helpless state. This gallant deportment of the males is continued thro' the whole season of incubation.

Young Rooks which have left the nest but are not able to fend for themselves and hop awkwardly about in the branches are known as Perchers or Branchers.

Rooks are often spoken of under the general term 'crow', but there are instances where it is clear from the context that the Rook is the subject. It is to Rooks, with their steady undeviating flight, that the saying 'as the crow flies' refers. And it was to frighten Rooks rather than crows that scarecrows were erected. Crowkeepers (like young Jude in Hardy's last novel) were hired to scare the Rooks at least as far back as Shakespeare's time, for Lear, in his ravings remarks on a 'fellow' who 'handles his bow like a crowkeeper'. Yet, in fact, Rooks probably do as much good as harm in the fields. Although they are considerably more vegetarian than most crows, and will eat seeds, a large part of their diet is composed of insects and grubs and the larvae of creatures injurious to crops. Perhaps it was partly ignorance, partly the presence of big black 'crows', a sign of ill omen, that caused farmers to dislike them in their fields. Bewick in his *History of British Birds* has a charming picture of a Rook amiably regarding a scarecrow, while the field behind is blotted with the black shapes of a score or so of its companions. (This scene is placed by the text on the Carrion Crow, while the Crow picture follows the Rook entry.)

Rooks are also held to forecast rain, though the signs to look out for vary: − a tumbling flight; roosting at midday (Devon); flying to the hills (Isle of Man); standing on the *dead* branches of trees (Yorkshire). In Durham there is a saying that if the Rooks feed in the streets of a village a storm is close at hand. They have also been drawn into one or two Christian stories. It is a Shropshire tradition that Rooks do no work on Ascension Day, but sit quietly and reverently in the trees. It was also believed that if you failed to wear something new on Easter Day, the Rooks would 'spoil your clothes'.

The presence or the establishment of a rookery on your land was not thought to be a specially good omen, but the desertion of a rookery is most certainly a bad sign, corresponding to rats leaving the ship. On the whole the way 'rook' has passed into the general language reflects badly upon the bird. The *OED* quotes an interesting usage of the mid-nineteenth century 'a rookery of prostitutes'. The slang phrase, to rook somebody, meaning to cheat them, is still in use, but the use of 'rook' for 'crook' has passed out of currency.

Jackdaw
Corvus monedula

from the cry:
Jack (General)
Daw (General)
Caddaw (East Anglia)
Cadder; Caddy (Norfolk)
Carder (Suffolk)
Cawdaw (Suffolk; North Country)
Caw (Banffshire; Kirkcudbrightshire)
Kya (Wigtown)
Jakie; Jaikie (East Lothian; Berwickshire; Midlothian)

various:
Grey Head
Grey Neck (Midlothian)
Pate; Paiet (Kirkcudbright)

The word Daw for Jackdaw may be traced back only so far as the fifteenth century but, since it corresponds in form to the Italian, French and Spanish names for the bird, they are all probably rooted in an Old High German and fundamentally echoic of the Jackdaw's cry, which sounds something like 'kow'. The local names Kya and Caddaw (or Kye-daw) and Caw are variations on the same sound.

The Jackdaw also makes a 'tchack' call. One could explain the name Jackdaw simply in terms of the sound it makes. I think this would, though, be losing much of the richness of language for the sake of a single clarity. If there were ever a single

225

identifiable origin, this has been enriched and reinforced by the other meanings and associations. Though Shakespeare always refers to Jackdaws as Daws, the name 'Iacke Daw' in two words was already in use by the beginning of the sixteenth century. Jack is a familiar name, often given to birds and other animals and conjoined with their names. Usually it denotes a smallness in size, as in Jack Snipe, or the local name Jack Doucker for the Little Grebe or Dabchick. Jack in the sense of knave (as in a pack of cards) meant small, and it came also to mean a rogue. The Jackdaw is considerably smaller than a Rook or Crow and is renowned for its 'theiving' habits. During the sixteenth century, the word daw was used synonymously with knave to mean someone held in very low esteem, and later it acquired connotations of stupidity as well.

The appearance of Jackdaws in one circumstance or another is given in several parts of Britain as a prognostication of rain, for instance in Norwich an old rhyme goes:

> When three daws are seen on St Peter's
> vane together
> Then we're sure to have bad weather.

There is also a belief in the North of England that a Jackdaw down the chimney may be considered to portend the death of someone in the house. Here we have a typical corvid-like prediction of death, but falling down a chimney would be typical only of the Jackdaw. The Jackdaw's method of building a nest is to bring up a continuous flow of sticks which it will drop into a hole or crevice (sometimes a chimney) until a few of them lodge and form a basis on which to construct the rest of the nest. I know of a bird whose nest became displaced and while a gas fire was burning beneath fell down a chimney on to the hearth. Incredibly it got away unscathed, apart from signs of mild shock, but often there are casualties. In Gloucestershire, a solitary Jackdaw is also said to be a sign of death, but as the species is highly gregarious, this is a generally unlikely occurrence.

Pie (General)
Piet (Westmorland)
Pianate; Pyenate (West Riding)
Piannot (Cheshire)
Mag; Madge
Maggot (Worcestershire; Gloucestershire; Lincolnshire)
Magot Pie (E. England)
Nanpie (Craven)
Longtailed Nan
Ninut (Nottinghamshire)
Mock-a-pie
Margaret's Pie; Marget
Miggy (North Country)

from its voice:
Chatternag (Somerset)
Chatterpie (Norfolk; Somerset)
Chattermag
Haggister

various:
Cornish Pheasant (Cornwall)
Tell Pienot; Tell Piet (N Riding)
Bush Magpie

Magpie
Pica pica

The word pied originally denoted a mixture of colours. Over the centuries it has narrowed its meaning to mean simply black and white rather than parti-coloured, though it is used in the latter sense by Gerard Manley Hopkins in his 'Pied Beauty', as it was in Shakespeare's lovely song 'When daisies pied and violets blue . . .'. The word pie indicating a mixture continues through to the present day in the pie that we eat, which can contain a mixture of contents, and also in the 'printer's pie', a jumble of assorted type. The Magpie has another association with printing in that its Latin name 'Pica' (used synonymously with pye or pie in the fifteenth century) is also the name for a type size (measuring about six lines to the inch).

The first syllable of Magpie is a familiar name, a diminutive form of Margaret. There are a number of other variations as well as Mag; Madge, Marget, Margaret, Margot and Miggy. The Magpie has a very loud chattering voice and in the late eighteenth century Mag or Meg was used for somebody who chattered a great deal. The Magpie itself is called Chatterpie and Chatternag and also Haggister, which comes via Old High German *Agalstra* = chatterer. Today calling someone a Magpie is more likely to signify that they collect and hoard things in the 'Thieving Magpie' tradition which Rossini characterized so well in the sprightly music of his overture of that name. The Magpie 'chatter' is in fact not dissimilar from the cackling noise that a person might make and like a number of birds (see Yellowhammer) whose voices ressemble those of a human being, the Magpies are said to have a drop of the devil's blood in them.

Pied plumage also has diabolic associations, so the Magpie is doubly ominous. The Reverend Swainson records that if he saw a Magpie, a North Shropshire friend of his used to take off his hat, spit in the direction of the bird and say 'Devil, devil I defy you' (a phrase rather similar to the rhythm of the Magpie's own cackling call). Eating a mixture of ground–up Magpie used to be thought to cure epilepsy, on the basis that consuming a chatterer could neutralize the chattering disease (see Swallow and Yellowhammer).

In common with others of the crow family, there are resonances of pagan symbolism in Magpie lore where, as illustrated in these three tales from the North of England, Magpies fail to comply with the requirements of Christianity. The Magpie, it was said around Durham, was the only bird which refused to go into the ark with Noah and all the other animals. It preferred instead to perch on top of the roof of the ark and chatter and swear as the world drowned. And because they still enjoy the sight of bad fortune, it is best to turn back from a Magpie or you will come across bad luck. Another story says that the Magpie is a hybrid between a Raven and a dove (an interesting mating of the Celtic and the Christian) and so, unlike other birds, it had never been baptised by the waters of the deluge. Another tale says that at the time of the crucifixion, the Magpie did not, like all the other birds, go into full mourning.

In the West Riding, crossing oneself is thought to mitigate the evil effects of a Magpie crossing your path — a nice play on the word cross, as is contained in the old rhyme:

> I cross the magpie
> The magpie crosses me
> Bad luck to the magpie
> Good luck to me.

It was also said that the sight of a crow soon after would neutralize the evil of the Magpie. In the same way, in the Magpie rhyme, though one is for sorrow — two is for joy. The oldest versions of this rhyme were short and simple, one from the West of England, from about 1750, goes:

> One for sorrow, two for joy
> Three for a wedding, four for death.

Later versions substitute 'a boy' for four, or 'mirth' and 'a birth' for two and four, and there are also many other additions which prognosticate the effects of up to ten Magpies.

Jay
Garrulus glandarius

Gae (Scotland)
Jay Pie (Cornwall; Devon; Midlands)
Jay Piet (Perth)
Blue Jay (Linlithgow)
Jenny Jay (North Riding)
Kae
Devil Scritch (Somerset)
Scold (Somerset)
Oak Jackdaw
Schreachag choille = screamer of the woods (Gaelic)

Though it is so beautifully coloured, the word Jay has nothing to do with 'gay', nor has the French name *geai* any etymological connection with *gai*. One rather homely suggestion from Sargent and Potter is that *Gaius,* the latin name for the Jay, was a personal name in the same way as Robin is, or Jackdaw, or Margot Pie. Other names such as Gae and Kae (and perhaps Jay itself) echo that harsh sound which is captured in the name Devil Scritch.

The Gaelic *Schreachag choille* means 'Screamer of the woods' and Chaucer speaks of 'the screaming jay' in the *Parlement of Foules*. When one looks at the way the word Jay is applied to other birds, it becomes clear that it is on account of the voice rather than the plumage. The Chough, which has a ringing caw, is the Cornish Jay, and the Mistle Thrush, which has a quite astonishingly loud call, is also the Jay Thrush.

The 'pie' and 'piet' of Jay Pie and Jay Piet refers to the many shades of plumage, brown, black, white and grey with a splash of blue on the forewings. The Jay is the most arboreal of the crow family and the most retiring in its native habitat. You are far more likely to hear the formidable screech than to catch sight of the Jay, or if you do, to see more than the flash of white on the rump as it makes its swift retreat. It has, however, in recent times shown itself to be completely adaptable to town parks which have a certain amount of woodland and in this habitat it is actually quite bold. There are breeding Jays in the Royal Parks almost in the centre of London. Jays, the Oak Jackdaws, are particularly partial to acorns and to beech mast (the second part of the scientific name *glandarius* means precisely that – 'eating acorns and beech mast') and some quite serious authorities consider that the Jay plays a part in the spreading of oak forest, through its habit of burying acorns (especially when the range of forest is extended uphill).

Chough
Pyrrhocorax pyrrhocorax

from its geographic haunts:
Cornish Daw; Cornish Jack; Cornish Chough; Cornish Kae; Cornish Jay
Market Jew Crow (Cornwall)

from its appearance:
Red-legged Crow
Long-billed Chough

from its cries:
Daw; Chauk Daw
Chauk
Tsauha

habitat names:
Cliff Daw
Sea Crow (Ireland)
Hermit Crow

others:
Killigrew
Palores (Cornwall)

It seems likely that in ancient times Choughs, along with other corvids, figured importantly in religious beliefs of the Celtic parts of Britain. There are myths which tell of King Arthur returning in the form of a Chough (also a Crow or a Raven) though not as an Eagle, which is mostly a bird of southern and eastern cultures and whose importance gradually spread from Mediterranean regions to eclipse the Celtic black birds. There may be a connection with this and the legend that Arthur lies in a cave in a mountain, guarded by eagles.

Those who know the Chough invariably regard it with affection. Dr J. T. R. Sharrock in the *Atlas of Breeding Birds* introduces it as 'a crow of great character and charm' and goes on to describe the few western stretches of coastline to which Choughs are now restricted. Sadly, this bird with so many Cornish names, is no longer to be found in that county; in fact, there may be only one place in the whole of the south-west peninsula where Choughs might possibly be breeding.

The range and population of the Chough used to be much greater than now. 'Sea Crows' used to be seen inland in East Scotland and Yorkshire as well as on the coasts of Dorset, Devon and Sussex. There are several indications that they used also to colonize the Dover cliffs, though by 1850 this was no longer so. Dunkin's *History of Kent* (1857) chronicles that 'before the war of extermination was ruthlessly waged against the Chough or Red-legged Crow, Cornish Chough . . . Red-legged Jack Daw . . . Cliff Daw, Gesner's Wood Crow, this bird was very plentiful among the Dover cliffs.'

> How fearful
> And dizzy 'tis to cast one's eyes so low?
> The crows and choughs that wing the midway air
> Show scarce so gross as beetles;

says Edgar in *King Lear*, trying to create in words the scene on Dover cliffs for the blind and despairing Gloucester who intends to throw himself from the clifftop. In order to save his father's life, Edgar has to convince him that they are at Dover. To this purpose, it seems quite likely that Shakespeare is not using the word Chough in the loose sense but as an image he knows to be peculiar to the cliffs at Dover.

Choughs have another Kentish association in that the coat of arms of Canterbury has upon it five Choughs. This device commemorates the city's most famous archbishop, the 'holy, blissful, martyr' Thomas à Becket, whose own coat of arms features three Choughs. Later the heraldic Choughs became known as 'beckits'.

The word Chough used, it seems, to be pronounced 'chow' echoing the wheezy 'kee-argh' cry. The Old English words *Cio* and *Ceo* and the Middle English *Co, Coo, Chogh* and *Chough* refer to both Choughs and Jackdaws, and it is difficult to say with any certainty which bird is being referred to in some older writings. However, it looks as if the 'war of extermination' recorded by Dunkin must have been aimed against Choughs (though possibly against other corvids too) as the Chough, alone among the crow family, possesses red legs and is known as the Cornish Daw or Cornish Chough.

from the black on its head:
Black Cap, Black Capped Lolly (Northamptonshire; West Riding)
Black-headed Bob (Devon)
Black-headed Tomtit (Shropshire; Stirling)

from its rasping, short-phrased song:
Saw Sharpener (Roxburgh)
Sharp Saw (Norfolk)
Sit ye Down
Pridden Pral = tree babbler (West Cornwall)
Sawfinch

other names:
Big Ox-eye (Forfar; East Lothian; Roxburgh)
Ox-eye (Midlands; Shropshire; North Riding; Ireland)
Joe Ben (Suffolk)
Heckymal (Dartmoor)
Tom Noup (noup = bullfinch) (Shropshire)

It is said that if you hear a birdsong you can't identify in the woods, it is a Great Tit. It has an astonishing variety of different songs and variations which it obligingly performs during most of the year. Even in winter you can hear its wheezy 'tee-cher, tee-cher' as it moves through the trees. It is this most typical call that gives it the many call-names including the word saw, such as Saw Sharpener.

Like the Blue Tit, the Great Tit is a frequenter of birdtables, sometimes dropping its fear of human beings to the extent that it will feed from the hand. It is an extremely handsome little bird, its colours bright and very clearly defined. Its glossy black cap has given rise to a substantial group of names. The large white patch on the cheek, outlined in black, is probably the reason for the Ox-eye names, which are widely used (see Ringed Plover).

The word Tit is an abbreviation of Titmouse, the family name for this species. Titmouse had nothing to do with mice in its original meaning, though the name is very apt for the way these little birds scurry along the branches. This 'mouse' comes from the Old English *mase*, a word used generally for a small bird. Tit came into Middle English from the Icelandic *tittr*, which means small, so Titmouse really means a small, small bird. However, by the sixteenth century, the original meaning had been forgotten and *mase*, which by this time had become *mose*, was altered to mouse; this development was probably influenced by the mousey movements of the Titmice.

Blue Tit

Parus caeruleus

plumage names:
Blue Cap; Blue Bonnet (Shropshire; West Riding; Scotland)
Blue Ox-eye (Forfar)
Blue Yaup (Scotland)
Blue Spick (North Devon)
Nun (from the white fillet round its head)

from its repeated sharp, shrill cry:
Pedn-play; Pridden Pral = tree babbler (West Cornwall)
Pinchem (Bedfordshire)
Tidife; Tinnock
Yaup (Renfrew)

other names:
Bee Bird (Hampshire)
Billy Biter (Shropshire; North Riding)
Allecampagne (Cornwall)
Jenny Wren (Craven)
Ox Eye (East Lothian)
Pickcheese (Norfolk)
Stonechat (Ireland)
Tom Nouf (Shropshire)
Tom Tit
Hickmall; Hackmal, Heckymal, Hagmal, Titmal (Devon; Cornwall)

These tiny acrobatic creatures are a familiar sight in garden and woodland and, it seems, were as tame and friendly centuries ago. A sixteenth century round-song by William Wagner was based on a catch which began:

> I have a pretty titmouse
> Come pecking at my toe . . .

Blue Tits are beautifully marked birds and are so confiding in their behaviour that they are easy to observe. The blue colouration which has given rise to a large group of local names is at its purest in the azure of the crown, which is encircled by a nun-like fillet of white. The Blue Tit also has the white 'ox-eye' cheek patch. The nape, wings and tail are a darker shade of blue-grey. High pitched raspy cheeps are a continuous accompaniment as Blue Tits fly about, usually in company, from branch to branch, seeking food. John Clare describes the bustling activity of the Blue Tits

> . . . The bluecap tootles in its glee
> Picking the flies from orchard apple tree

behaviour also observed by the chair-ridden B. J. Massingham, whose time was brightened by watching the journeys of parent Blue Tits between nest and apple trees in his orchard. He calculated, as a conservative estimate, that the brood received something in the region of 1,500 meals a day, consisting of grubs of the apple blossom weevil and maggots of the Apple Sawfly. He became more and more impressed as he watched:

> It was beautiful to see them swoop down from the telegraph wire and infallibly swing up to it again. Every motion of these jewelled atomies of life was a flash of certainty. Every feather in the fiery furnace of the sun had the metallic sheen of a humming bird. Everything they did was as purposive as an arrow . . . There was nothing blurred nor fumbling nor meaningless in their lives. What acuity of the senses and brilliance of execution . . .
>
> (*An Englishman's Year*)

Its flight is indeed rapid and straight and parent birds become extremely annoyed if the direct line of flight to the nest is impeded. Small as they are, they will hiss and bite at anything which intrudes on the nest, which is how they came by the name Billy Biter. They deeply resent any disturbance, even the mildest. In my own experience of last summer, during the period when eight Blue Tit youngsters were being fed, it was uncomfortable to do any work in their part of the garden. The adults, their tiny beaks crammed with titbits, would perch nearby and, full beaks regardless, swear loudly and precisely until they were allowed free access. The scold has a dry pebbly sound to it which is probably why Blue Tits have borrowed the name of the Stonechat in Ireland. There is also something of a scolding sound in the Hickmal and Heckymal group of names. These derive from the Old English name for the Blue Tit, *Hicemase*.

Coal Tit
Parus ater

Black Cap (Shropshire; Stirling)
Black Ox-eye (Forfar)
Coal; Coaly Hood (Scotland)
Coal Hooden (East Lothian)
Tomtit (Ireland)
Little Blackcap (Yorkshire)
Coalmouse (Ireland)

The black cap or coaly hood of the Coal Tit is not as strikingly glossy black as those of the Marsh or Willow Tits. But the *Colemase* has been known since Anglo-Saxon times and the coal referred to is not the shiny black mineral we know today, but the grey-black charcoal. More than any other tit, the Coal Tit is closely associated with conifers and it will cling acrobatically to cones, picking out the seeds and eating them. It also feeds on the insects and larvae which live upon the trees. The white smudges on the cheeks and nape of the neck are very conspicuous as the birds move actively over the trees, often hopping up a trunk like a Treecreeper. The population of Coal Tits has increased greatly over recent years, trebling itself since 1964. It may now be seen in almost any situation which can boast a few conifers, not only commercial plantations, but parks, churchyards and cemeteries, and suburban gardens.

Marsh Titmouse
Black Cap (Nottinghamshire)
Joe Ben (East Anglia)
Saw Whetter (Staffordshire)
Willow Biter (Nottinghamshire)
Black-headed Tit (Somerset)

Marsh Tit
Parus palustris

Willow Tit
Palus montanus

There is no choice of names for the Willow Tit. It was only distinguished as a separate species in Britain in 1897, and was the last native British breeding species to achieve recognition. The discovery was made, not by ornitholigists in the field, but by systematists Otto Kleinschmidt and Ernst Hartert who were going through a tray of specimens marked 'Marsh Tit' at the British Museum and noticed two birds which were decidedly a different species. But one should not be too surprised at such a long anonymity for a fairly common and widespread species. These two 'Black Cap' birds are remarkably similar, and even today accomplished ornithologists admit that surveys probably confuse the two species. It is very likely that, especially since there is a good deal of overlap in their habitat, most of the Marsh Tit's names belong also to its close cousin, though the people who used them would most probably have been unaware of this, regarding them as one species.

The Marsh Tit, the commoner bird, out-numbers the Willow quite considerably in broad-leaf woodland, less so in farmland habitats. It has a harsh, clear song with seven or so notes, all at the same pitch; it also has a 'scold' which makes Saw Whetter definitely a Marsh Tit name. The Willow Tit has a vocabulary which includes curious buzzing calls and a loud plaintive song with fewer but much longer notes than the Marsh Tit, almost like a Nightingale. It is the only tit which excavates its nests out of tree trunks, leaving little heaps of chippings beneath. (The Marsh Tit may sometimes enlarge an existing hole.) On the face of it, one would imagine that this habit earned it the name of Willow Biter, but it is worth remembering that the Blue Tit is known as Billy Biter. The Marsh Tit

Marsh Tit
Willow Tit

and the Willow Tit will also peck furiously at any intrusion to their nest (the Willow Tit is reputed to be less demonstrative) so it would seem likely that it was this habit which gave rise to the 'Biter' names.

Long-tailed Tit

Aegithalos caudatus

from its plumage:
Long-tailed Mag; Long-pod (Midlands)
Long-tailed Pie; French Pie; Dog-tail (Cheshire)
Long-tailed Capon (Hampshire; Norfolk)
Long-tailed Chittering
Long-tailed Mufflin
Mumruffin, Hedge Mumruffin (Worcestershire; Shropshire)
Ragamuffin
Juffit; Fuffit (East Lothian)

from the shape and construction of the nest:
Jack-in-a-bottle; Bottle Tom
Bottle Tit (West Riding; Berkshire; Buckinghamshire; Shropshire)
Bag (Northamptonshire)
Poke Pudding, Poke Bag (Gloucestershire; Shropshire)
Pudding Bag (Norfolk)
Puddney Poke (Suffolk)
Feather Poke
Oven Bird; Oven Builder (Stirling)
Oven's Nest (Northamptonshire)
Bum Barrel (Nottinghamshire)
Bush Oven (Norfolk)
Can Bottle (Shropshire)
Hedge Jug

other names:
Bum Towel (Devon)
Bellringer (Kirkcudbright)
Millithrum = Miller's Thumb
Nimble Tailor
Prinpriddle

It is rare to see a Long-tailed Tit on its own. They are gregarious birds and usually travel around together in family parties or small bands. It is not unusual for a group of birds to attend a nestling family, sharing parental duties such as feeding and protection. The tail is the most remarkable feature of this otherwise very tiny bird, and accounts for more than half of its total length. During their short, undulating flights, the tails dips up and down. A small flock typically moves in rapid surges through the trees or across a hedge in restless waves.

The nest is a work of considerable beauty and many of its features have attracted vernacular names. Shredded wool, moss, spider silk and lichens are worked into a 'felt' and shaped in an oval or bottle shape. The ten or so eggs rest softly upon a lining of feathers (more than 2,000 feathers have been counted in a single nest). When brooding, the parent birds holds the tail erect over its back and the top of the head and the tail block the nest entrance.

Long-tailed Tits are slightly fluffy in appearance, which is the reason they have been given some 'muffler', 'muffin' names. Muffin is also a term of affection and aptly bestowed on such an appealing little bird. But for all their attractive fluffiness, Mumruffins are very susceptible to cold. Finding insect food is more difficult during a hard winter and the birds have a hard time in keeping up adequate energy supplies. As a means of conserving heat, Long-tailed Tits will huddle together inside a suitable hole, warming each other with their body heat.

Nut Topper
Nutcracker (Shropshire)
Nut Jobber (Somerset; Sussex; Berkshire)
Nuthack
Woodcracker
Woodhacker (Surrey)
Woodjar (Gloucestershire)
Woodpecker (Surrey)
Jobbin (Northamptonshire)
Mud Dabber (Somerset)
Mud Stopper (S England)
Blue Leg (Sussex)
Jar Bird

Nuthatch
Sitta europaea

Nuthatch is an unlikely kind of a name if you take it literally; an earlier version was Nut Hacker, both tougher and more practical. Nuthatches are small birds (only as big as a Great Tit) but their strong beaks can deal with food as large and as hard as hazel nuts and acorns. The nut is jammed in a crevice of wall or tree and the whole body swings, bringing the beak hammering down until the shell is broken and the sweet kernel exposed. Nut Jobber and Jobbin are virtually synonymous with Nuthatch. The old meaning of 'job' (from at least the fifteenth century) was 'to peck, stab or prod at something with a sharp instrument'. The *OED* gives the origin as 'apparently echoic', and the Reverend Swainson notes that the Gaelic for beak is '*gob*'. The Nuthatch will also tap tree trunks, in the manner of a woodpecker (possibly crushing large insects for consumption), which earns it the names Woodhacker and Woodcracker. The discordant jarring sound of its hacking has given rise to the names Woodjar and Jar Bird, the name used by Gilbert White.

The Nuthatch is an attractive, solidly built little bird, less eye-catching in the forest with its grey back, peachy underneath and severe black eye-stripe, than one would imagine. It scutters about the trees of thick woodland; upwards, downwards, or sideways with equal facility, sometimes doing its 'hacking' from an upside-down position. The Nuthatch is in fact the only British bird which can travel *down* a tree. (It used to be thought that they roosted head down.) Nuthatches choose holes in tree trunks or walls as places to nest in, making the entrance smaller by stopping it up with mud, until it is exactly the right size – hence the names Mud Dabber and Mud Stopper.

Creeper
Tree Climber; Tree Climmer (Surrey; Sussex)
Tree Crawler (Sussex)
Tree Clipper (Oxfordshire)
Creep Tree (Norfolk)
Climb Tree (Somerset)
Creepy Tree (Yorkshire)
Tree Speiler, Bark Speiler (speiler = climber) (East Lothian)
Bark Creeper; Bark Runner (Suffolk)
Brown Treecreeper; Brown Woodpecker
Woodpecker (Ireland; Perthshire)
Little Woodpecker (Yorkshire)
Tree Mouse (Somerset)

various:
Daddy-ike, Eeckle (Gloucestershire)
Cuddy (Northamptonshire)
Tomtit (Ireland)
Ox-eye Creeper

Treecreeper
Certhia familiaris

The Somerset name Tree Mouse is perhaps the most descriptive name for the Treecreeper which is extremely mouse-like in its movements. Scurrying up tree trunks and long branches, it points its long, scimitar curved bill into holes and crevices to find the insects upon which it mainly feeds. There is a large and widespread resident population of Treecreepers all over the British Isles, but they are small birds, easily missed, their brown backs merging against the bark of trees. Nearly all the names allude to its creeping, crawling, scurrying and climbing habits. Of the remaining names, Cuddy (see Moorhen) may have something to do with the fact that the Treecreeper makes use of the stout feathers of its tail for support as it climbs up trees. Occasionally it will feed, clinging tit-like, upside down and its undulating flight also resembles that of the tits and it is accorded two 'tit' names – Tomtit (more commonly used for the Blue Tit) and Ox-eye Creeper (Ox-eye, usually the Great Tit). The Treecreeper is midway between these two tits in size, and it has a silvery white stripe above the eye which could account for the Ox-eye name. Treecreepers often travel in company with tits in the winter time.

241

Wren

Troglodytes troglodytes

Wranny (Cornwall)
Wrannock; Wirann (Orkney)
Wran (Ireland; Scotland)

from its short tail:
Cutty; Cut (North and West England)
Cutteley Wren; Cuddy (Somerset)
Scutty (Sussex; Hampshire; Somerset)
Skiddy (Gloucestershire)
Stumpy Toddy (Cheshire)
Stumpit (Lancashire)

from its diminutive size:
Tiddy Wren, Tidley Wren (Essex)
Tom Tit (Norfolk; Craven)
Titmeg; Titty Todger (Devon)
Titty Wren (Gloucestershire; Suffolk; Wiltshire)
Tintie (Nottinghamshire)

familiar names:
Bobby Wren (Norfolk; Suffolk)
Kitty Wren; Jenny Wren (General)
Sally (Ireland)
Kitty-me-wren (N England; Scotland)
Jenny (Lancashire; Lincolnshire; Yorkshire)

from the voice:
Crackadee; Cracket; Crackeys (Devon)
Chitty Wren (Ireland)
Jitty (Cheshire)
Crackil (Devon)
Juggy Wren (Surrey)

various:
Gilliver Wren (Lincolnshire)
Tope; Stag (Norfolk; Cornwall)
Guradnan (Cornwall)
Our Lady's Hen (Scotland)
Puffy Wren; Puggie Wren (Surrey)

This tiny bird, estimated at the time of writing to be the most abundant nesting bird in Britain and Ireland, plays a large part in a very ancient tradition of folk ritual. The Wren is recorded as *magus avium* (*magus*, a magician or sorcerer) in Irish hagiology and it is mentioned also as a Druidic bird of prophesy. It was known as God's Bird and Our Lady's Hen and it was said that harm would inevitably befall anyone who hurt a Wren. An old

Scots rhyme heaps curses (malaisons) on the offender:

> Malaisons, malaisons mair that ten
> That harry Our Lady of Heaven's wren

and a Cornish rhyme also gives warning:

> Hunt a robin or a wren
> Never prosper man or boy.

However, in seeming contradiction to the protective feeling, one of the most widespread and elaborate folk rituals surviving in Britain, and in parts of Europe, is the Wren hunt which takes place in the depths of winter in the days between Christmas and Epiphany. The Wren hunt seems to be part of the observations peculiar to this period (which also had a place in ancient calendars) entailing a reversal of the accepted order of things. Another tradition was that a Lord of Misrule should be appointed king for this time and an insignificant boy was accorded all the dignities of a king. Similarly the little Wren, normally a sacred bird, was hunted and sacrificed at this one festival. In Pembrokeshire, a boy bedecked in ribbons comes around with a Wren in a cage, singing:

> Come and make your offering
> To the smallest yet the king

. . . and he sets the Wren free. There is enormous variety in the style and form of the ceremonies and in the rhymes and songs. Often the Wren is killed, and in most cases, much is made of the disparity in the size of the bird and the importance accorded to it. In the Marseilles district, four strong men affect to labour under the weight of the slaughtered Wren carried between two poles, and in Devon, two men play the same part, singing a song about the heaviness of their burden. Play is also made on the Wren's small size in the Greek story of the Wren and the Eagle, where the Wren deviously wins the title King of the Birds (see Eagle).

There has been a considerable study made of the variety and significance of the Wren hunts. Edward Armstrong concludes, taking into account the form of the hunts and the geographical evidence, that the Wren cult reached the British Isles during the Bronze Age, proceeding from the Mediterranean along prehistoric trade routes. Its significance, he suggests, is that at this time of the New Year the Wren hunt represents the death of the dark earth powers and the beginning of a new season of light and life.

There are a number of explanations which have overlaid the original tradition. The most widely known is that it was a Wren which alerted guards to the attempted escape of Saint Stephen from imprisonment, and so indirectly brought about the death of the first English martyr. Here, as in many other instances, Christianity takes over a pagan tradition, offers its own explanation and sets a ceremony of its own on the same date. Saint Stephen's day is 26 December, the date of many Wren hunts, and falls well within the ancient period of Misrule. In the Christian tradition, as in the pagan, the Wren is respected for the rest of the year and there are two stories of Wrens which endeared themselves to holy men, Saint Malo and Saint Calasius, by making a nest in their cloaks. Saint Malo, it is said, refrained from wearing his cloak until the birds had fledged.

The Wren who betrayed Saint Stephen raised the alarm by flying in the face of a guard. A number of other 'warning' stories in circulation in Ireland involve the Wren 'drumming' an alert. (It hopped up and down on a drum to tell the Danish of an impending Irish attack at Doolinn, and later by the same means warned Cromwell of an attack by the Irish.) This drumming is a reference to the alarm call of the Wren, a rush of sharp loud notes following thick and fast one after the other and resembling a rapid drumming. It was these sounds which gave rise to the Crackil and Cracket group of names.

The song of the Wren, a clear, high-pitched musical succession of phrases, is often overlooked in favour of those of other birds such as the Robin, Thrush or Blackbird. To Wordsworth however, the Wren's song had a special meaning. In Book II of *The Prelude*, he describes a poignant occasion when hearing a Wren composed his boisterous spirits:

> . . . that single wren
> Which one day sang so sweetly in the nave
> Of that old church, – though from recent showers
> The earth was comfortless, and, touched by faint
> Internal breezes, sobbings of the place
> And respirations, from the roofless walls
> The shuddering ivy dripped large drops – yet still
> So sweetly 'mid the gloom the invisible bird
> Sang to herself, that there I could have made
> My dwelling-place, and lived for ever there
> To hear such music.

Bessie Ducker
Water Ouzel
Water Blackbird (Scotland; Ireland)
Water Crow (Westmorland; Lowlands)
Water Thrush (Cornwall)
Brook Ouzel

colour names:
Piet (Scotland)
Water Piet (Scotland)
River Pie (Ireland)

various:
Ess Cock (Aberdeen)
Water Peggie (Dumfries)
Water Colly (Somerset)
Gobha uisge = water smith (Gaelic)
Gobha dhubh nan allt = blacksmith of the stream (Gaelic)
Colley (Cheshire)
Bobby

Dipper
Cinclus cinclus

'River' and 'water' are commonly part of Dipper names, and the bird is rarely seen away from the fast moving upland streams where it lives and feeds. Its diet consists mainly of land and water beetles and insect larvae and it can walk or fly underwater to catch them. As it patrols the banks and rocks it engages in a dipping, bobbing movement which has given it the comparatively recent name of Dipper. This name was first recorded in Tunstall's *Ornithologica Britannica* (1771), though as Water Ouzel it was described by Turner (1544) and a number of other early writers. There are three subspecies of Dipper which appear in Britain, but they are all fairly similar in behaviour and the appearance varies principally in the amount of chestnut brown in the lower breast. All Dippers have dazzling white shirtfronts and the brown on the top of the head merges with a slatey-grey back, fully qualifying them for their various 'pied' and 'pie' names. The Dipper used to be classified along with the Thrush family and it shares Ouzel and Colley names with the Blackbird and Ring Ouzel. Colley, which means 'dark as coal', was probably descriptive of the dark plumage of the wings, back and tail of these three species.

Bearded Tit
Panurus biarmicus

Bearded Pinnock
Reed Bunting (Essex)
Reedling (Norfolk)
Beardmanica
Reed Pheasant, Pheasant (Norfolk)
Water Pheasant (Sussex)
Least Butcher Bird
Lesser Butcher Bird

Some ornithological papers on the Bearded Tit refer to this bird as the Bearded Reedling a name both apt, as it is virtually never seen away from its reedy habitat, and accurate, since this species is related not to tits but to the family of Babblers, not otherwise represented in Britain. Never a common bird, its popularity with cagebird collectors, taxidermists and egg collectors led to an increase in names and a decrease in the numbers of the living birds. Numbers declined disastrously in the nineteenth century, but recently they have shown a rise, despite the way that suitable reedbed habitat is being destroyed by drainage and reclamation.

It may seem odd that a bird which some-times feeds upon insects but which lives mainly upon the seeds of reeds, especially its favourite phragmites, should attract two Butcher Bird names. However, when you see that it shares the name Lesser Butcher Bird with the Red-backed Shrike, which also has a distinctive black facial streak, the mystery resolves itself. The shrike has a broad straight-back moustachial stripe; the Bearded Tit's moustaches drop down into the mandarin beard of its standard name. It is also the Bearded Pinnock, a name which makes reference to its ear-catching, sharp 'chink-chink' call. Along with many other birds with long tails, this little bird is also called Pheasant.

Hollin Cock (Yorkshire)
Holm Thrush; Holm Cock; Holm Screech (Cornwall; Devon; Dorset)
Muzzel Thrush (Roxburgh)
Mizzly Dick (Northumberland)

from its harsh voice:
Screech
Skirlock (Derbyshire)
Skrike; Skrite (South of England)
Squawking Thrush (Isle of Wight)
Gawthrush (Northamptonshire)
Jay (N Ireland)
Jay Pie (Wiltshire)
Jercock; Chercock (Westmorland)
Stormcock
Jeremy Joy

from its size:
Big Mavis (East Lothian)
Big Felt (Ireland)
Bull Thrush (Hampshire)
Horse Thrush (Northamptonshire)

others:
Corney Keevor (Antrim)
Crakle
Bunting Thrush
Butcher Bird

Mistle Thrush
Turdus viscivorus

247

Felfit (E Suffolk)
Fulfer (Norfolk)
Hillan Piet (Aberdeen)
Fen Thrush (Northamptonshire)
Marble Thrush (Northamptonshire)
Norman Thrush (Craven)
Stone Thrush (Dorset)
Wood Thrush (Dumfries)

Viscivorus the second part of the scientific name coined by Linnaeus is basically the same as its standard English name, *viscum* = mistletoe and *voro* = devour. The Mistle Thrush and its fondness for berries was mentioned by Aristotle in his *History of Animals* written in the fourth century BC. Mistletoe berries are an important food for the bird in Mediterranean countries where a species of mistletoe with red berries grows abundantly upon olive trees, but in the British Isles, it has not been proved that mistletoe is part of its diet at all. But the name, derived from Aristotle's early description, has been carried through to the standard name of the present day. In the West Country, however, they have their own group of names for the Mistle Thrush based not on mistletoe, but on holly, the Old English *holen* which became *holm,* thus Mistle Thrush is the Holm Thrush or Holm Cock. (The holm oak is so called because its foliage resembles that of holly.) Mistle Thrushes are in fact omnivorous, eating insects, worms and snails, and with a special partiality for berries of all kinds, including holly and perhaps mistletoe, but also ivy, hawthorn, yew, rowan and juniper. A classical belief, reiterated by Thomas Bewick in his *British Birds,* that mistletoe would only germinate if passed through the body of a Mistle Thrush, may be partially true. Some seeds, such as those of fat hen *(Chenopodium album)* germinate much more quickly for having been eaten by birds, the hard outer coating having been dissolved by the abrasive action of the bird's gizzard and gut. Another old belief, that Mistle Thrushes can speak seven languages, seems less likely to be substantiated.

The name Thrush, or rather the Anglo-Saxon *thysce,* was in use over a thousand years ago and the Mistle Thrush and the Song Thrush had been distinguished as different species by the eighth century. The Mistle Thrush is among those birds with the greatest multiplicity of names, and in general such birds (which also include the Hedge Sparrow and Chaffinch) lack anything considerable in the way of folklore, but the names, clearly observant of a number of different features, point to a close acquaintance and a certain affection. The Mistle Thrush is known as Bull Thrush. Bull and horse, as adjectives, are often used to signify size; in this case, that the Mistle Thrush, the Big Mavis is larger than the Song Thrush. Sometimes, perhaps with popular use, the 'thrush' in compound names is dropped, and the bird, with that piercingly loud alarm cry, becomes simply the Screech or the Skrite, and possibly because the repeated screech from high raised an echo in people's minds of the cockerel, a variety of screech words were suffixed with 'cock', giving Skirlcock, Chercock and Shrillcock.

Another noticeable feature of the Mistle Thrush's behaviour is that, unlike most other birds, who seek shelter from stormy weather, this bird seems to be stimulated by approaching storms and will sing or call lustily before and through bad weather. As a solitary singer it is particularly conspicuous. This may account for the large number of voice names it has in addition to those directly linking it with the weather, such as Stormcock and Storm Thrush. The Stormcock will also sing very early in the year; Coward reports hearing the 'exultant and ringing song' during a driving snowstorm and one of the names, Jeremy Joy, is said to be a corruption of January Joy.

Not normally an aggressive bird, the Mistle Thrush is fearless in defence of its nest and will drive off marauding Jackdaws and Rooks, and will even attack and beat a Kestrel or Sparrowhawk. As well as being bigger than the Song Thrush, it is also greyer in appearance and the marks on the breast

249

are more blotched and spotted, which is nicely described in the name Marbled Thrush. The French have a word *'grievelé'*, from *Grieve*, a thrush, which means 'speckled like a thrush'.

Fieldfare

Turdus pilaris

from the Anglo-Saxon felde-fare = *the traveller over the fields:*
Feltyfare; Feldefare (Midlands; Ireland)
Fellfare (Northamptonshire)
Fildifire (Shropshire)
Feltiflier (Scotland)
Felfer (Yorkshire; Lancashire)
Felfaw (Yorkshire)
Felfit
Felt; Cock Felt (Northamptonshire)
Velverd (Wiltshire)
Hill Bird

alluding to the slatey-grey of the head and rump:
Blue Back (Lancashire; Shropshire)
Blue Bird (Devon; West Cornwall)
Blue Tail (Midlands)
Blue Felt, Big Felt (Ireland)
Grey Thrush (Scotland)
Pigeon Felt (Berkshire; Buckinghamshire; Oxfordshire)

from its cry:
Jack Bird
Screech Bird, Screech Thrush (Stirling)

other names:
Snow Bird (Shropshire)
Storm Bird (Norfolk)
Storm Cock (Shropshire; Scotland)

Fieldfares are above all the birds of winter. In *The Parlement of Foules* Chaucer introduces them in a memorable phrase 'the frosty feldefares'; they are also Snowbirds. A few pairs breed in Britain, but these are very small in number compared with the winter flocks which fly in from Scandinavia as the autumn weather begins to get chill. Though omnivorous like most thrushes, Fieldfares show a preference for berries and in a good season will feed on hawthorn, rosehips, rowan and other berries to the exclusion of insects. These winter flocks are nomadic, moving from place to place depending on the food supply. Fieldfare means literally the traveller over the fields. John Clare knew them well; and included them in his 'March' poem for the *Shepherd's Calendar*.

> . . . flocking fieldfares, speckled like the thrush,
> Picking the red haw from the sweeing bush
> That come and go on winters chilling wing
> And seem to share no sympathy with Spring.

Matthew Arnold also mentioned the Fieldfares feeding on berries: 'Hollies . . . with scarlet berries gemmed, the Fell-Fares' food'. Wordsworth, too, refers to them as Fellfares. The Arnolds had a country house in Westmorland, near to the Wordsworths. Matthew Arnold grew up almost literally in William's shadow and had both affection and admiration for him. Possibly the two poets watched Fellfares together on the fell country walks they shared, and later recalled their observations using the dialect name they both knew. In parts of Scotland the Fieldfare is known as the Hill Bird.

Many of the Fieldfare names allude to the blue-grey head and rump, and the predominant impression of the birds as they fly is grey. The Fieldfare flocks chatter sociably as they make their progress through trees and bushes, a gentle 'chacking' and 'chucking' from which comes the name Jack Bird. The Fieldfare alarm cry is loud but it is probably not this alone which gives it the names Screech Bird or Screech Thrush, but its family resemblance to the Mistle Thrush with whom it shares these names.

Dirsh (Somerset)
Drush (Dorset)
Grey Bird (Sussex; Devon; Cornwall)
Mavis (East Anglia; Ireland; Scotland)
Mavie (SW Scotland)
Throstle (Midlands; Ireland; North of England)
Thrush; Thrusher (Berkshire; Buckinghamshire)
Thrushfield (Shropshire)

Song Thrush
Turdus philomelos

Song Thrush

Thirstle (Devon; Cornwall; Shropshire)
Whistling Thrush; Whistling Dick (Thames Valley)
Garden Thrush
Throggie (Cheshire)
Trush Drush (Somerset)

The Song Thrush is a bird of rare distinction. For centuries it has been tenderly observed by common people and by poets. Today it is one of the most frequent and welcome of the birds which visit our gardens, and it is quite as widespread (if not more so) in suburban areas as in woodland. A modern poet Adrian Stokes devoted a poem to 'The Suburban Songthrush' singing in a place where there are

> . . . houses gaunt
> But for the bird-chant pressing out
> To penetrate and sublimate the brick.

Long ago, it may also have been subject of one of the Anglo-Saxon riddle poems in The Exeter Book written down in the eighth century but probably of older tradition than that.

> An old evening poet, I bring to men
> bliss in the cities. When I cry out
> in a voice of varying pitch, they sit quiet
> in their dwellings, listening.

The Song Thrush's tolerance of people in close Proximity, its open manner and prowess as a singer, have all drawn attention towards this common and widespread bird.

The song is sweet and loud, with full-toned, clear notes, scattered with repeats and ornaments. It is Robert Browning's rapturous thrush that 'sings its song twice over', Shakespeare's 'Throstle with her note so true', Skelton's 'Mavis with her whistell'. Like the Blackbird, the Song Thrush seems to improve its song year by year as it reaches maturity; augmenting the basic tunes and adding extra notes, through the season and as it grows older. It is a considerable mimic and will copy the songs of other birds including those of the Lapwing, Redshank, Nightingale and Great Tit. It has also been recorded giving an absolutely perfect 'note so true' reproduction of a GPO trimphone.

The name Mavis which appears in Chaucer and other Middle English poets comes to us via the French *mauvis* and could be of Celtic origin, possibly from Brittany. Sometimes Mavis and the Anglo-Saxon Thrush or Throstle are used interchangeably (Shakespeare does this). In East Anglia Mavis is generally reserved for the Song Thrush, Throstle referring to the Mistle Thrush, while in Southwest Scotland, in a contrary usage, Mavis seems most usually to be applied to the Mistle Thrush.

Redwing Mavis (Forfar)
Redwing Thrush; Red Thrush (Midlands)
Redwing Throlly (Yorkshire)

others:
Wind Thrush (Somerset)
Windle; Windle Thrush (Devon)
Winnard
Felt (Northamptonshire)
Little Feltyfare (East Lothian)
Pop
Swine Pipe

Redwing
Turdus iliacus

The first time the name Redwing appears in print is in the Willughby/Ray *Ornithology* of 1678 though it is hard to imagine that such a simple descriptive name was not in use before that time. One of the most charming birds in the thrush family, migrant Redwings usually begin to arrive in late October, in softly twittering flocks. They are very vocal birds and they chatter conversationally to each other, particularly in the evening when they go to roost; often the air is full of their musical babble, a winter subsong, part gentle churr, part lilting warble. An explanation offered for the name Swine Pipe by Alfred Newton is that it refers to 'the soft inward whistle which the bird often utters, resembling the sound of the pipe used by the swineherds of old when collecting the animals under their charge.' They remain in flocks throughout the winter months and these may often be seen spreading over a field or feeding in the hedgerows, standing out from the Song Thrushes, who often feed alongside them, by the pale eyestripe and the red flanks and underwing.

Turner (1544) calls Redwings Wyngthrushes and also quotes *Weingaerdsvogel* (vineyard bird) as the German name. A name still current in Germany is similar to this and the standardized name in Denmark is *Vindrossel* (the bird which feeds in the vineyards). However, in Britain, a country lacking in vineyards, this name became mistranslated as Wind Thrush. The explanation that the migratory Redwing flocks were aided by the winter winds, was proposed by Charleton (1668). This name not only held good, but gave rise to a new group of derivatives such as Windle and Winnard.

Ring Ouzel
Turdus torquatus

Ring Blackbird
Ring Thrush

from its favoured haunts:
Heath Throstle
Hill Chack (Orkney)
Moor Blackbird, Mountain Blackbird (N Riding; Scotland)
Mountain Ouzel; Mountain Thrush (Kirkcudbright)
Mountain Colley (Somerset)
Rock Blackbird (Stirling)
Rock Starling (Roxburgh)
Tor Ouzel (Devon)
Rock Ouzel; Crag Ouzel (Craven)

others:
Cowboy (Tipperary)
Ditch Blackie (East Lothian)
Michaelmas Blackbird (Dorset)
Blackbird (Shropshire)
Flitterchack (Orkney)
Whistler (Wicklow)
Round-berry Bird (Connemara)

The Ring Ouzel is intimately associated with mountain and moorland and is rarely seen away from these habitats. Local names for these habitats are reflected in the names for the bird; so in Devon it is Tor Ouzel; in Craven, Crag Ouzel and in other parts of Scotland, Craigie Easlin and in Orkney, Hill Chack. The 'chack' part of this name, and of Flitterchack, echoes the alarm call, which is similar to that of the Jack Bird, the Fieldfare. The most regular song of the Ring Ouzel is a triple or quadruple repeat of one clear, flutey note, perhaps with some quieter introductory notes, which accounts for Whistler (and possibly, the Reverend Swainson thinks, for Cowboy, because the bird whistles along with the cowherds).

Swainson also offers an explanation for another Irish name Round-berry Bird, as possibly once 'Rowan-berry Bird' indicating the Ring Ouzels' liking for these berries. Ring Ouzels are summer visitors and they spend the spring and summer feeding largely on insects, but as the summer progresses, they turn to the ripening berries of blaeberry, cranberry, bird cherry and elder as well as rowan. They are seen in large numbers around South Dorset on their spring and autumnal, or Michaelmas, flights: hence Michaelmas Blackbird. They are striking birds, slightly smaller than a Blackbird, dark plumaged with a contrasting gorget of white which gives rise to the 'ring' names. The name Ring Ouzel goes back to at least 1450 and most of the early ornithologists used it as a standard name.

There has been a notable decline in the Ring Ouzel population over the last century, but recently it seems that there may have been a local spread in breeding Ring Ouzels in Shetland and Orkney. J. W. H. Trail recorded a belief in Orkney, that a Flitterchack seen near a house foretold that one of the household would die or move away. Ring Ouzels do not normally venture near to human habitation, so this in itself would be unusual – and therefore sinister. It could be also that in this superstition the Ring Ouzel's own behaviour was transferred to the people who saw

255

it. Until recent years, all of the Ring Ouzels seen in Orkney would have been birds of passage, themselves moving away after only a brief stay.

Blackbird
Turdus merula

Blackie (N Riding; Scotland)
Amsel
Black Uzzle (Craven)
Merle (Ireland; Scotland)
Ouzel; Ouzel Cock
Woofell
Colley (Gloucestershire)
Zulu (Somerset)

> The ouzel cock so black of hue
> With orange tawny bill . . .

sings Bottom in *A Midsummer Night's Dream:* unmistakably the Blackbird. Shakespeare prefers Ouzel to Blackbird and so does Spenser, though the name Blackbird was certainly known by the seventeenth century as an alternative name. The bird is Black Bride in the *Boke of St Albans* (1486). Turner (1544) gives Blak Byrd or Black Ousle and Willughby, Merrett and Bewick all follow the tradition of giving two names. Blackbird derives quite obviously from the Anglo-Saxon *blac* plus *brid*. Ouzel may also be traced back to its Anglo-Saxon root, *osle*. The name Merle, sometimes used in poetry (also the French name), and Amsel (also the German name), the Latin second name *merula, mesula* in its ancient form, and Ouzel itself, together with its Northumbrian variation Ewesley, are all distantly related words.

Nowadays, the Blackbird is a noted suburbanite and this population added to those of woodland habitats make it one of the most common birds of Britain and Ireland. The glossy black of the cock with its golden bill gives it a most distinctive character. Thomas Hardy found perhaps the best description of it in his 'crocus coloured bill' which exactly catches the warmth and intensity of the colour. Like other thrushes, the Blackbird is omnivorous. Particularly characteristic is the way it makes its rustling progress through the leaves of a

256

forest, picking the leaves up and throwing them about as it searches for insects. Disturbed, it will utter a startlingly loud shriek and make off, flying low, into the undergrowth, like the villain of a melodrama, its wings held low like a dark cloak, keeping up a continuous flow of imprecations as it retreats.

The Blackbird is justly loved for its beautiful song, an easy 'laid-back' flow of mellow notes. C. E. Hare quotes a proverb, 'to whistle like a Blackbird', meaning to do something easily.

The Blackbird does not have a great wealth of folklore attached to it. In Meath, it is said that 'when the blackbird sings before Christmas, she will cry before Candlemas'. It is possible that this may refer to abnormally early nesting, when nestling mortality would be very high. Blackbirds tend to suffer much less than thrushes from severe winters probably because their feeding habits are more flexible. In 1962–63, when there was a 57 per cent thrush mortality, Blackbirds declined by only about 18 per cent.

One of the nicest stories about Blackbirds comes from Ireland and concerns St Kevin, a seventh century saint who, like many Irish saints, had a strong feeling for wildlife. It is said that one day, as St Kevin was praying in the temple of the rock at Glendalough, one hand stretched upwards, a Blackbird flew down and laid her eggs in his palm. The compassionate saint remained with his arm thus outstretched until the eggs were hatched, and the brood flown.

White Rump (Norfolk)
White Tail
White Ass (Cornwall)
Wittol = white tail (Cornwall)
Wheatears

from its pebbly note:
Chock; Chuck (Norfolk)
Chack; Chacks (Orkney)
Check Bird; Chickell (Devon)
Chat (Northamptonshire)

Wheatear
Oenanthe oenanthe

Wheatear

Clocharet (Forfar)
Horse Smatch; Horse Musher (Hampshire)
Snorter (Dorset)
Stanechacker (Lancashire; Aberdeen; N Ireland)
Steinkle (Shetland)
Stonechat (Northamptonshire; Westmorland; West
   Riding)
Hedge Chicker (Cheshire)

from its habitat:
Fallow Finch; Fallow Smirch; Fallow Lunch; Fallow
   Chat; Fallow Smith
Fallow Smiters (Warwickshire)
Clodhopper (Northamptonshire)
Furze Chat, Fuzz Chat (Sussex)

others:
Cooper (S. Pembroke)
Dyke Hopper (Stirling)
Jobbler (Dorset)
Coney Chuck (Norfolk)
Straw Mouse (Cheshire)

Francis Willughby in his *Ornithology* (1678) explains that in Sussex the Wheatear is so called because 'at the time of Wheat harvest they wax very fat', implying that the birds feast themselves on the harvest. Some years earlier in 1654, John Taylor, in an elegiac poem devoted to the tastiness of a roasted Wheatear, also notes the name was bestowed on them 'because they come when wheat is yearly reaped'. The real explanation is that the name Wheatear, and the other similar local names which come from several regions, is derived from 'White Arse' alluding to the flashy white rump, which contrasts brightly with the black wings and tail-tip and grey back. And to lay the last part of the false myth, the Wheatear is insectivorous with a few worms and snails thrown in. It is much more interested in searching out insects in the fallow and ploughed fields as suggested by the names Fallow Finch and Clodhopper than it would be in full ears of wheat.

The song of the Wheatear is sweet and quite musical like that of 'the Skylark in its beginning' (as T. A. Coward quotes his friend Miss Turner as saying), but the numerous 'Chock', 'Chuck' and

'Chack' names leave us in no doubt that its call note is a typical 'Chat' explosion. Horse Smatch and Horse Musher, as distinct from the directly echoic names, probably represent the clicks of encouragement people make to urge on horses. Clocharet, also a 'pebble-sound' name, comes from *Cloich*, Gaelic for stone. The Norfolk Coney Chuck is an interesting diversion from the mainstream names; Wheatears not only use rabbit holes as nesting sites, but may bolt into them when frightened.

Stonechat
Saxicola torquata

from the alarm note:
Stone Clink; Chickstone (Yorkshire)
Stanechacker (Craven)
Stone Clocharet (Forfar)
Stonepricker (Cheshire)
Stonesmith
Stane Chapper

plumage names:
Blacky Top; Blacky Cap (Ireland)
Blackcap

habitat names:
Furze Chitter (Cornwall)
Furze Hacker (Hampshire)
Bushchat
Moor Titling; Moretetter (Yorkshire)
Gorse Chat; Gorse Jack (Gloucestershire)
Heath Tit (Sussex)

'A restless bird', Wordsworth called it, aptly, for it rarely stays still for more than the space of a few seconds, but will fly, usually a short distance along a hedge or fence, pose there a few moments, then make another short hop. Every time it halts, it flicks its tail and shrugs itself a little, and often utters a short burst of song or its sharp alarm call which sounds just like two pebbles striking each other. This characteristic 'chacking' gives rise to the largest group of names which echo the sound of the stones 'chatting', 'chinking', 'chacking' and 'chapping'.

Stonechats are very open in their habits. If you miss the 'chat' no doubt your eye will be caught by

259

its restiveness, and it perches conspicuously upon bushes or posts, showing off its bold plumage. It has a glossy black head (Blacky Top, Blackcap) set off by a white collar and shoulder patch and rich chestnut coloured breast. It seems to prefer a heath or moorland habitat as indicated by names such as Furze Chitter and Moor Titling, although recently Stonechats have taken to young forestry plantations – but there are as yet no new names to mark this move.

Whinchat
Saxicola rubetra

other habitat names:
Furze Hacker (Hampshire)
Gorse Hopper (Cheshire)
Gorse Chat (Westmorland)
Gorse Hatch
Grass Chat (West Riding)
Bush Chat
Furze Chat (Worcestershire)
Furr Chuck (Norfolk)
Whinchacker (Craven)
Whincheck (Lancashire)
Whin Clocharet (Forfar)
Whin Lintie, Fern Lintie (Aberdeen)

from the alarm note:
Utick, Tick (Nottinghamshire; Shropshire)
Uthage (Shropshire)

other names:
Horse Smatch
Dock Topper (Somerset)

Whinchats share several names with the Stonechat to which they are not dissimilar, though the Whinchat is readily distinguished by its buff-coloured eyestripe and the white sides to its tail in flight (as well as by the absence of the black cap and white collar of the Stonechat). The note of the Whinchat is less grating and insistent than that of the Stonechat, more of a 'tic' which may be where the Utick, Uthage names arose. Whinchats like a grassy habitat, but they display considerable variation in their choice of locality. Rough grassland, almost anywhere from hillsides to watermeadows; railway embankments or roadside verges can afford a suitable environment for feeding and nesting for the Grass Chat. Like Stonechats, they need posts or bushes from which to sing their loud and distinctive song, but unlike them they do not nest in gorse, but usually upon the ground in the rough grass. As with the Linnet, note how the local variation in the words for gorse gets incorporated into the bird names (see Linnet).

Redtail (Norfolk; Oxfordshire; Scotland)
Fanny Redtail; Jenny Redtail (Yorkshire)
Nanny Redtail
Redrump (Yorkshire)
Redster; Redstare
Fiery Redtail, Fiery Brantail (Shropshire)
Bessy Brantail; Katie Brantail (Shropshire)
Fire Tail (Hampshire; Norfolk; Nottinghamshire;
   Somerset; Warwickshire; Scotland)
Fire Flirt; Flirt Tail (Yorkshire)
White Cap (Shropshire)
Woh Snatch (Cheshire)

Redstart
Phoenicurus phoenicurus

The Redstart has been so called since Anglo-Saxon times. The male bird is more dramatically coloured than the female with his full black throat and white forehead, but both birds possess the most striking feature, a red-brown tail which like a train begins at the rump and, contrasting with the greyish wing, projects fierily behind them. The 'start' comes from *steort,* the Old English for tail. Interestingly, the verb startle and the usage to start doing something, meaning to move impulsively into the action, derive from the same root and also suit the Redstart. An active bird, it is always moving about from branch to branch inside its woodland habitat, shooting into the air now and again to catch the flies or other winged insects upon which it feeds. As it hops it flirts its marvellous tail and during the courtship the bobbing and flourishing is specially pronounced. Shropshire people caught the picture well in their Brantail or brand-tail names, and gave it a double emphasis in

261

Fiery Brantail, but nobody would quibble at such a poetic and apt tautology.

Black Redstart

Phoenicurus ochruros

Blackstart
Tithy's Redstart
Black Redtail

The Black Redstart is a rare breeding bird in Britain and it is unusual in its choice of habitat. You will look in vain for this species in the mature woodland in which the Redstarts make their home. The Black Redstart clearly favours industrial complexes: railway sidings, riverside warehouses, bombed sites and other typically urban places. Power stations come out top; of sixty-five breeding pairs observed in London over five years in the late sixties, twenty chose these as a nesting place, gas works came a close second in popularity with eighteen pairs. Industrial society holds no fears for these birds; in the summer of 1973, a Black Redstart sang his short warbling song from a jumbo jet hangar at Heathrow.

The male Black Redstart is, suitably, sooty-black in colour, the female, grey-brown. Both have the typical Redstart 'firetail'. Black Redstarts have only begun to be seen in Britain in any numbers since the war, when they began to colonize bomb sites. Prosaic though it is, Black Redstart is probably the most correct name. Blackstart is also quite widely used, though strictly speaking it is an inaccurate short form: though black elsewhere, the 'start' is decidedly a red one. Tithy's Redstart (from an earlier scientific name: *Phoenicura tittys)* is altogether too academic a name for this soot and rust coloured bird of our industrial landscape.

Nightingale
Luscinia megarhynchos

There are so many Nightingales of Poesy that one tends almost to forget that the bird has a real physical presence, an impression aggravated by the fact that the bird is not at all open in its habits, secreting itself inside clumps of foliage even when singing. T. A. Coward, who can be relied upon to be faithful to the real bird, in his *Birds of the British Isles* introduces the Nightingale as 'a large handsome brown robin'. But it is difficult to get away from the beautiful voice. The Latin name *Luscinia* is from *luctus* = lamentation and *cano* = sing, the Old English is *nihte* = night and *gale* = singer. John of Guildford in his *The Owl and the Nightingale* (1225) saw the bird was eclipsed by the song, and has the Owl insult the Nightingale by saying that she is nothing but voice, a nonsensical 'galegale'. The Nightingale is predominantly a literary figure and appears very little in the oral tradition, though it is a little surprising that there is no more than one local name (and that one is shared with several other birds). There is very little background known even about the East Anglian name Barley Bird. The obvious deduction is that the bird arrives on the southeast coasts at about the time that something important occurs relating to barley. Around April time the young shoots will be showing. An oral tradition links the arrival of the two migrants, the Nightingale and the Cuckoo:

> On the third of April
> Come the cuckoo and the nightingale.

A fourteenth century poem (in the past mistakenly attributed to Chaucer and 'modernised' by Wordsworth) 'The Cuckoo and the Nightingale', links these two birds, but uses them exclusively as symbols, the one for romantic love, the other for adultery. John of Guildford's poem, *The Owl and the Nightingale* also has an allegorical content, but there is a considerable amount of nicely observed detail as well in this witty and racy

263

poem. The poem takes the form of a furious debate between the two birds each of whom represents a traditional complex of values, and argues its superiority over the other's. In the course of the argument there are remarks about the migration of the Nightingale, its song and the places it chooses to sing, and its appearance. Of the latter the Owle says of its opponent:

> . . . Besides, you're filthy dark and small
> Like a sort of sooty ball
> You have no loveliness or strength
> And lack harmonious breadth and length.
> Beauty somehow passed you by
> Your virtue too is in short supply.

Izaak Walton had considerable reverence for the exquisite song of the Nightingale who, he wrote, 'breathes such sweet lowd music out of her littel instrumentall throat that it might make mankind to think miracles are not ceased.' Chaucer and Coleridge stepped out of poetic convention when they heard 'that marvellous crescendo on a single note' as a 'merry' and exultant song. The classical interpretation coming down through most ancient poets is that the Nightingale's song is a lament, and most British writing follows this. The Nightingale is often called Philomel in poetry, alluding to the classical myth of Philomel and Procne, two sisters. Procne was married to Tereus, King of Thrace, who ravished and imprisoned Philomel and had her tongue cut out so she should not tell the tale. She managed to convey the story of her seduction to her sister in the form of a tapestry. The two sisters reunited, take revenge upon Tereus by killing his son and serving him for dinner. Tereus is about to kill them both when they are all turned into birds by divine intervention. In early versions, Procne is turned into a Nightingale, Philomel into a Swallow, but Ovid reverses them (Tereus becomes a Hoopoe). This was the story which was the major influence in creating a sorrowful image for the Nightingale. If not every poet who wrote about the Nightingale had actually heard her song (the poetic Nightingale, contrary to nature's, is always female) nonetheless, the notes of the song could be said to have a sad lilt to them.

Another strong theme of poetic imagery insists that the Nightingale always sings with her breast against a thorn. This is another mournful image, and there are many fanciful stories which give account of it, the earliest one on record being in a poem by Aneau published in 1571 which says that the Nightingale stays awake by singing against a thorn, fearful that she will be seized by a serpent if she lets herself sleep. This accords with a folk tale told in parts of France and Germany, in which it is said that the Nightingale borrowed eyes from the serpent and then refused to return them and has to be ever watchful or the snake will steal them back. Shakespeare in 'The Rape of Lucrece' as usual bends the tradition to his own purpose; suitably choosing the image of Philomel for a ravished wife. Lucrece contemplates stabbing herself, comparing herself with the Nightingale:

> And whiles against a thorn thou bear'st thy part
> To keep thy sharp woes waking, wretched I
> To imitate thee well, against my heart
> Will fix a sharp knife . . .

Robin
Erithacus rubecula

Ruddock (North)
Reddock (Dorset)
Redbreast
Robinet
Robin Ruck = Ruddock (North)
Broindergh = red belly (Gaelic)
Yr hobel goc = red bird (Wales)

familiar names:
Robin Redbreast
Bob (Nottinghamshire)
Bob Robin (Stirling)
Thomas Gierdet
Tommy-liden
Ploughman's Bird (Yorkshire)

Robin is a nickname, the affectionate diminutive of Robert. It is a name associated with at least three particular favourites: Robin Hood, Robin Goodfellow and Robin Redbreast. It carries with it connotations not just of fond familiarity but also of a certain spirited contrariness; thus, a generous hearted outlaw, the mischief-making Puck and a distinctive bird who sings all through the winter. Satirical verse has taken the figure of the bird to represent several favourite Roberts of history. Elizabeth I's Robin was Robert Devereux, Earl of Essex; James I favoured Robert Carr, Earl of Somerset and during the reign of Queen Anne, satirists went so far as to coin the word 'robinocracy' in a poem abusing Robert Harley, Earl of Oxford.

The Anglo-Saxons called the Robin *Rudduc* for the ruddyness of its breast, a usage which still survives today in some parts. In the first half of the fifteenth century the compound name Robin Redbreast was current, (the name chosen by David Lack for his book which sought out and celebrated so many different aspects of Robin lore and literature). This was shortened first to Robinet or Robeen, then, during the nineteenth century to Redbreast. Robin only returned to fashion comparatively recently; the British Ornithologists Union formally accepted Robin as an alternative to Redbreast as late as 1952. Wordsworth, who mentions Robins in no less than fourteen of his poems, refers to them always as Redbreasts. In a note to his poem 'The Redbreasts', he related how, when his sister Dorothy was ill, a Redbreast accommodated itself in her sickroom, where 'it used to sing and fan her face with its wings in a manner most touching'.

It is perhaps as well that the literary Wordsworths were not acquainted with the folk tradition that a Robin's appearance to a sick person might presage death. There is a widespread belief that to harm a Robin brings evil consequences: continuous trembling of the hands, sickness, broken limbs and a number of unpleasant visitations upon animals belonging to the aggressor. It is as if for centuries the Robin has been a 'protected' species in Britain. It has never been eaten or caged here on anything like the scale that this happened on the continent. Another old tradition says that the Wren was the Robin's wife and that together they were blessed as 'God's cock and hen'. Perhaps it was an echo of this that led Blake to single the Robin out as a special case for protest, 'a robin in a cage, puts all heaven in a rage.'

In nearly all the stories (except where harm is done them) Robins are benefactors. In the legend of the bringing of fire, the Robin sometimes replaces the Wren as the firebringer; sometimes it is said that the Robin takes the fire from the burning Wren for the last part of the journey, burning his breast on the way. Another 'red breast' legend describes how the Robin, plucking thorns from Christ's crown of thorns, wounded himself and was blessed by the Saviour.

There is also perhaps something of a Christmas tradition in the idea of the 'charitable robin', first recorded in writing in Drayton's 'The Owle' (1604):

> Covering with moss the dead's unclosed eye,
> The little redbreast teacheth charity.

This theme occurs also in the 'Babes in the Wood' story, when the children have died of cold:

> No burial this pretty pair
> From any man receives
> Till robin redbreast piously
> Covers them with leaves.

There are several early references to Robins which have this distinctly funereal overtone, but the origins of this theme are obscure as are those of the most famous Robin rhyme 'Who Killed Cock Robin?' This ballad was first published in 1744, but it is almost certain that folk versions of the story are very much older.

An early Christian legend concerns not only death but resurrection. (It is interesting that three birds with prominently red markings have resurrection associations: Robin, Swallow and Goldfinch.) St Kentigern was a Scottish bishop who founded Glasgow cathedral in the sixth

267

century. As a boy he was a pupil of St Serf at Culross and was greatly favoured by his teacher. Fellow students in jealousy killed a Robin which was very much loved by the master. They blamed Kentigern for the deed, but Kentigern's piety was such that he restored the Robin to life. It is to commemorate this miracle that the Glasgow coat of arms has a 'robin proper' as one of its features.

The Robin, the Ruddoc of the red breast, is almost always associated with the colour red. The Robin's Flower or Herb Robert has not only a red flower but red stems. Robin Goodfellow references from the sixteenth century say that he was a hairy goblin who wore a red suit. The first postmen, whose uniform included a bright vermilion waistcoat, were known as 'robins' and this is one of the reasons why Robins are not only featured on Christmas cards, but often shown with a letter in the beak, actually delivering mail.

Grasshopper Warbler

Locustella naevia

from its vibrating song:
Cricket Bird (Norfolk)
Grasshopper Lark
Reeler

as it keeps itself to the centre of bushes:
Brake Hopper
Brake Locustelle (*locusta* = grasshopper or cricket in Latin)

In looks, and in its habits generally, this warbler is immensely shy and retiring, well deserving the epithet Brake Hopper. It is easy to overlook the bird when it is silent, quietly making its concealed progress through bush and bracken to seek out insects. But when it sings you cannot ignore the Grasshopper Warbler's insistent voice, unmistakably announcing its presence. It is no accident that nearly all of this warbler's names, Latin and common, draw attention to its chirrupy song. As early as 1678 Willughby described 'the Titlark that sings like a grasshopper', but it is Gilbert White who really brings the character of this retiring little warbler before us:

The grasshopper-lark began his sibilous note in my fields last Saturday. Nothing can be more amusing than the whisper of this little bird, which seems to be close but though at an hundred yards distance; and, when close at your ear, is scarce any louder than when a great way off. Had I not been a little acquainted with insects, and known that the grasshopper kind is not yet hatched, I should have hardly believed but that it had been a *locusta* whispering in the bushes. The country people laugh when you tell them that it is the note of a bird. It is a most artful creature, skulking in the thickest part of a bush; and will sing at a yard distance, provided it be concealed. I was obliged to get a person to go on the other side of the hedge where it haunted; and then it would run, creeping like a mouse, before us for a hundred yards together, through the bottom of the thorns; yet it would not come into fair sight: but in a morning early, and when undisturbed, it sings at the top of a twig, gaping and shivering with its wings.

(Letter to Thomas Pennant, 18 April 1768)

The song, it is reckoned, is audible from up to a kilometre away but it is pitched so high that some people fail to catch it altogether. It is sad to think that Gilbert White himself might sometimes have missed the voice of the bird he knew so well, troubled as he was by fits of deafness during the last twenty years of his life.

Although still hardly a common bird, the Grasshopper Warbler population is on the increase, thanks largely to conifer afforestation. The tangle of grasses, willowherb, bracken and bramble typical of new plantations is splendid Brake Hopper territory, and the policy of clear-felling and replanting ensures them security of habitat.

Reed Warbler

Acrocephalus scirpaceus

from its reedbed haunts:
Reed Wren; Reed Tit; Reed Chucker; Reed Sparrow
Water Sparrow (Shropshire)
Fen Reedling
Marsh Reedling
Rush Warbler
Small Straw (Yorkshire)

other names:
Night Warbler
Babbler
Smastray (Cheshire)

Our plainest, brownest warbler, the Reed Warbler is rarely far away from the reedbeds with which it is so completely associated and which, fittingly, form part of most of its names. Reed Warblers usually arrive in Britain during late April, and by mid-spring the reedbeds of the southeast are 'achurr' with Reed Warblers. Often the bird sings unseen and it is as if the sound were coming from the tall reeds themselves.

The song itself consists of a series of high-pitched notes, interrupted at intervals by a fast churring descant. It is an insistent, headlong sound, full of pace and urgency. In late summer Reed Warblers sometimes sing after dusk. Then, with nothing but the quiet rustle of reeds in the background, the sound takes on a strange and poignant clarity.

The nest of the Reed Warbler, like everything else about the bird, is intimately bound up with the reeds. The birds usually begin building around a few young stems of reed growing just above the water. As they grow higher, the nest rises on its supports, strong, compact and shapely. It holds fast when the winds blow the reed beds and it is so deep as sometimes to hide, not only the clutch of green-marbled eggs, but the sitting bird as well.

as a frequenter of sedgy and watery places:
Sedge Bird, Sedge Wren, Seg Bird (Yorkshire)
Sedge Marine (Norfolk)
Sedge Reedling
Water Sparrow (Shropshire)
Sally Pecker, Sally Picker (sally = willow) (Ireland)
Reed Fauvette (*fauvette* = French name for Orphean
    warbler)
Pit Sparrow
Thorn Warbler (Yorkshire)
Willow Lark

as a night singer:
Irish Nightingale (Ireland)
Night Singer (Ireland)
Scotch Nightingale (Roxburgh; Stirling)
Night Sparrow

others:
Chat; Chitter Chat (Northumberland)
Hay Tit (Oxfordshire)
Leg Bird
Chamcider (Hampshire)
Fantail Warbler
Grey, Grey Bird (Yorkshire)
Lesser Reed Warbler

Sedge Warbler
Acrocephalus schoenobaenus

It was Gilbert White again who, in May 1769, wrote the first exact description of a Sedge Warbler, clearly discriminating it from the Reed Warbler, whose song is similar and whose habitat it shares. He describes the characteristic features: the dark brown back, the dusky legs and the distinctive 'milk white stroke' above each eye.

It is possibly the streaky brown of the back which gave rise to the several 'Sparrow' names of the Sedge Warbler. This warbler tends to roam further afield from sedge and reedbeds than Reed Warblers do, which may account for the variety of habitat adjectives aside from the basic 'sedge'. It has recently been reported that the Sedge Warbler has begun to nest away from its usual waterside haunts, usually at no great distance from damp ground, but sometimes in places such as young forestry plantations, arable fields and, in Lincolnshire, among sea-buckthorn scrub. Sedge Warblers have also adapted to new man-made sites such as clay workings and gravel pits.

271

Like the Reed Warbler, the Sedge Warbler may sometimes be heard to sing in the evening. Unlike the Reed Warbler, the Sedgie may be heard over most of the British Isles and several of the 'nightsong' names come from Scotland and Ireland. The basic song is something like that of the Reed Warbler but easily distinguished from it. The 'chitter chat' of the Sedge Warbler is loud and brisk, much shorter in its phrasing than the attenuated churring of the Reed Warbler and it often adds in snatches of song imitated from other birds. Though not a melodious voice, it is attractive and evocative in its own way and adds its particular contribution to our experience of summer. A poem by Edward Thomas called 'The Sedge Warblers' captures exactly the right note. The poem is too much of a piece to quote an extract, its twenty-nine lines all too subtly integral to remove any without breaking the sense of wholeness of the poem, so I will simply recommend it.

Blackcap
Sylvia atricapilla

from black crown:
King Harry Black Cap (Norfolk)
Coal Hoodie (North Riding)
Black-headed Hay-jack (Norfolk)
Black-headed Peggy

from nesting materials:
Jack Straw (Somerset)
Hay Bird (Northamptonshire)
Hay Chat (Northamptonshire)
Hay Jack (Northamptonshire)

from the song:
Mock Nightingale
Northern Nightingale

other names:
Nettle Creeper
Nettle Monger

Blackcap sings sweetly, but rather inwardly: it is
a songster of the first rate. Its notes are deep &
sweet. Called in Norfolk the mock nightingale.
(Gilbert White's *Journal*, 19 May 1770)

The Blackcap has probably been one of our best-
loved summer songbirds for a thousand years or so.
The Anglo-Saxon scholar Aelfric, Abbot of
Eynsham, probably refers to the Blackcap with the
name 'Swertling' in an Anglo-Saxon/Latin vocabulary written about 998.

The names of the Blackcap which are personal
to the bird itself, and not held in common with
other warblers, are either descriptive of its striking
black crown or of the clear piping song. John Clare
wrote two poems for the Blackcap, 'The March
Nightingale', in which he celebrates 'such a rich
and early song', and 'The Blackcap', which ends on
that individual note which marks Clare out as an
acute observer as well as a poet. He writes of the
birds singing early in the season from ivy-covered
trees with 'berries black as jet' and muses to himself
as to whether Blackcaps eat ivy berries. In fact,
Blackcaps, though mainly insectivorous, are
considerably more vegetarian in their diet than
most other warblers. They tend to feed on ivy
berries and tree flowers when they first arrive early
in spring. In summer and autumn they also relish
soft fruits and berries. There are many records of
Blackcaps overwintering and this ability to feed *à
la carte* may be of considerable importance to their
survival in the cold months.

Garden Warbler

Sylvia borin

Billy Whitethroat (East Lothian)
Garden Whitethroat
Greater Pettychaps
Peggy (Yorkshire)

from nesting material:
Small Straw (West Riding)
Strawsmear, Smastray (Cheshire)
Streasmear (Westmorland)
Haychat
Juggler (Surrey)

It would be rather daunting to set out to look for this bird, 'best recognised by its lack of field characteristics,' if its song did not help to single it out. The song of the Garden Warbler resembles that of a Blackcap, to which it is a near relative, but the notes are more mellow and flow more rapidly and evenly. Garden Warblers and Blackcaps favour the same kind of habitat, though the former will sometimes choose scrub or conifer plantation territory as well as the traditional mature woodland. The Garden Warbler seems to recognise the similarity of the two songs and will be aggressive towards any Blackcap, as well as to another Garden Warbler, which intrudes upon its territory.

The Garden Warbler rewards observation. As if to compensate for the drab grey-browny appearance, it has a spectacular courtship culminating in a 'moth-flutter' with spread tail and wings. But it is not by any means an obvious bird and its lack of striking features has meant that it has had to share most of its common names with other species of warbler. Even the adjectival 'garden', which is its one claim to originality, is something of a mistake for it is not a bird commonly associated with gardens, unless they happen to be near a wood or to possess an invitingly overgrown shrubbery which might be a good nesting site. Nevertheless, it has a respectable history of ornithological observation. The Garden Warbler was one of the four warblers to be studied in the field by John Ray in the third quarter of the seventeenth century (though it was one warbler not mentioned by Gilbert White).

from its throat colour' and the thick tufts of feathers beneath its chin:
White Lintie (Forfar)
Whitecap; Billy Whitethroat (Shropshire)
Charlie Muftie; Muffit (Stirling)
Whey Beard; Wheetie Whey Beard; Whittie Beard;
    Wheetie Why
Beardie (Scotland)

from the deft way it moves through dense undergrowth:
Nettle Creeper; Nettle Monger (North Riding;
    Hampshire)
Nettle Bird (Leicestershire)
Hedge Chicken

from its choice of nesting materials:
Feather Bird (Northamptonshire)
Flax (Shropshire)
Hay Jack (Norfolk; Suffolk)
Haysucker (Devon)
Hay Tit (Oxfordshire; Shropshire)
Hazeck (Worcestershire)
Strawsmall (West Riding)
Strawsmear (Westmorland)
Winnel Straw; Jack Straw (Shropshire)
Cut-straw

other names:
Great Peggy (Leicestershire)
Peggy (Nottinghamshire)
Muggy, Meggie (North)
Jennie, Meg Cut-throat (Roxburgh)
Caperlinty
Bee Bird (Devon)
Blethering Tam (Scotland)

Whitethroat
Sylvia communis

The wide number of different county names for the Whitethroat reinforces the evidence of ornithological records which state that Whitethroats penetrate into nearly every British county during the months of summer. But as anyone will know who regularly listens out for the brisk, warbling phrases of its song, the years following 1968 have seen a disastrous decline in the Whitethroat population. The number of birds in Britain fell, it is estimated, from a very healthy 5 million in 1968 to less than fifteen per cent of that figure. Very severe droughts in the southern Sahara, where Whitethroats spend their winter months, are held responsible for this decline, which shows little sign of improvement.

The Whitethroat is one of the more easily recognisable warblers, generally unshy in its habits. It has a very characterstic way of displaying itself, usually from a hedgetop, puffing out its white-feathered throat and singing lustily, and then slipping down unobserved into dense hedge, nettle or bramble scrub, and reappearing somewhere quite unexpected. It often sings on the wing, a brief and repetitive little burst of notes, not at all displeasing to the ear (to call the Whitethroat a Blethering Tam seems a little over censorious).

The Whitethroat is a bird very much associated with scrub and will feed, sing from, and nest in hedges and bushes alongside lanes, fields, woodsides and overgrown orchards and gardens, and a large proportion of the common names, such as Winnel Straw, Hay Jack and Strawsmear, refer straightforwardly to its habitat and nesting materials.

Lesser Whitethroat

Sylvia curruca

Babbling Warbler
Haychat
Hazel Linnet
Mealy Mouth (Yorkshire)
White-breasted Warbler

The first reference to the Lesser Whitethroat identifying it as a separate species was made less than two centuries ago. It was another original observation from that singularly acute warbler watcher, Gilbert White. 'A rare and I think a new little bird frequents my garden,' he wrote in *The Natural History of Selbourne* (letter LVII). 'This bird much resembles the white-throat, but has a more white or rather silvery breast and belly; is restless and active, like the willow wrens, and hops from bough to bough, examining every part for food . . .'

Now, as in the late eighteenth century, the Lesser Whitethroat is not a common bird. England is right on the edge of its range. The species was not, however, affected by the conditions which decimated the Whitethroat numbers because of the rather unusual migration route it takes, flying southeastwards towards the eastern Mediterranean, which does not entail passing through the Sahara.

The most striking feature of the Lesser Whitethroat is the set of very dark, bandit-like patches which cover both eyes and ears, quite distinct from the grey of the cap and contrasting sharply with the white of the throat and breast – which may have prompted the name White-breasted Warbler. It is a bird of high scrub and thick copse, and the song usually comes from a patch of dense cover. The most conspicuous song is a kind of rapid rattling (probably alluded to in the name Babbling Warbler) but it also has a subsong, a very much quieter, musical warble like a wistful version of the Whitethroat.

Willow Warbler
Phylloscopus trochilus

from its haunts:
Ground Isaac (from Old English *Hege-sugge*) (Devon)
Ground Wren
Sally Picker (sally' = willow) (Ireland)
Willow Sparrow; Willow Wren (General)
Fell Peggy (Lancashire)

from its colour and size:
Miller's Thumb
Tom Thumb (Roxburgh)
Golden Wren (Ireland)
Yellow Wren
White Wren (Scotland)

from various qualities of the nest:
Bank Jug (Bedfordshire)
Ground Oven; Oven Tit; Oven Bird (Norfolk)
Grass Mumruffin (Worcestershire)
Feather Bed (Oxfordshire)
Feather Poke (West Riding)
Hay Bird; Strawsmeer
Mealy Mouth (Craven)
Willie Muftie (Scotland); Muffie Wren (Renfrew)

Willow Warbler

other names:
Huck Muck
Bee Bird
Sweet Billy (Nottinghamshire)
Peggy, Peggy Whitethroat (West Riding; Shropshire)
Smeu; Smooth; Smeuth (Stirling)

The Willow Warbler is the most abundant and widely distributed warbler in Britain. It is a very small, yellow-green bird (hence Tom Thumb, and Golden and Yellow Wren) but in appearance it is virtually undistinguishable from the Chiffchaff. (The Scots name White Wren is a bit of a puzzle, unless this refers to the northern race of Willow Wren, *Phylloscopus trochilus acredula,* which is a distinctly brown and white bird and is a bird of passage over Britain − on its way to Norway and Sweden.)

Oddly enough, there is no name descriptive of the single most characteristic feature of the Willow Warbler: the beautiful falling trill of its song. Coward quotes one of the best verbal descriptions: 'a tender delicious warble' with 'a dying fall . . . It mounts up round and full, then runs down the scale, and expires upon the air in a gentle murmur.' Another insight into this 'silvery cadence' is represented more mundanely, but with careful accuracy, in Witherby's *Sound Guide to British Birds* as 'seep-seep tye-tye-tye tyay-tyay weriwi weer'. (Try it, you have to have heard the song to get an idea of the pitch, but once you have it works very well.)

The names Feather Poke and Feather Bed probably result from a confusion with the Chiffchaff; the Willow Warbler does not normally include feathers in the construction of its nest which, partly domed like an old-fashioned oven, is neatly concealed upon the ground (Ground Oven) and is usually made of grasses (Hay Bird and Grass Mumruffin) perhaps with a little moss and dead bracken.

from its two-note song:
Chip Chop, Huck Muck
Choice and Cheep (Devon)

referring to the domed nest, lined with feathers:
Bank-bottle; Bank Jug (Bedfordshire)
Feather Poke; Feather Bed (Oxfordshire)
Wood Oven

other names:
Least Whitethroat
Least Willow Wren
Lesser Pettychaps
Peggy (West Riding)
Sally Picker (Ireland)
Thummie

Chiffchaff
Phylloscopus collybita

The earliest entry that Gilbert White has in his *Journal* for the sound of the first migrant Chiffchaff of the year is 18 March. This occurred in the year 1780 which had a fine warm spring.

> The uncrested wren, the smallest species, called in this place the *Chif-chaf,* is very loud in the Lythe. This is the earliest summer bird of passage, & the harbinger of spring. It has only two piercing notes.

With those 'two piercing notes' this bird names itself: Chiffchaff or Chip Chop or even Choice and Cheep. Now, no less than in 1780, it is a sound of early spring. Over the last few years with a series of mild winters there have been many records of Chiffchaffs overwintering, but nonetheless, from the middle of March onwards, there is an obvious busyness as migrant birds arrive and begin seeking out breeding territories. The song, though limited, can be very expressive and at this time of year is uttered with tremendous vitality. It is much more subtle than plain 'chiffchaff'; an initial double note may be elaborated into a series of reiterations and embellishments: double and treble 'chiffs' and 'chaffs', and fluting high 'chiffies'.

A number of the Chiffchaff's names play on the shape and construction of its nest. Made out of dead leaves, moss and grass, it is domed, and therefore nicknamed bottle, jug, oven and poke.

279

Chiffchaff

Inside, the nest is lined with soft grasses, rootlets and a profusion of feathers, a Feather Bed for a brood of five to seven small Chiffchaffs.

Wood Warbler

Phylloscopus sibilatrix

from its favoured habitat:
Wood Wren

from its colouration:
Green Wren
Linty White
Yellow Wren

from its nesting material:
Hay Bird (West Riding)

The Wood Warbler or Wood Wren is well-named. Its distribution coincides closely with that of mature woodland, particularly old oak woodland. On the face of it, it seems as if the three colour names must be contradictory. But from above the plumage looks distinctly green, the throat and eye stripes are yellow, gradually merging into the soft white of the underparts. So the Wood Warbler can simultaneously be, like the answer to a riddle, a Green Wren, a Linty White and a Yellow Wren. The Wood Warbler is the most greeny of the warblers. C. B. Ticehurst looked for a more exact description in his *Systematic Review of the Genus Phylloscopus* (that is the leaf warblers, or literally, the 'leaf-explorers') and finally fixed upon a range of shades from 'mignonette green to écru olive'.

The Wood Warbler is not a particularly common bird and since it tends most of the time to be concealed behind the foliage of trees, it is usually the song which draws attention to its presence. Both male and female have a piping call note which is heard continuously during the height of courtship. The song itself is loud for such a little bird, a far-carrying and sustained trill, in W. H. Hudson's words 'long and passionate . . . the woodland sound which is like no other'.

Golden-crested Wren
Golden Wren (Stirling)
Golden Cutty (Hampshire)
Marigold Finch
Tidley Goldfinch (Devon)
Kinglet
Wood Titmouse (Cornwall)
Moon; Moonie; Muin (Roxburgh)
Miller's Thumb (Roxburgh)
Thumb Bird (Hampshire)
Tot o'er Seas (East Anglia)
Woodcock Pilot (Yorkshire coast)
Herring Spink (East Suffolk)

Goldcrest
Regulus regulus

Most of the local names for the Goldcrest make some reference to its diminutive size. Along with the Firecrest, it is the smallest bird to be found in Britain – a mere nine centimetres. A creature of conifer forest, it shows a preference for exotic conifers and in Montgomeryshire specially favours the coast and sierra redwoods: our tiniest bird on the tallest known tree species.

Many of the local names (and the double *regulus* of the scientific name) make a play on the distinctive head markings: orange-yellow in the cock bird; lemon yellow in the hen, offset by a line of black. During courtship, the male droops his wings, and puffs out his feathers, expanding the black border to display the orange crown to best effect to the female. Being insectivorous, and so small, Goldcrests are extremely susceptible to severe winters and their numbers have been decimated at least three times in living history (in the winters of 1916–17, 1946–47 and 1962–63).

There is, however, with the increase in conifer plantations, considerably more suitable habitat for Goldcrests than in the eighteenth century when Gilbert White wrote of them that they were 'almost as rare as any bird we know'. They seem to have the capacity for recovering from population disasters. In 1920, T. A. Coward wrote that the Goldcrest 'could have little more than an obituary notice', but within a short time it had made up its numbers, and since the crash of 1962, they have increased their population more than tenfold, and their characteristic 'sisi' song is now a familiar voice in conifer woodland.

The song, 'the smallest of small songs' as W. H. Hudson put it, consists of 'two notes, almost identical in tone, repeated rapidly without variation, two or three times, ending with a slight quaver, scarcely audible, on the last note.' (Witherby's *Sound Guide* renders it as accurately as is possible with such an indefinable quantity as bird song: 'cedar-cedar-cedar-cedar stitch-i-pee-so'.)

The name Tot o'er Seas comes from the East Suffolk coast to which many tired migrating continental Goldcrests come in autumn *en route* for their winter quarters. On the Yorkshire coast the Goldcrest migration is said to precede that of the Woodcock by two days, which gave rise to the name Woodcock Pilot.

Firecrest
Regulus ignicapillus

Fire-crested Wren
Fire-crested Kinglet
Fire-crowned Kinglet

For the Firecrest there is, as yet, no equivalent to affectionate popular names such as Golden Cutty or Tidley Goldfinch, not surprisingly, because until recently it was a fairly rare winter visitor. The first pair definitely known to have brought off young nested in the New Forest in 1962. Since that time both the population of passage birds and breeding birds has increased considerably – how far is not known exactly, but a Buckinghamshire wood, which has been extensively studied, holds a population of at least forty-three singing males, and others have been heard in areas as far flung as Wales, Yorkshire and Worcestershire. The song is slightly harsher than that of the Goldcrest, a 'zit-zit' repeated without the terminal flourish characteristic of the Goldcrest. The Firecrest has a distinctive black and white eyestripe, and is fractionally smaller than the Goldcrest.

Bee Bird (Norfolk)
Lead-coloured Flycatcher (Northamptonshire)
Grey Flycatcher
Spider Catcher
Cherry Sucker; Cherry Chopper; Cherry Snipe
Post Bird (Kent)

from its nest sites:
Beam Bird; Wall Bird (Berkshire; Buckinghamshire;
  E Anglia; Hampshire)
Rafter; Rafter Bird
Wall Plat (plat = a flat beam lying on top of a wall) (Devon)
Wall Robin (Cheshire)
Wall Chat (Yorkshire)
Wall Bird

various:
Cobweb (Northamptonshire)
White Baker; White Wall (Northamptonshire)
Chait (Worcestershire)
Chancider
Miller (Shropshire)

Spotted Flycatcher

Muscicapa striata

The word Flycatcher came into written usage at the beginning of the seventeenth century and the first records of the Spotted Flycatcher date from 1662. This is a fairly late name, descriptive of the bird's food-finding activities: it feeds mainly upon dipterous flies which it hunts on the wing in marvellously adroit, twisting flights. The Spotted Flycatcher is a quiet bird, rarely singing, and with a little high note of a call which might be the foundation of the Chait and Chancider names. The young birds have more of a claim to being called spotted than the adults whose breast and head would better be described as lightly streaked. The Spotted Flycatcher gives a predominantly grey-brown impression with a contrast in the white of its underparts. This is probably why it was given the names of Miller and White Baker. Plants with a dusty, floury appearance often attract names like Miller and Dusty Miller.

The Spotted Flycatcher is among the latest arrivals of our summer migrants, generally not present in any number until early May by which time flies and flying insects are becoming plentiful.

Spotted Flycatcher

Characteristically, a Post Bird will adopt a fencepost or tree stump, on which vantage-point it sits, upright and alert, watching for flies, moths, butterflies or beetles, flinging itself into the air at intervals in acrobatic pursuit and returning in a few moments to its perch. Bees and wasps are also eaten. (However, as the Flycatcher is almost exclusively insectivorous, the 'cherry' group of names don't seem to fit the pattern of feeding.)

In its woodland haunts, Flycatchers will tuck their nests inside a thick cover of ivy, or find a cleft in a tree or an old nest belonging to another kind of bird. But this species also shows marked favour towards human dwellings as nesting sites. As one sees from the names, holes in walls, ledges, projecting beams and rafters are favourite positions. The soft nest lining is composed of fine grasses, feathers or cobweb (Cobweb is a Northamptonshire name). Having found a good nesting place, the birds will often return year after year. Gilbert White tells a moving story about a pair of Flycatchers who used regularly to nest at the Wakes.

> The flycatcher . . . builds every year in the vines that grow on the walls of my house. A pair of these little birds had one year inadvertently placed their nest on a naked bough, perhaps in a shady time, not being aware of the inconvenience that followed. But an hot sunny season coming on before the brood was half fledged, the reflection of the wall became insupportable, and must inevitably have destroyed the young, had not affection suggested an expedient, and prompted the parent-bird to hover over the nest all the hotter hours, while with wings expanded, and the mouths gaping for breath, they screened off the heat from their suffering offspring.
>
> (*Natural History of Selborne*)

Coldfinch
Colefinch (Northumberland; Cumberland; Westmorland)

Pied Flycatcher
Ficedula hypoleuca

The Pied Flycatcher is considerably less common than the Spotted Flycatcher; its habitat is mainly confined to deciduous woodland areas in Wales, and in Southwest England, and a few counties north and south of the Scottish border. It is a conspicuously pied bird, black on the upper plumage except for the wingbars and forehead which, like the breast and underparts, are white, but the 'pied' seems not to have been brought in until about the fourth edition of Pennant's *British Zoology*. A century before, Willughby's *Ornithology* introduced the Pied Flycatcher 'as a bird called "Coldfinch" by the Germans', and this appears to be the first written record in Britain of the bird. From this evidence it would seem that names for this bird are entirely bookish. However, the Reverend Swainson quotes Coldfinch and Colefinch as provincial names in several northern counties, so there may have been some vernacular usage of this early name.

---

colour names:
Black Wren (Ireland)
Blue Dunnock; Blue Isaac (Gloucestershire)
Blue Jig; Blue Jannie; Blue Tom; Blue Sparrow (Scotland)
Blue Dickie (Renfrew)
Doney (Lancashire)
Smokey (Northumberland)

Hedge Sparrow or Dunnock
Prunella modularis

habitat names:
Bush Sparrow (Stirling)
Dykesmowler; Dykie; Dyke Sparrow
Fieldie; Field Sparrow (Roxburgh)
Hedge Chat (Northamptonshire)
Hedge Betty (Warwickshire)
Hedge Chanter, Hedge Creeper (Yorkshire)
Hedge Spick; Hedge Mike (Sussex)
Hedge Spurgie (spurgie = *sporr* = flutterer) (Aberdeen)
Isaac, Hazock (Worcestershire)
Segge (Devon)

Hedge Sparrow or Dunnock	Hedge Scrubber (Suffolk)
	Whin Sparrow (East Lothian)
	Hedge Warbler; Hedge Accentor; Hedge Chanter
	Hedge Dunny (Lancashire)

behaviour names:
Creepie (Scotland)
Shufflewing (Craven)
Blind Dunnock
Foolish Sparrow

various:
Billy (Oxfordshire)
Cuddy (Craven)
Cudgie (Nottinghamshire)
Dickie (Lancashire)
Hempie (Yorkshire; Scotland)
Sparve (Cornwall)
Titlene; Titling (North)
Reefouge (Ireland)
Winter Fauvette
Pinnock; Philip; Phip

This bird is unusual in having two common names of ancient lineage in more or less equally widespread use. The Old English word for Hedge Sparrow was *Hegesugge,* meaning 'flutterer in the hedges' (*hege* = hedge; *sporr* = flutterer, from the Icelandic, the same as for House Sparrow). From *Hegesugge* come the Worcestershire names Isaac, Hazock and Haysuck. The other main stream of names is drawn from the bird's grey-brown colouration; the Old English *dunn,* itself possibly derived from the Celtic *dwn* giving us Dunnock.

Chaucer refers to the Hedge Sparrow as *Heysugge* and remarks particularly on the way the Cuckoo, then as now, makes very wide use of Hedge Sparrow foster parents. A Cuckoo's eggs often mimic the colouration of those of the most frequently selected foster species (some species will reject dissimilar eggs). But the Hedge Sparrow seems to be an exceptionally tolerant host, which has led to it being characterized as Blind Dunnock and Foolish Sparrow.

The Blind Dunnock's own eggs are quite remarkable. Usually to be found in a group of four or five in a neatly made, hair-lined nest wedged in a hedge, they are of a wonderfully deep pure blue. The blue group of names may be taken to refer to these beautifully coloured eggs, or to the slatey-blue in the plumage, or maybe, as is often the case, a combination of both attributes. The Hedge Sparrow gait is also quite individual; it advances in a series of short low hops, one foot held before the other and with its legs slightly bent. Almost exclusively a ground feeder, it scurries around in the undergrowth in this creeping attitude, with a sharp eye for the insects which form the major part of its diet. As the courting season approaches, each hop is accompanied by a little shiver of the wings, from which we get that perfectly descriptive name Shufflewing.

Linnaeus gave the Hedge Sparrow the rather stilted latinate name of Accentor, literally, 'one who sings with another'. Hedge Chanter and Hedge Warbler also celebrate the short but musical song which sounds to my ear like a snatch of tune from a ragtime piano. The call note is a shrill, piping note which possibly gave rise to the names Phip, Pinnock and Titlene.

Hedge Sparrow or Dunnock

---

from its note:
Titling, Tit (General)
Tietick (Shetland)
Titlark
Cheeper
Peep (Forfar)
Teetan (Orkney)
Wekeen (Kerry)
Chitty (Lancashire)

habitat names:
Meadow Titling; Meadow Lark (Hampshire)
Field Titling; Earth Titling (East Lothian)
Moss Cheeper (Scotland)
Moss Cheepuck (Northern Ireland)
Heather Lintie (Cumberland; Westmorland)
Ling Bird (Cumberland; West Riding)
Moor Titling (Craven)
Moor Tit
Hill Sparrow (Orkney; Shetland); Hill Teetick (Shetland)
Banks Teetick (Bressay)
Ground Lark (Yorkshire)

Meadow Pipit
Anthus pratensis

Meadow Pipit

various:
Cuckoo's Sandie; Cuckoo's Titling (Durham)
Gowk's Fool (North of England)
Gwas y Gog = Cuckoo's knave (Welsh)
Glasian = grey bird (Gaelic)

Tree Pipit
Anthus trivialis

Pipit Lark
Tree Lark (Nottinghamshire; Somerset; Yorkshire)
Wood Lark (Cheshire; North of England; S Scotland)
Short-heeled Field Lark (Scotland)
Titman (Sussex)
Blood Lark (Cheshire)
Lesser Field Lark; Field Lark

Rock Pipit
Anthus spinoletta

Rock Lark
Sea Titling; Sea Lark (East Riding)
Sea Lintie (Scotland)
Rock Lintie (Aberdeen)
Tangle Sparrow (Orkney; Shetland)
Gutter Teetan; Shore Teetan (Orkney)
Teetuck, Teetan (Shetland)
Dusky Lark
Sea Mouse

The identification of Pipits can be a tricky task. The *Bulletin* of the British Museum published a few verses on the subject of Pipit taxonomy some years ago which began:

> It's a pity pipits have
> No diagnostic features
> Specifically they are the least
> Distinctive of God's creatures.

Pipits are indeed the ultimate in 'little brown birds', but very engaging ones. It is virtually impossible to tell one pipit from another when they are quiet and seen from a distance, and the different species share many names; Lark and Tit crop up in many compound names. Pipits resemble Larks in their browny streaked appearance and Tit and Titling signify a creature small in size.

There are of course differences. The Rock Pipit (the Sea Titling, Sea Lark or Sea Lintie) is a coastal bird and very slightly larger than the other species, and darker and greyer. It will hop familiarly about on rocks and shore making its 'phist' call. In Orkney its most commonly used name is Tangle Sparrow for it is usually to be found briskly searching the seaweed or 'tangle' for insect or vegetable food. All three species have a distinctive song flight; they fly upwards beginning the song, and then 'parachute' down, wings held still and outspread, singing vigorously. The Tree Pipit is the strongest singer with a loud and extended song and it usually starts its song flight from high up in a tree, climbing upwards and then descending in a lyrical spiral, often returning to the same perch. Meadow Pipits have a thin, tinkling song. They launch themselves from the ground to sing and return to earth at the end of it. The Rock Pipit song is midway between the two, its flight rather more like the Meadow Pipit's. The name Pipit echoes the 'peep' of the call which the birds make as their call note. (The Latin *pipio* means chirper.)

There are several Cuckoo names for Pipits and the contrast in size between the large Cuckoo and the small Pipit gave rise to the phrases 'like the cuckoo and the titlark' and 'like the gowk and the titling'. The Meadow Pipit is second only to the Dunnock in playing host to Cuckoo's eggs; one estimate giving a toll as high as one in five nests so parasitised. An Irish story says that the Pipit is always trying to get into the Cuckoo's mouth, but that if it should ever succeed the end of the world would come. This superstition could easily have come from life, though it puts an unexpected slant on it. Watching the diminutive pipit trying to feed the large young Cuckoo one might easily fear that it would be swallowed.

Pied Wagtail
Motacilla alba yarrellii

Wagtail; Quaketail
Waggie (East Lothian)
Nannie Wagtail (Nottinghamshire)
Willie Wagtail (Orkney)
Lady Wagtail (Somerset)
Piedie Wagtail (Cheshire)

habitat names:
Water Wagtail (General)
Wattie; Wattie Wagtail (Westmorland)
Watitty (Cheshire)
Wattertiwagtail (Cumberland)

'washer' names:
Dishwasher (Gloucestershire; Somerset; Sussex; Home
    Counties; Craven; Shropshire)
Dishwipe; Dishlick (Sussex)
Lady Dishwasher (Gloucestershire)
Molly Washdish (Hampshire; Somerset)
Polly Washdish (Dorset; East Anglia; Somerset)
Nanny Washtail
Scullery Maids (Wiltshire)
Ditchwatcher (Surrey)
Dish-dasher (Somerset)
Washdish; Washerwoman; Washtail

various:
Devil's Bird; Deviling (Ireland)
Seed Bird (Yorkshire)
Seed Lady (Peebles)

Grey Wagtail
Motacilla cinerea cinerea

Barley Bird (General)
Barley-seed Bird (Yorkshire)
Winter Wagtail (S England)
Oatseed Bird (Yorkshire)
Dishwasher (Sussex)
Yellow Dishwasher (Somerset)
Yellow Wagtail (Ireland; Somerset; Sussex)
Dun Wagtail (Sussex)

Barley Bird (Nottinghamshire; Surrey; Sussex)
Barley-seed Bird (Yorkshire)
Cow-klit; Cow-bird (Sussex)
Dishwasher (Sussex); Golden Dishwasher (Somerset)
Ladybird (Sussex)
Potato Setter; Potato Dropper (Cheshire)
Maw-daw (Sussex)
Oat-ear (General)
Oatseed Bird
Spring Wagtail (Yorkshire)
Summer Wagtail; Sunshine Bird
Yellow Molly (Hampshire)
Yellow Waggie
Quaketail

Yellow Wagtail
Motacilla fiava fiavippima

Wagtails of various species and subspecies are to be found all over Europe, Asia and India. The Pied Wagtail, Grey Wagtail and the Yellow Wagtail (each with three parts to their scientific names which signifies that they are separate 'races' or subspecies) are those most common in Britain and Ireland. The Pied Wagtail is the most abundant of the three and breeds in every county. Many of the birds are resident, though those in more northerly places tend to move southwards in winter and back again in spring. Two northern names, Seed Bird in Yorkshire and Seed Lady in Peebles, recognise this seasonal movement and are not 'food-names'. Wagtails are insectivorous.

Though it is commonly known as the Water Wagtail and has several other 'water' names the Pied Wagtail is, in fact, the least restricted to a watery environment of the three species, particularly where it has adopted an urban or suburban way of life. However, where there is any amount of fresh water, the Pied Wagtail can usually be relied upon to make an appearance, whether it is a country lake, gravel pit, reservoir or the settling tank of a sewage farm. Even small and temporary collections of water seem to delight them and they are often to be seen after a rainstorm, dipping and wagging vigorously in park puddles. They are bright handsome little birds, the most conspicuous feature being, of course, the long tail which is constantly dipped up and down. They are quick and alert in their movements, running this way and that as they search for food, stopping every so often to peer, head tilted, at some potentially tasty morsel. John Clare caught the manner of their gait and habit in his childlike rhyme about them:

> Little trotty wagtail, he went in the rain,
> And tittering, tottering sideways he near got
>   straight again
> He stooped to get a worm, and look'd up to
>   catch a fly
> And then he flew away ere his feathers they were
>   dry.

The Wagtail's plumage is black and white in summer, a greyer tone in winter. (Pied plumage has diabolic associations which may be why there are the isolated names Devil's Bird and Deviling in Ireland.) The Pied Wagtail has the typical wave-like, bounding flight of the wagtail and while in flight it utters a brisk cheerful double note 'chissik chissik'. A prominent ornithologist, interviewed on the radio, said that he privately called the Pied Wagtail the 'Chiswick flyover' because of its habit of 'leapfrogging' past you as you walk, calling loudly.

Grey Wagtail is a confusing standard name for a bird most conspicuous for its bright yellow breast and underparts. It does however have a slatey-grey back. The breeding male has a striking glossy black bib which extends over its chin and throat. The Grey Wagtail is very much a bird of fast-flowing water and it is to be found alongside turbulent brooks and streams. Its distribution is accordingly much more upland and mountainous than that of the Pied Wagtail. Some birds are resident in winter but in hard weather they suffer badly and move to the warmth of towns, or further south to milder weather in Europe. Their spring return is, like that of the Pied Wagtail, marked by 'seed' names such as Barley Bird and Oat-seed Bird, though in Southern England it is the Winter Bird or Dun Wagtail because of the migrants in their dull winter plumage who come down South during the cold months.

The Yellow Wagtail is slightly smaller than the

other two species, a brightly coloured and very welcome summer visitor. They return to their summer haunts quite early in spring. T. A. Coward conveys the excitement of seeing the first arrivals on a cold day of early spring.

> All Wagtails are dainty, delicate birds, but the Yellow is the most graceful and fairy-like of them all; in March and April when the flocks appear in our pastures, the males are wonderfully brilliant. As they run nimbly through the growing herbage their slight bodies are often hidden, but the bright colours, gold as the dandelions, catch the eye.

The spring return of the Yellow Wagtail has not only produced the usual names of Spring and Summer Wagtail, and Oat-seed Bird, but also Sunshine Bird which makes a nice reference to both the season and to the bird's seasonal colour.

All of the Wagtail species have 'washer' names and these seem to have arisen from the similarity between the constant up-and-down movement of the tails and the action of dipping and lifting made by a person washing or scrubbing clothes (or dishes) by the waterside. It is interesting to see how, on one case, the name has become generalized to Scullery Maids and in another, the old meaning has been forgotten and the name rationalized into Ditchwatcher. The exclusive association of women (in the past) with washday activities, together with a certain feminine lightness and grace, is probably what led to the feminization of many Wagtail names. There is, for instance, not only Washerwoman, but Molly and Polly Washdish, and Ladybird and Seed Lady.

Great Grey Shrike

Lanius excubitor

Butcher Bird (General)
Great Shrike
Murdering Pie; Murdering Bird
White Whiskey John
Sentinel Shrike
Wierangle (Derbyshire)
Shreek; Skriek; Skrike

Red-backed Shrike

Lanius collurio

Butcher Bird (Gloucestershire; Suffolk; Surrey;
    Worcestershire)
Butcher Boy (Surrey)
Murdering Bird
Nine Killer
Wierangle (N England)
Wurger; Worrier (Yorkshire)
Granfer (Somerset)
Flesher; Flusher Shrike (Surrey)
Cheeter (Somerset)
Horse-match (Gloucestershire; Surrey)
Cuckoo's Maid (Herefordshire)
Jack Baker (Hampshire; Surrey)
Pope (Hampshire)

Shrikes are strong, fierce creatures, well-built with hooked predatory beaks. They catch their prey by striking with the feet and carrying the prize to a suitable place to consume it. Victims such as bees and grasshoppers are eaten at once. Small mammals, lizards and birds are impaled on a thorn or barb. On a blackthorn bush with its vicious extended thorns or on the spikes of a barbed wire fence, there may be a large group of small rotting bodies. It is this undelectable habit which gives both these species of Shrike the title Butcher Bird. With the evidence of their deeds so much more openly displayed than, for instance, a hawk's, Shrikes have also been given names such as Murdering Pie and Murdering Bird.

There is a superstition recorded by both Turner (1544) and Willughby (1678) that the Red-backed Shrike kills nine creatures before it even begins to feed. The name Nine Killer comes from the German *Neunmoder*. Wierangle, Wurger, and Worrier also come to us from Germany where both the Great Grey and Red-backed Shrikes are much more abundant. These names are based upon *Wurchangel* which means 'Destroying Angel' and *Wurger,* 'Worrier' or 'Throttler'. Chaucer knew the Shrike by a Germanic name 'Wariangle', and used it in his *Friar's Tale* as a simile for the Summoner, an unpleasant and lecherous character, never short of harsh words (jangles).

> This Somnour which that was as ful of jangles
> As ful of venim been thise wariangles
> And ever enquering up-on every thing . . .

The name Shrike itself comes from the Old English *Scric* which was principally applied to the Mistle Thrush, and for the same reason: the loud shrieking cry. The Flesher, Flasher and Flusher group of names are probably all based on the North Country name for a butcher which was 'flesher'.

Both these Shrikes are heavily handsome birds. The Great Grey is a winter visitor. When perching sentinel-like on a high branch, letting not the slightest movement in the surrounding land escape its eye, its aspect is predominantly grey. In flight it looks more black and white, for the wings and the long tail are a rich black with white markings. Its breast and underparts are pearly pale grey to white and it may be this colouration which gave it the name White Whiskey. The black of the beak continues in the feather colour of the thick eyestripe. The Red-backed Shrike has no white markings on its chestnut brown back. It is a smaller bird than the Great Grey, and not dissimilar in its black-moustachioed face and tail markings, and the grey of the forehead and nape. The Red-backed Shrike comes to us as a summer visitor and breeds in Southeast England. Over the past hundred years, however, the numbers of Red-backed Shrikes to breed in Britain have shown a marked and consistent decline and it looks as if they may within a relatively short time cease to breed here altogether.

Starling
Sturnus vulgaris

Stare (Ireland; W Cornwall; Dorset; North Riding)
Starnel (Northamptonshire)
Starn (Shetland)
Staynil; Gyp Starnill (N Riding)
Black Starling (East Lothian)
Black Steer (Worcestershire)

from the way it perches on the backs of sheep to feed off ticks:
Sheep Stare (Somerset)
Sheeprack (Northamptonshire)
Shepster; Sheppie (Cheshire)
Shepstarling; Shepstare (Craven)

various:
Black Felt
Gyp (N Riding)
Jacob (Sussex; Northamptonshire)

When the autumn sky of dusk is blackened prematurely by a mass flight of Starlings in their pre-roost congregation, it is difficult to believe that they were in a state of severe decline at the beginning of the nineteenth century. But, over the last hundred and fifty years, the birds have more than made up their numbers and are now among the most widespread and common birds in the British Isles, familiar in towns, parks, gardens, farmland and even moorland and woods. The evening flights are quite extraordinarily dramatic. A few months ago an autumn roost, usually situated several miles from where I live, spent three weeks in small wood nearby. Every night tens of thousands of starlings patterned the sky with their barbed shapes and filled the air with skreeling and twittering. The Starling beats its wings rapidly, then glides wings outstretched, each individual like a dark wide arrowhead. Together, they form a fluttering, pulsating mass which divides and rejoins, drops down to smother trees and bushes, or to rope themselves along telegraph wires and cables.

The word Starling, with the related Stare, Starnel, Starn and other similar names, are very close to the Anglo-Saxon *Staer* and *Staerlinc*. There are similar forms of this name to be found all over Europe (the German *Star*, Swedish *Stare*, as well as the Latin *Sturnus*). The old Greek *psaros* means 'spotted or flecked' and it is possible that the Stare names allude to the white flecked winter plumage of the Starling. These white flecks on the feather tips wear off gradually and by early spring, the Starling has a glossy, almost oily, browny-black breeding plumage with hidden irridescences of green and purple.

The group of names which include sheep, Sheep Stare, Shepster, or Chepster and Sheppie, refer to the Starling's habit of alighting upon the backs of sheep to pick off the ticks with its long sharp beak. I have also seen them doing this to deer. Starlings are formidable feeders and will, it seems, try almost anything. The ones who live near me feed mostly in the fields round about, ignoring my birdtable, but on the days I put out the remains of a curry, I can guarantee a band of Starlings. But tastes seem to be regional; Tony Soper notes that Starlings cannot resist Cheshire cheese, but this does not recommend itself to the birds here.

There are several 'Gyp' names for Starlings, possibly a use of the word as a synonym for black, in the same way as people used to be called gypsy for their dark complexions.

Hawfinch
Coccothraustes coccothraustes

Cherry Finch (Yorkshire)
Berry Breaker (Hampshire)
Grosbeak (Yorkshire)
Black-throated Grosbeak; Haw Grosbeak; Grosbeak Haw
Coble
Kate
Pie-finch

It is not established whether the Hawfinch is so called from the haw, the fruit of the hawthorn, a favourite food, or from the fact that the bird is a frequenter of 'haws' or hedges. Both versions are in fact quite appropriate, being derived from the Old English *haga* = hedge or enclosure. The Hawfinch also eats the seeds of wych elm, hornbeam, beech, sycamore and maple, but its *tour de force* is the cherry stone. Cracking cherry stones is quite a feat for a small bird, only about eighteen centimetres from bill to tail. Sir Thomas Browne, the Norfolk antiquarian, naturalist and scientist (1605–1682), made the first written notes on the Hawfinch

> . . . a kind of *coccothraustes* called a coble bird . . . finely coloured and shaped like a Bunting. It is chiefly seen in summer, about cherrietime.

The word *coccothraustes* (still found in the scientific name for the Hawfinch) was used by the Zurich naturalist Conrad Gesner for the Hawfinch in 1555 and comes from the Greek meaning nut-cracker.

Guy Mountford, who has written a book on the Hawfinch, describes it as 'a staunchly individualistic bird', and points out that 'fossil remains dating back a million years reveal no trace of recent change in its evolutionary history.' It is certainly a very distinctive bird to look at. The most conspicuous feature is the large and powerful beak. Blue-grey in colour, it becomes brighter during courtship and a smart snapping shut of the beak is part of the courtship display. It is certainly a fomidable instrument. Mountford enlisted the help of R. W. Sims of the British Museum's Zoology Department, and very careful experiments were carried out to ascertain the amount of pressure needed to crack the cherry stones on which British Hawfinches feed, and also olive stones, food for Hawfinches in Mediterranean areas. Mr Sims simulated the mandibles and pressure pads of horn which made up the Hawfinch bill and discovered that cherries required a pressure of 60–95 pounds to fracture the shell, and olive stones 106–159 pounds. Both these results were over a time of twenty seconds. (It was established that a greater force was needed to crack the stones more quickly, and in fact a Hawfinch takes considerably less time than twenty seconds.)

The 'Grosbeak' names of course refer to the *gros - bec* = large beak. But though large, it is not at all ugly, following the line of the forehead in a continuous curve. The Hawfinch has a nicely blended mixture of colours: pink, grey and chestnut, with black wing tips and bib at the throat, and a wide white wing bar. Pie-finch here means not simply black and white but 'particoloured' finch. The different colours all tone with each other in a nicely balanced pattern, and the whole effect is of a strong, sleek and handsome little bird. Though by no means common, it appears rarer than it is because it is so shy and retiring in its habits.

Greenfinch
Carduelis chloris

Green Linnet (Norfolk; Lancashire; Scotland)
Green Bird; Greenbull (Lancashire)
Green Olf = *Alpe* early name for Bullfinch (Norfolk)
Green Grosbeak
Greeney; Green Chub
Greenick; Green Lennart (Northumberland)

from its call:
Peasweep

The long drawn out wheeze of the Greenfinch (usually rendered 'dweep') is now a familiar sound of town as well as countryside. Of all finches it is the least bothered by proximity to man and is a regular and frequent visitor to birdtables. So much so, in fact, that in the lean the months before spring arrives, the survival of many birds depends almost entirely upon garden feeding tables, and peanuts can form by far the largest item of diet. Greenfinches have large bills (whence Green Grosbeak) with which they can feed on a wide range of different sized seeds of woodland plants and trees, crops and weed-wildflowers. As they feed, clinging to plants, or scanning the ground, Greenfinches keep up a rapid twitter interspersed with a thin 'pee wee' call, which seems to be the reason that this bird has borrowed the name Peasweep from the Lapwing.

From research done on the Greenfinch it seems that normally a bird will tend to live in the same general area for most of its life, though food foraging will be carried out over the whole of the home territory, perhaps a radius of five kilometres (which takes in an area of about eighty square kilometres). Local movement between feeding places and roosts is considerable; at one small garden roost, where a bird ringing programme was practised, over a thousand Greenfinches were ringed during two months, although there were never more than twelve birds there at any one time.

Until recently the Greenfinch was placed in a separate genus and bore the Latin name *Chloris chloris chloris,* from the Greek *khloros* meaning green. Most of the local names too call attention to the greeny colouration though none of them goes quite so far as 'Green-green-green'.

Goldfinch
Carduelis carduelis

plumage names:
Goldie; Gold Spink
Goud Spink, Gooldspink (Scotland)
Gool French (Devon)
Gold Linnet (North)
Redcap, King Harry Redcap, King Harry (Shropshire; Suffolk; N Riding)
Seven-coloured Linnet; Spotted Dick (Shropshire)
Lady with the Twelve Flounces (Shropshire)
Sheriff's Man
Foolscoat

various:
Thistle Finch (Stirling); Thistle Warp

Sweet William
Proud Tailor (Derby; Nottinghamshire; Somerset;
    Northamptonshire; Warwickshire)
Las air-choille = Flame of the Wood (Gaelic)
Linnet (Shropshire)
Jack Nicker (Northamptonshire; Shropshire; Cheshire)
Draw Bird; Draw Water
Moleneck (Cornwall)

immature:
Grey Kates, Grey Pates (North)
Brancher (London fanciers) *one-year-olds*

Goldfinch

The Anglo-Saxons of the eighth century knew this brightly coloured little finch as *Thisteltuige* or Thistle-tweaker. Twelve centuries later we still have Thistle Warp and Thistle Finch, and now as ever flocks of Goldfinches dance and dip to and fro over their favourite seed plants. Their beaks are proportionately longer and sharper than those of most finches and very good for tweaking out the seeds of thistles, teasels and knapweeds. The association with the thistle plant is ancient and widespread; the Latin for thistle is *Carduus* and today this forms the first part of the scientific name for a genus of thistles which includes the musk thistle. The French for Goldfinch is *Chardoneret,* the Italian *Cardello,* but the association is not always through Latin, as we know from the thistle names and the German *Distelfink*.

For a bird so prettily coloured there is of course a preponderance of plumage names, Goldfinch itself being the one most widely used. This name too has a long history and goes all the way back to the Old English *Goldfinc*. The wide strip of yellow-gold on the wing is very apparent, especially when the birds are flying. By association the word goldfinch came to mean a golden guinea at the beginning of the seventeenth century. George Farquhar in *The Constant Couple* puns on this with reference to the immense popularity of Goldfinches as cagebirds: 'Here is a nest of the prettiest goldfinches that ever chirped in a cage, twenty young ones, I assure you madam.'

The craze for keeping caged Goldfinches came

301

to a peak in the second half of the nineteenth century. In 1860 it was reported that 132,000 birds were caught at Worthing alone, and by the end of the century the numbers of wild Goldfinches was becoming very seriously affected. The Society for the Protection of Birds, later the Royal Society for the Protection of Birds (see Great Crested Grebe), made this wretched depletion one of their foremost concerns, for although the Protection of Birds Act of 1880 technically gave the Goldfinches protection, it was widely ignored.

Several new names came into the language purely on the basis of their popularity as cagebirds. Draw Bird and Draw Water from the unpleasant whimsy of teaching the birds to pull a thread to draw up a small bucket of water (also widespread in France and Holland). Among so-called Goldfinch fanciers, a Brancher was the term for a one-year-old bird, and Grey Pates or Kates for juvenile birds, who as the names suggest, have much more sombre head colours than the adults.

By the beginning of the eighteenth century a new slang meaning of the word Goldfinch was coming into use, meaning someone very wealthy (possessing gold or 'goldfinches'). Perhaps the cagebird was also in mind with this usage, with the implication of a rich dandy, perhaps flashing his gold pieces about, ready to be trapped by robber or seducer. This association of wealth with the Goldfinch is found again in the popular rhyme 'The Marriage of Cock Robin and Jenny Wren'. There is no direct evidence that this rhyme was written after 'The Death of Cock Robin' (see Robin), but to my thinking, the texture of the verses and the rather arch voice signifies a much later period. This is from an early nineteenth century version:

> Who gives this maid away?
> I do says the goldfinch
> And her fortune I will pay.

The only Goldfinch in early English art occurs in a miniature from the Psalter of Robert de Lisle (c 1300), a work directly influenced by French art. Compared with this, the symbolic significance of the Goldfinch in Italian and French painting is quite overwhelming. About three-quarters of European devotional paintings figure a Goldfinch. Excluding the white dove which represents the Holy Spirit, the Goldfinch is the most widely painted bird. Usually pictured with the Madonna and Child, it has a complex of meanings, at once a symbol of the resurrection and of fertility, and with miraculous healing powers also attributed to it. Sometimes the Goldfinch is centrally placed in the picture, often with the Christ child or another important figure holding it as in the Spanish painter Francisco de Zurbaran's *Madonna and Child with St John* (and Goldfinch), but it is quite easy to overlook the little figure of the bird, as in the well-known *Nativity* by Piero della Francesca in the National Gallery.

John Keats, towards the end of his life confined by illness to the cage of his room, had perhaps more than a little sympathy for the Goldfinch. His poem about them ('I Stood Tip-toe upon a Little Hill') is more about Goldfinches as birds and less about the thoughts they inspire in him than most bird poetry of that era.

> Sometimes goldfinches one by one will drop
> From low-hung branches; little space they stop;
> But sip, and twitter, and their feathers sleek;
> Then off at once, as in a wanton freak:
> Or perhaps, to show their black and golden wings
> Pausing upon their yellow flutterings.

It is not only their appearance which makes this little finch so attractive. As they fly they make light tinkling sounds, as delicate as Chinese bells, and the same 'conversational' twittering goes on as they feed together. The collective name for a number of Goldfinches is a charm. The word 'charm' is defined as 'a blended sound of many voices; as of birds, schoolchildren, etc' and the modern meaning of 'charming' comes from the same roots: the Middle English *charme* and the Latin *carmen* meaning a magic song or spell. Nor did this feature go unnoticed by poets, for while Keats watchfully described the Goldfinches' appearance, the listening Burns rejoiced in: 'The gowdspink, music's gayest child'.

Siskin
Carduelis spinus

Aberdavine
Blackheaded Thistlefinch
Golden Wren (Cheshire)
Tea Leaves (Sussex)

The name Siskin, like Brambling, is a diminutive form. It seems to have come ultimately from a Slavic origin via the Middle Low German *ziseke*, meaning something like 'whistler' or 'chirper'. Modern German is *Zeisig*, Swedish *Gronsiska*. The Siskin's breeding range in the West extends over Scandinavia and Russia, southwards to Central Europe, Yugoslavia, Bulgaria and Asia Minor. There is another major breeding population in the Far East, covering much of China and Japan. Despite this split population however there seems only to be one Siskin race; no subspecies have been observed. The Siskin is about the same size as the Goldfinch and has a similarly narrow, pointed bill. It is a dark-streaked yellow-green in colour with a black forehead and little bib. Its call note, from which its most widely used name is derived, is a high 'tsy-zi' (which seems to have been interpreted in Sussex as Tea Leaves). Like many of the finches it is conversational in habit and flocks keep up a constant music of flight calls and twittering song as they move about.

Siskins are very much birds of conifer forest. With the fashion for planting ornamental conifers and recent commercial afforestation, they have greatly increased their breeding range in the British Isles. The largest population of breeding Siskins is still concentrated in Scotland though, and in most of the rest of Britain and Ireland it is known only as a winter migrant. During the winter months Siskins rely largely upon alder seeds for food and are very adroit and acrobatic in withdrawing them. They 'leapfrog' through the scrub or forest from tree to tree, 'tzeeting' as they go, rising in a flock after only a short, rapid search over each tree, taking only the tastiest and ripest fruits. In this way they can feed from alder as it ripens for over five months from October to March. The *OED* marks the introduction of the alternative name Aberdavine as 1735, but confesses ignorance as to the origin. The Reverend Charles Swainson, doing some detective work, came to the conclusion that this name was a version of 'Alder Finch', *Erlenzeisig* or *Che d'aune; erle* and *aune* being the German and French respectively for alder. As a coda to his explanation, the Reverend Swainson quotes a nice sentence from J. Thompson's *Natural History of Birds, Fishes etc of Ireland* (1849–55) 'They [the Siskins] fed wholly on the alder, and looked beautiful, hanging like little parrots, picking at the drooping seeds of that tree.'

Linnet
Acanthis cannabina

summer plumage:
Red Linnet (Hampshire; W Riding)
Greater Redpole
Blood Linnet (Norfolk)
Rose Linnet, Rose Lintie (North)
Red-breasted Linnet
Red-headed Finch
Lemon Bird (W Riding)

winter plumage:
Grey Linnet (England; S Scotland)
Grey; Grey Bird (Westmorland; N Ireland)
Thorn Grey (Ireland)
Whin Grey (N Ireland)
Brown Linnet (Norfolk)

habitat names:
Gorse Bird, Gorse Hatcher (Shropshire)
    Gorse Thatcher
Whin Linnet (Stirling)
Furze Bird (Northamptonshire)
Gorse Linnet (Northamptonshire)
Furze Linnet (Oxfordshire)
Heather Lintie (Scotland)
Thorn Linnet (Yorkshire)
Whin Lintie (Scotland)

Like the Goldfinch, the Linnet has a very musical and appealing song, and like the Goldfinch it used to be popular as a cagebird; during the nineteenth century the population seriously declined for this reason. The numbers seem now to have recovered and Linnets are today a familiar sight over most of Britain and Ireland. Linnets are mostly a streaked brown-grey in colour, the cock's rosy crown and breast turning to a warm red in the breeding season. In common with Twite and Redpolls, Linnets do not have to moult to bring out their red courtship colours. Those feathers which eventually appear red start off with dullish browny tips and, as these tips wear down, the bright red beneath, which gives rise to so many rose-red names, is exposed. Perhaps more surprising is that there seem also to be so many names which refer to the quiet winter plumage of the cocks, and to the hens and young birds.

The word Linnet comes to us via the Old English *linece*, from the Latin *linum* = the flax family, though none of the flaxes now plays an important part in the diet of British Linnets who survive almost entirely upon the seeds of arable weeds and wildflowers. The Orkney name Lint White is a form of the Old English *linetwige* or flax tweaker, referring to the way that the little beaks of the Linnets twist the seed pods to get at their food. Linnets have short, broad bills which can't cope with very big seeds or those difficult to extract, so they feed mainly from plants whose seeds are attached to the stem, such as dock or chickweed, or they pick up the seeds from the ground.

Commons with gorse on them, rough ground with gorse or hawthorn, even suburban waste ground or railway banks provide nesting places for Linnets. The earliest nests are usually in gorse bushes for the Linnets begin nest building early in the season, before other bushes come into leaf. Although they do not actually feed upon the large seeds of gorse, there is good reason why Linnets should be called Gorse, Furze or Whin Linnets, making use of the several country names for this common shrub, and which themselves indicate locality. Gorse (from Old English *gorst*) is used generally in the Midlands, Furze (Old English *fyrs*) in the southwest and in Ireland, and Whin in eastern and northern counties, Scotland and Ireland.

Linnets nest socially, as do a number of other finches, with usually four to six pairs making their nests in close proximity (though as many as forty pairs have been counted in the space of two hectares). Outside the breeding season, Linnets will roost together, again usually in gorse bushes. The company assembles together at dusk, calling and singing to each other and they will circle around for perhaps over an hour in noisy aerial display, before settling down to roost. Although some birds use several roosts, some perches in the roost are used night after night, and there is a certain amount of squabbling over perches. If disturbed, a bird will return each time to its chosen perch.

Twite
Acanthis flavirostris

from its call:
Twite Finch (N Riding)
Moor Peep (Cheshire)
Little Peewit (Yorkshire)
Peepie Lannart (Northumberland)

habitat names:
Heather Lintie (Borders; Shetland; Orkney)
Hill Lintie (Orkney)
Rock Lintie; Rockie (Forfar)
Ling Linnet (Yorkshire)
Moor Linnet (Cheshire)

various:
Lintie (Orkney)
Grey Linnet
Trice Finch (Lancashire)

The Twite is similar in appearance to the Linnet, though of slighter build and with red on the rump; its forehead and breast are a streaky brown. It is not nearly so numerous as the Linnet. Its distribution is mainly north-westerly, apart from a population in the Pennines, and this is more or less mirrored by the counties of origin of the local names. The actual names give us a good idea of the kind of open windswept environments that are frequented by Twite: hill, heather, rock and moor. The name Twite itself probably comes from the bird's call, also rendered 'peep' and 'peewit'.

Redpoll
Acanthis flammea

plumage names:
Rose Lintie (Lowlands)
Red Linnet (West Riding)
Red-headed Finch
Redcap (Yorkshire)
Little Redpole Linnet

various:
Chevy Linnet (West Riding)
Chippet Linnet
French Linnet
Chitty; Chaddy (Cheshire)
Chivey Linnet (Yorkshire)

The natural habitat of Redpolls is in the wide areas of tundra and forest of the northern hemisphere. Seven different forms of Redpoll have been identified, but only one, the Lesser Redpoll, *Acanthis flammea disruptes,* lives and breeds in Britain. In the past they were more typically birds of northern areas, as may be guessed by the origins of the local names; but the 1970s have brought a population increase, and Redpolls are now coming further south. By no means restricted to land which resembles the birch scrub of their northern habitats, Redpolls will not only nest in willows, hawthorn and alder, but are attracted by the new conifer plantations. The Redpoll was introduced to New Zealand and has become one of the commonest birds there, having taken to a variety of habitats from mountain tundras to lowland farms.

The British Redpoll is smaller and darker in colouration than the other forms, but the characteristic bright red poll and little black bib show up distinctly. It has the smallest bill of all the finches, with which it can pick the tiniest of seeds such as those of grasses. It will eat willow flowers as well as seeds, but does not usually feed from fruit trees in Britain, though it does in New Zealand.

As they feed from one spot to another, and in the courtship display flight, they sing a rattling little 'chi-chi-chi' song by which they became known as Chivey and Chippet Linnets.

Bullfinch
Pyrrhula pyrrhula

from 'Alpe' the old name for this bird:
Hoop; Hope (Somerset; Cornwall; Devon; Dorset)
Olf (E Suffolk)
Nope (Stafford; Shropshire)
Mwope (Dorset)
Mawp (Lancashire)
Pope (Dorset)

from its large head and stocky form:
Bull Finch; Bull Flinch (Yorkshire)
Bull Head
Bulldog
Bull Spink, Bully (Yorkshire)
Thick Bill (Lancashire)

colour names:
Red Hoop (Dorset) *male*
Blood Olp (Surrey; Norfolk) *male*
Tawny (Somerset) *female*
Tony Hoop; Tonnihood (Somerset) *female*
Black Cap (Lincoln)
Billy Black Cap; Black Nob (Shropshire)
Monk

from its partiality to fruit buds:
Bud Bird, Bud Finch, Bud Picker (Devon)
Plum Bird, Lum Budder (Shropshire)

The first written appearance of Bullfinches is in the beautiful garden, a true harbour for birds, in Chaucer's *The Romaunt of the Rose*. There, 'Alpes'

309

(Bullfinches) other Finches and many other 'joly briddes smale' are described filling the air of a May morning with 'the sweetness of hir melodye'. 'Alpes', the oldest name we know for Bullfinch, still exists in varied forms such as Olf, Hoop and Mawp. And if we read on through Chaucer's poem, we find that Alpes in particular should have found the Romaunt garden a very agreeable habitat. For not only did it have plenty of ash trees, whose seeds play an important part in their diet, but also 'many hoomly trees there were' among them apple, plum, pear, medlar and cherry.

In the course of his studies of finches Ian Newton has shown that when the seeds of nettle, dock, bramble and ash are plentiful, Bullfinches tend to ignore the buds of fruit trees, but in years where the seed stocks give out before the end of the winter, they will turn to orchards. They have distinct preferences as to variety, favouring James Grieve and one or two other dessert apples to cookers. Among cherries, only Morello buds are really appreciated; Conference, Williams and Dr Jules pears are eagerly sought, though Comice and Hardy are ignored. All kinds of plum seem to be relished, gages in particular. Bullfinches are very methodical in their fruit bud feeding, working all the way through a tree, branch by branch, in small flocks. However, unless the late winter months have been very low in other seeds, and Bullfinches are forced to survive on fruit trees, the crop of fruit may be virtually unaffected. A pear tree for instance, can lose at least half of its buds without the eventual crop of fruit being reduced, so it is only in certain years that these Bud Birds do really significant damage.

Bullfinches, particularly the cock birds, are very striking in appearance with their glossy black cap, bib and tail, setting off the colour of the breast – the gentle buff-pink of the female and the deeper warm red of the male – which gives them the names Blood Olp and Red Hoop.

Crossbill
Loxia curvirostra

Though the Crossbill is not a common bird in Britain, it is a distinctive one with its askew beak and the male's bright crimson colouration. The upper part of the bill curves downward, the lower upward and may twist either to the right or left of the upper. Such bills are exactly the instrument for dealing with pine or larch cones which form the main diet of Crossbills. T. A. Coward observed the manner of their feeding:

> Their attitudes and actions were more parrot-than tit-like; they climbed along the branches, often walking sideways, and swung head downwards to wrench at a cone. This was first carried in the bill to a firm perch, where it was held, sometimes with one, sometimes with both feet, whilst the bird wrenched back scale after scale, picking out then eating the seeds with head raised. When enough had been secured the cone was dropped and the bird hunted for another; about five minutes was spent on each cone.

Looking at things literally, it is easy to see why the Crossbill is so called. However, there is an alternative legend of the name which, like the catechism of the passion flower, draws on a certain number of correlations: the cross of the Crossbill and the cross of Christ; the crimson colouring and the Blood of Christ, to make a religious story of it. The Crossbill is one of several red-fronted birds (the Swallow and Robin are others) who are credited with having tried to assist Christ on the cross. The Crossbill, it is said, bent its beak in trying to withdraw the nails piercing Christ's hands and feet. Other versions (including that in verse of Longfellow) leave out this feature but agree that the bird was marked with the Saviour's blood. As Longfellow relates it:

> Stained with blood and never tiring
> With its beak it does not cease
> From the Cross t'would free the Saviour
> Its Creator's Son release.

And the Saviour speaks in mildness
'Blest be thou of all the good,
Bear as token of this moment
Marks of blood and holy rood.

And that bird is called the crossbill
Covered all with blood so clear . . .

Longfellow's poem was based directly on a German work by Julius Mosen. Like most of the other birds around the cross and the bird-and-Saint legends, this story was imported from the continent where such traditions were very much stronger than in Britain, where they circulated much more in written than oral form.

The first record of Crossbills, and a very good description of them, was made by Matthew Paris in 1251, and it looks to me as if this early piece of writing gave rise to another 'book-name' for the Crossbill, that of Shell Apple. The plot goes as follows:

At the turn of the year, at the season of fruits, certain wonderful birds never before seen in England appeared, particularly in orchards. They were a little bigger than larks and ate the pips of apples and nothing else from the apples. So they robbed the trees of their fruit very grievously. Moreover they had the parts of the beak crossed and with them split the apples as if with pincers or a pocket knife.

A similar record, this time of the year 1593, described a 'greate plenty' of . . .

strong birds, that shewed themselves at the time the apples were full rype who fedde upon the kernells onely of those apples, and haveinge a bill with one beake wrythinge over the other . . . they were of the bigness of a Bullfinch . . . the cock a very glorious bird, in a manner al redde or yellow on the brest, backe and head.

There is yet another reference in 1602 to the coming of . . .

a flocke of birds into Cornwall, about Harvest season, in bignesse not much exceeding a sparrow, which made a foule spoyle of the apples. Their bills were thwarted crosswise at the end . . .

As we have seen, the usual diet of Crossbills is the seeds of spruce or pine and these European Crossbills normally make one major migration each year in the summer, when the crops are forming, to areas rich in cones where they will settle, moult and breed. In certain years, perhaps because of widespread failure of cone crops, perhaps because of overcrowding, 'eruptions' of Crossbills, in enormous numbers, occur and the birds may leave their regular range to end up in places devoid of conifers, where they have to find what food they may. These eruptions may be such as are described in these early records, and Willughby, Merret, Pennant and Bewick all write of the Crossbill as Shell Apple.

At this point, it looks as if two different streams, the oral and the written, cross each other. I can find no record of the name Shell Apple as a local name in the oral tradition, yet there are a number of districts in which the Chaffinch has this title (see Chaffinch). Now, Chaffinches live on small seeds and insects, and not by any stretch of the imagination could their little beaks cope with something as large as an apple. The derivation is not what it seems, but in its own way it is quite appropriate. The 'Shell' means variegated or parti-coloured (as it does in Shelduck). The 'Apple' part of the name is not a reference to the fruit, but a corruption of 'Alpe', an old name for the Bullfinch. So the name 'Shell Apple' literally means something like 'a parti-coloured-Bullfinch-like-bird'. This is perhaps not so appropriate for the Crossbill as for the gaily coloured Chaffinch, but we have seen the species described as 'very glorious birds' and the male has a red head, breast and rump. So the less common Crossbill shares the Chaffinch's name, Shell Apple and this usage is reinforced by the historical 'Apple-cropping' reports.

Chaffinch

Fringilla coelebs

from its call note:
Chink Chaffey (Hampshire)
Chink Chink (Shropshire)
Binkie (Ross and Cromarty)
Chy (Aberdeen); Chay (Moray)
Pinkety (Northamptonshire)
Pink Twink (Devon; Somerset; Shropshire)
Prink Prink (Inverness)
Sheely (Northamptonshire; Kinross)
Shilfa, Sheelfa, Shelfie (Scotland)
Shiltie; Sheltie (Fife)

plumage names:
Copper Finch (Devon; Cornwall)
Blue Cap (Aberdeen)
Pea Finch; Pied Finch; Pine Finch (Midlands; Shropshire)
Shell Apple; Apple Sheller (Northumberland)
Apple Sheelie; Shieler Applie (Northumberland)
Apple Bird (Cornwall)
Whitewing (Donegal; Armagh)
White Wingie (Lanarkshire)
White Finch
Flackie; Fleckie Wings (Lancashire)
Fleckiewing

various:
Boldie (Kincardine)
Brisk Finch; Brichtie (Wigtown)
Snabbie (Dumfries; Fife)
Scobb; Scop, Scoppie (Cumberland; Northumberland)
Wet Bird (Rutland; Stirling) Wet Chaff (Angus)
Wheatsel Bird (Norfolk)
Charbob (Derbyshire)
Treeack; Tree Lintie (Moray)

The Chaffinch has had a long association with man, and it perhaps is because of this familiarity that its history is very thin on folklore. Maybe we knew this attractive and confiding little finch too well for it to acquire supernatural or even superstitious significance. Local names for the bird come from all over Britain and Ireland, and nearly all of them are literal. Phonetics never do more than approximate to the sound of a bird's voice, but with the Chaffinch there is a wide choice of similar sounds, from Chink in Hampshire, Pink Twink in Devon all the way up to Chy in Aberdeen and Prink Prink in Inverness. The variety of colours in the Chaffinch's plumage is appreciated in the 'shell' names (Shell or Sheld =

variegated) and in Pied Finch. (For the derivation of the 'Shell Apple' names, see Crossbill.) The cheeks, throat and breast of the male are pink-red, and the head in the breeding season is slate blue. In both sexes and the back is copper brown and the wings a dramatic black and white, as described with considerable care and tenderness by the Scots poet, Grahame:

> When not a strain is heard through all the woods
> I've seen the shilfa light from off his perch
> And hop into a shallow of the stream,
> Then, half afraid, flit to the shore, then in
> Again alight and dip his rosy breast,
> And fluttering wings, while dew-like globules
> coursed
> The plumage of his brown empurpled back.

The song of the Chaffinch is short but pleasing to the ear. It consists of a few piping little introductory notes, followed by a twittery trill ending in a small flourish. In his poem 'The Lover and the Birds' William Allingham interprets this as:

> Sweet, sweet, sweet.
> Pretty lovey, come and meet me here.

Bramble Finch
Mountain Finch
Furze Chirper; Furze Chucker
Cock o' the North (E and S Scotland)
Kate (Kent)
Bramble Cock (Cheshire)
Flat Finch (Cheshire)
Tartan Back (Scotland)
Goldie-wing; Yallawing (Northumberland)
French Linnet (North Riding)

Brambling
Fringilla montifringilla

This very handsome finch is a winter visitor to Britain and Ireland. It is a northerly counterpart to the Chaffinch. In regions more northerly than Britain there is a certain overlap in breeding territory, but the last confirmed case of Bramblings breeding in Britain was of a single pair in 1920. (*The Atlas of Breeding Birds* notes a few places where Brambling song has been heard in spring which may indicate breeding and it also quotes an instance of a Chaffinch/Brambling hybrid.) Migrant Bramblings are often seen in the company of Chaffinches in the winter months, though they are more specific in their food requirements. Whereas Chaffinches eat more or less whatever seeds or insects are available, Bramblings far prefer beech mast to seeds and berries and they will range widely to find it. The size of Brambling flocks will vary according to the mast. An amazing *seventy million* birds assembled in some heavy-laden beechwoods near the Swiss town of Huniback, for a few weeks in the winter of 1951–52.

Both Bramblings and Chaffinches feed on insects in the summer and mostly seeds during the winter months. As they feed Bramblings utter chuckling flight calls which has probably earned them the names Furze Chirper and Furze Chucker. Bramblings roost in thorny bushes such as furze or bramble. The name Brambling itself is a diminutive form of bramble. Tartan Back from Hett's *Glossary of Popular, Local and Old-fashioned Names of British Birds* (1902) seems rather contrived for a popular name but nonetheless is aptly descriptive of the chestnut, black and white divided symmetry of the Brambling's mantle and wings.

Corn Bunting

Emberiza calandra

from a passing resemblance to the Skylark:
Bunting Lark, Buntling Lark (Scotland)
Bunt Lark (Norfolk)
Horse Lark (Cornwall)
Lark Bunting (Somerset)
Bush Lark (Ireland)
Ground Lark; Chub Lark (Yorkshire)

various:
Common Bunting
Ebb
Corn Bird (Ireland)

Hornbill Bunting (Ireland)
Briar Bunting (Northern Ireland)
Skitter Brottie (Orkney)
Thistle Cock (Orkney)
Whisker Bird

Corn Buntings were originally known simply as Buntings; in Middle English, *Buntyle* or *Bountynge*. The word has been known since at least 1450 but it is possible that it may be older if Buntingford in Hertfordshire comes from the word (spelt *Buntingeford* in 1183). These birds are much associated with the agricultural landscape. Called Corn Birds as well as Corn Buntings they like arable fields, in and around which they can find both vegetable and insect food, with hedges, posts and fences from which they can sing. They nest sometimes in cornfields but also in gorse, bramble and briar; hence Briar Lark. The song of the Corn Bunting is oddly distinctive, a high-pitched jingling of notes rather like a trill on a harpsichord. Many of the names make allusion to Larks, to which Corn Buntings, the largest of the Buntings, bear a resemblance. The Corn Bunting is in fact about as big as a Lark and streaky brown in colouration, but more solid in its build, which is why it has been given the name Horse Lark.

A seventeenth century meaning of 'bunting' is plump or stocky, but it is possible this derives from the name of the bird rather than vice versa. 'Bunting' is also a term of endearment as in the nursery rhyme 'Bye baby bunting', perhaps because babies at their most endearing are plump and chirpy. 'Bunting' as used for the decorative flags which go up in the streets at festivals, seems to be from an eighteenth century word for a material used for making flags. 'Bunt' was also used a century earlier as a verb, 'to bunt' meaning to belly out in the wind like a sail. Here we have an allusion to plumpness again; perhaps people saw a similarity in the way a sail fills with wind and the puffing out of the Corn Bunting's breast before it sings.

Yellow-hammer

Emberiza citrinella

Yellow Amber; Yellow Omber (Shropshire)
Yellow Bunting (Renfrewshire)
Yellow Yorling (Bewickshire; E Lothian; N Ireland)
Yellow Yoit (Wigtown; Kircudbrightshire)
Yellow Yowlie (Northumberland)
Yellow Yite (Scotland)
Yellow Ring; Urin (Lancashire)
Gold Spink (North)
Gouldie (County Down)
Goldie (Nottinghamshire; Craven; North Riding)
Gladdie from Anglo-Saxon *gladde* = bright (Devon;
  Cornwall)
Buidheag-Bhearaidh = yellow broom bird (Gaelic)
Bessie Blaceling (Westmorland)
Bessie Buntie (Cumberland)
Yedda Yeldern (Antrim)
Guler (Norfolk)

from its song:
Little-bit-of-bread-and-no-cheese (Devon; Cumberland;
  Inverness)
Cheeser (Northamptonshire)
Pretty-pretty-*creature* (Gloucestershire)
May-the-devil-take-you (Cumberland)

from the irregular lines on the egg:
Writing Master (Shropshire)
Scribbling Lark; Writing Lark (Northamptonshire;
  Northumberland)
Scribblie; Scribbler (Northumberland)

various:
Blacksmith (Shropshire)
Scotch Canary (Scotland)

The Yellowhammer is one of the brightest and most conspicuously yellow birds. Nor does it hide its light; it is a bird of open country, a common and well-distributed resident and a fairly widespread winter visitor. It is particularly a hedgerow bird where it usually chooses a high twig as a singing perch. Its bright colouring which forms an element of so many of its names, led to the name Yellowhammer becoming a slang synonym for a gold piece during the eighteenth century. Similarly the Breckland name Guler may come from the *Gulden,* a gold coin of Germany and the Netherlands. It is not certain, but seems likely that the Anglo-Saxon *Amore* actually meant Yellowhammer and that over the centuries the memory of the original meaning was lost and the prefix 'yellow' added, making the bird literally a 'Yellow-yellowhammer'.

The rhythmic lilt of the Yellowhammer's song has coined for it the names A-little-bit-of-bread-and-no-cheese and, in Scotland, May-the-devil-take-you. As the Devil's Bird, the Yellowhammer was reputed to drink a drop of devil's blood every May morning

> The brock and the toad and the yellow yorling
> Tak a drap of the devil's blood ilka May
>   morning.

Like the badger (whose name, used as a verb, has become a synonym for harrassment), the Yellowhammer was cruelly persecuted in many parts of northern Scotland. A parallel 'devil's blood' superstition was reported by Grohmann (1864) in Czechoslovakia in the region of Prague, where the bird was similarly harried.

The eggs of the Yellowhammer are more or less covered with irregular lines, hence Scribbling Lark and Writing Lark, two names which the Reverend Swainson reports as hailing from Netherlands. It is not certain, but seems likely that the Anglo-Saxon *Amore* actually meant fanciful notions than is characteristic of him:

> Five eggs, pen scribbled o'er with ink their shells
> Resembling writing-scrolls, which Fancy reads
> As Nature's poesy and pastoral spells –
> They are the yellow hammer's and she dwells
> Most poet like, 'mid brooks and flowery weeds.

Reed Bunting
Emberiza schoeniclus

habitat names:
Reed Sparrow; Riverside Sparrow
Water Sparrow; Bog Sparrow; Pit Sparrow (Cheshire)
Seave Cap (Yorkshire)

from its white collar:
Ring Bird
Ring Bunting
Ring Fowl (Aberdeen)

Reed Bunting

from the black head:
Black-headed Bunting
Black Bonnet (Scotland)
Coaly Hood (Scotland)
Black Coaly Hood (S Scotland)
Colin Blackhead (Renfrew)
Black Cap (Hampshire; Craven)

various:
Chink (Scotland)
Toad Snatcher (Yorkshire)
Spear Sparrow (Hampshire) *female*
Bodkin (Lancashire)

Reed Buntings are little birds of the waterside. Depending on the local landscape, they are called Reed Sparrows, Fen Sparrows, Bog Sparrows, Riverside Sparrows and, in Cheshire where they frequent old marl pits, Pit Sparrows. The hen and young Reed Buntings (and in winter the male) are streaky brown in colour, paler on the breast, which disguises their presence in the reeds. They are not unlike Sparrows though they are taller and slimmer. Seave Cap is another habitat name; 'seave' is a dialect name meaning reed. Another reed connection is made in the specific part of the scientific name *schoeniclus* which is derived from the Greek *skhoinos,* a reed. Turner in 1544 knew this species by the name Reed Sparrow, and it seems it was not until 1813 that the title Reed Bunting was introduced by George Montagu in his *Ornithological Dictionary.*

The cock Reed Bunting in breeding plumage is a handsome figure, with a black head and bib, a white moustachial stripe and a white collar. The features, especially the collar and the black 'Coaly Hood' form the basis for a large group of common names. The Reed Bunting has a small staccato song, but several call notes, one of which is a 'ching' sound, probably gave rise to the Scottish name Chink.

variations on Sparrow:
Spadger
Spurdie (Aberdeen; Banffshire)
Spuggie (Cumberland; Northumberland)
Spurgie (Aberdeen)
Sproug (Caithness)
Speug (Ayr; Lanark; Stirling)
Sprug (East Lothian)
Grey Spadger (Antrim)

various:
Lum Lintie (East Lothian)
Craff (Northumberland)
Cuddy; Hoosie (Northumberland)
Row-dow; Roo-doo (Northamptonshire)
Thatch Sparrow; Thack Sparrow (Northamptonshire;
    Shropshire)
Easing Sparrow (Shropshire)

Stone Age man had Sparrows for companions.
The name Sparrow comes from the Anglo-Saxon
spearwa. In this passage from the Venerable Bede
(translated here by Wordsworth) a Sparrow is used
as the central simile:

> Man's life is like a Sparrow, Mighty King,
> That, stealing in, while by the fire you sit
> Housed with rejoicing friends is seen to flit
> Safe from the storm, in comfort tarrying.
> Here did it enter – there on hasty wing
> Flies out, and passes on from cold to cold;
> > But whence it came, we know not, nor
> > behold
> > Whither it goes.

In *The Parlement of Foules* a Sparrow is characterized as 'The sparow, Venus sone', in all likelihood
referring to the way Sparrows, then as now, take
advantage of every possible opportunity to breed.
Aristotle disapproved of this, calling the Sparrow
'of all birds the most wanton' (but Sparrow eggs
were nonetheless popular as an aphrodisiac). John
Donne treats the subject more delicately, as might
be expected from a poem entitled 'An
Epithalamion on Marriage on St Valentine's Day',
referring to 'The sparrow that neglects his life for
love'. Both *The Parlament of Foules* and the

Epithalamion are structured around the legend that on St Valentine's day all the birds meet together to choose their mates.

We meet the Sparrow as arch villain in the familiar rhyme 'Who Killed Cock Robin' but the origins of this story and the characterizations are enigmatic. A touching reversal of roles is described in John Skelton's 'Lament for Phyllyp Sparrowe' in the early sixteenth century, in which the Robin

> . . . shall be the priest
> The requiem mass to sing
> Softly warbeling.

This poem (modelled on Catullus) mourns the death of the author's pet and friend 'Phyp sparrow' not in heavy lugubrious lines but in sprightly verse which conveys all the restlessness and boldness of the bird, and, despite the liveliness of the metre, the real sadness of the loss.

> Phyp, phyp
> Phyllyp had leve to go
> To pyke my lytell toe
>
> . . . Phyllyp might be bold
> And do what he wolde
>
> . . . Phyllyp wolde deke and take
> All the flies blake
> That he could espy
> With his wanton eye.

It is a lovely poem, gay yet tenderly in keeping with its subject. After the Robin's rather serious requiem has been sung (in Latin and English) the poet makes a personal prayer to Jupiter for his 'wanton' pet who delighted in his sexual prowess as much as the next Sparrow.

> To Jupiter I call
> Of heaven imperial
> That Phyllyp may fly
> Above the starry sky,
> To tread the pretty wren
> That is Our Lady's hen
> Amen, amen, amen!

Sparrows have recently been redefined taxonomically and are now placed in the family *Ploceidae* which includes the African Weaver Birds, renowned for their beautiful nests. Sparrow's nests are on the whole not remarkable except for their makeshift quality, an untidy heap of straw stuffed into a hole or space under the eaves. They rarely nest away from human constructions: houses, factories or other buildings, (though when they do build nests in trees or hedges, these are large, domed, and well-constructed). Rather fittingly, numerous Sparrows nest in the warehouse of Penguin Books Ltd where they live happily among the Puffins, Peregrines, Kestrels and Pelicans as well as Penguins.

Sparrows will also use the nests of other birds, sometimes evicting the rightful owners, often Swallows, Martins or Blue Tits. Bartholomew de Glanville, the thirteenth century herbalist, in his *De Proprietatibus Rerum* observed that the uncouth Sparrow 'waileth and biteth for to have the nests of Swallows'. A folk tale, dictating poetic justice says that Martins and Swallows return to the nest which Sparrows have taken over and build over the entrance imprisoning the squatters. I had imagined the foundation for this belief to lie in indignation rather than fact, but Summers-Smith in his monograph on the House Sparrow quotes two references where this 'Walling up' actually seems to have taken place.

There are several mentions of Sparrows in the Bible, both in the Old Testament and the New. It is not, however, certain whether the word referred specifically to Sparrows, or to any small bird. But as Sparrows are fairly common in Israel, Sparrows could have it, either way. One notes that inflation has hit the Biblical Sparrows over the last few years. The King James version has 'two sparrows sold for a farthing', whereas the *New English Bible's* Matthew x 29 has 'Are not two sparrows two a penny?', a price for which one could formerly purchase no less than nineteen. That ironic eighteenth century Whig, Addison, observed one occasion of the purchase of Sparrows in 1771; he saw 'an ordinary fellow carrying a cage full of little birds upon his shoulder' and was told they were bought for the opera at Covent Garden where 'the sparrows were to act the part of singing birds in a delightful grove'. Unfortunately, 'there have been so many flights of them let loose in this opera that it is feared the house will never get rid of them; and that in other plays they make their interest in very wrong and improper scenes . . . besides the inconvenience which the heads of the audience may sometimes suffer from them.'

Tree Sparrow
Passer montanus

Copper Head (Cheshire)
Red-headed Sparrow (Yorkshire)
Rock Sparrow (Cheshire)
Tree Finch

In terms of the long history of observation of Sparrows, it is only comparatively recently, in 1713, that the Tree Sparrow was formally distinguished from the House Sparrow as a separate species. The reason for this may be partly that there is a considerable degree of variation in the House Sparrow's plumage and that the Tree Sparrow is, from man's point of view, reclusive, not always before the eye as the House Sparrow is. They are very similar at first glance, but whereas the House Sparrow has a grey pate, the Tree Sparrow has a rich brown 'Copper head'. Tree Sparrows also have a smaller but denser black bib and a small black patch on each cheek. As their name suggests they usually nest in the hollows of trees, but they also use crevices in rock, or other kinds of holes to give a solid form to their nests which are just as untidy as those of their grey-headed relatives.

Allen, David Elliston, *The Naturalist in Britain*. London,
  Allen Lane, 1976.
Alexander, Michael, *The Earliest English Poems*. London,
  Penguin Books, 1966.
Alexander, W. B., 'The Ornithology of Inn Signs', *Bird Notes*
  Vol XXXVI.
Armstrong, Edward, *The Folklore of Birds*. London and New
  York, Dover, 1970. *The Life and Lore of the Bird*. New
  York, Crown Publishers, 1977.
Bannerman, D. A., *The Birds of the British Isles*. Edinburgh,
  Oliver and Boyd, 1953–63.
Benson, C. W., *Our Irish Song Birds*. Dublin, Hodges Figgis
  & Co, 1901.
Bewick, Thomas, *A History of British Birds*. London,
  Paddington Press, 1976.
Brown, Leslie, *British Birds of Prey*. London, Collins (New
  Naturalist series), 1976.
Burns, Robert, *Poems and Songs* (ed J. Kinsley). Oxford,
  OUP, 1968.
Buckley & Harvie-Brown, *Fauna of the Orkney Islands*.
  Edinburgh, David Douglas, 1891.
Buxton, John, *The Redstart,* London, Collins, 1950.
Chaucer, Geoffrey, *Complete Works,* Oxford, OUP, 1912.
Clare, John, *The Shepherd's Calendar* (ed Geoffrey
  Summerfield & Eric Robinson) Oxford, OUP, 1964.
  Selected Poems and Prose (ed Geoffrey Summerfield & Eric
  Robinson) Oxford, OUP, 1967.
Colerdge, S. T., *Poetical Works*. Oxford, OUP, 1912.
Coward, Thomas, A., *The Birds of the British Isles*. London,
  Warne, 1950.
Cramp & Simmons, *The Bird of the Western Palearctic*.
  Oxford, RSPB/OUP, 1977.
Drayton, Michael, *Poly-Olbion*. Oxford, Basil Blackwell,
  1961.
Dryden, John, *Poems and Fables*. Oxford, OUP, 1962.
Fisher, James, *The Shell Bird Book*. London, Ebury
  Press/Michael Joseph, 1966.
Fitter, R. S. R., *London's Natural History*. London, Collins
  (New Naturalist Series), 1945.
Friedmann, H., *The Symbolic Goldfinch*. Washington,
  published for the Bolligen Foundation by Pantheon
  Books, 1946.

Gerard, John, *The Herball* 1597 (ed Johnson 1633). New York, Dover, 1975.

Gollancz/Mackie, *The Exeter Book*. Oxford, OUP, 1934.

Gordon, H. K., *Anglo-Saxon Poetry*. London, Dent, 1954.

Grant & Murison (eds), *Scottish National Dictionary*, Scottish National Dictionary Association, 1970.

Graves, Robert, *The Greek Myths*. Harmondsworth, Penguin Books, 1955.

Grieve, Mrs M., *A Modern Herbal*. New York, Dover, 1971.

✓Grigson, Geoffrey, *The Englishman's Flora*. London, Hart-Davis MacGibbon/Paladin, 1975.

Groundwater, William, *Birds and Mammals of Orkney*. Kirkwall, Orkney, The Kirkwall Press, 1974.

Gurney, J. H., *Early Annals of Ornithology*. London, Witherby, 1921.

Hamer, R. A., *Choice of Anglo Saxon Verse*, London, Faber, 1970.

Hare, C. E., 'Bird Lore'. London, *Country Life*, 1952.

✓Heinzel, Fitter, Parslow, *The Birds of Britain and Europe*. London, Collins, 1972.

✓Hollom, P. A. D., *Popular Handbook of British Birds*. London, Witherby, 1968.

Howard, Eliot, *A Waterhen's World*. Cambridge, CUP, 1940.

Hughes, Ted, *Season Songs*. London, Faber, 1976.

✗Jackson, Christine, *British Names of Birds*. London, Witherby, 1968.

Lack, David, *Robin Redbreast*. Oxford, OUP, 1950.

Lockley, R. M., *Letters from Skokolm*. London, Dent, 1947. *Shearwaters*. London, Dent, 1942.

McLeod, R. D., *Key to the Names of British Birds*. London, Pitman, 1954.

Mather, J. Y., *Linguistic Atlas of Scotland*. London, Croom Helm, 1975.

Mitchell, *Birds of Lancashire*. Gurney and Jackson, 1842.

Mountford, Guy, *The Hawfinch*. London, Collins, 1957.

Murray, Sir J. A. H., *Oxford English Dictionary*. Oxford, OUP, 1933.

Newton, Ian, *Finches*. London, Collins (New Naturalist Series), 1972.

North, Myles & Simms, *Sound Guide to British Birds*. London, Witherby, 1958.

Little, William, *The Shorter Oxford English Dictionary*. Oxford, OUP, 1968.

✓Peterson, Mountford, Hollom, *A Field Guide to the Birds of Britain and Europe*. London, Collins, 1965.

Potter, S. & Sargent, L., *Pedigree, Words from Nature*. London, Collins (New Naturalist Series), 1973.

Rawson, Jessica, *Animals in Art*. London, Trustees of the British Museum, 1977.

Shakespeare, William, *Complete Works*. Oxford, OUP, 1907.

Sharrock, J. T. R., *The Atlas of Breeding Birds in Britain and Ireland*. Berkhamsted, T. & A. D. Poyser, 1977.

Shelley, Percy Bysshe, *Complete Works*. Oxford, OUP, 1961.

Simms, Eric, *Birds of Town and Suburb*. Glasgow, Collins, 1975.

Skeat, W. W., *Etymological Dictionary of the English Language*. Oxford, OUP, 1910.

Spurgeon, Caroline, *Shakespeare's Imagery*. Cambridge, CUP, 1935.

Summers-Smith, J. D. *The Housesparrow*. London, Collins, 1963.

Swainson, Reverend Charles, *Provincial Names and Folk Lore of British Birds*. London, Trubner, 1885.

Swann, H. Kirke, *A Dictionary of English and Folk-Names of British Birds*. London, Witherby, 1913.

Thomas, Edward, *Selected Poems*. London, Faber, 1964.

Thomson, James, *The Seasons and Other Poems*. Oxford, Clarendon Press, 1972.

Walpole-Bond, John, *A History of Sussex Birds*. London, Witherby, 1938.

White, Gilbert, *Journals* (ed Walter Johnson), Newton Abbot, David and Charles, 1970. *Natural History of Selborne* (ed Richard Mabey). Harmondsworth, Penguin Books, 1977.

Williamson, Kenneth, 'The Antiquity of the Calf of Man Manx Shearwater Colony' *Bird Study* 20.

Willughby, Francis, & Ray, John, *The Ornithology*, 1678. Newport Pagnell, PPB Minet, 1972.

Wordsworth, William, *Poems*. Oxford, OUP, 1920.

Wright, Joseph, *Wright's English Dialect Dictionary*. Oxford, OUP, 1905.

Yarrell, William, *British Birds* (ed Saunders). London, John Van Voorst, 1871–1885.

Index

Standard and regional names are listed in this index, as well as general references and names of writers and poets. The names which are now used as the standard form appear in bold type for easy reference, and are followed by the scientific name in each case.